Words and Values

Words and Values
Some Leading Words
and Where They Lead Us

PEGGY ROSENTHAL

New York   Oxford
OXFORD UNIVERSITY PRESS
1984

Library of Congress Cataloging in Publication Data
Rosenthal, Peggy.
Words and values.
Includes bibliographical references and index.
1. Semantics. 2. Thought and thinking. I. Title.
P325.R67   1984   401'.9   83-13446
ISBN 0-19-503364-7

Printing (last digit): 9 8 7 6 5 4 3 2 1

Printed in the United States of America

To A. Marguerite Zouck
and the late Grace N. Cushman,
my first great teachers

Preface

This book is a collection of biographical sketches of some of the leading figures of our time, though the figures aren't people but configurations of words. The purpose of tracing their lives is to find out how they got to be where they are today (how they got into their leading position) and what difference their being there makes in our own lives (what attitudes, beliefs, behavior we're led into by them).

The book therefore conceives of the leading words it examines as "leading" in two senses: as being currently "dominant" words, words in positions of power; and as "directing" us, from this dominant position, to think and act in certain ways. Each of the four parts of the book focuses on a group of very common leading words: words like *individual, feelings, develop, growth, alternative, opinion, relationship*. The words are examined to see where they get their popularity and their power, what meanings and values they carry as they move into different areas of our lives, and where they seem to be carrying us as they move along.

This view of our relation to the words we use perhaps appears a bit alarming. We aren't seen as leading our own language anywhere at all, but as being led by it. Our words, even our common everyday ones, are seen as an active force in our lives; our own position with respect to them is seen as passive. This is indeed a disturbing position to find ourselves in, but as the analysis proceeds we'll see that the normal operations of language do put us in this passive position: language works to give us much less control over "what we mean" than we generally assume we have. Even when we think we're choosing our words with care and giving them precise meanings, they can mean much more (or less) than we think; and when we use them carelessly, without thinking, they can still carry thoughts. These thoughts we're not aware of, these meanings we don't intend, can then carry us into certain beliefs and behavior — whether or not we notice where we're going.

But though the workings of language tend to put us in a passive position, this doesn't imply that our position must remain simply helpless. It will be helpless as long as we let ourselves remain blind to what our language is doing. But we have powers of critical detachment that we're always free to exercise with respect to any of our activities: so instead of letting ourselves be pulled along by the going terms of the day, we can always step back from them and look, from a position of critical detachment, at where they've come from and where they're going. Examining them from this distance, we'll be in a position to resist some of their pull if we want to; seeing more clearly where a certain set of words is going, we'll be able to decide how far we want to go along with it and where we'd perhaps rather switch to a different set of terms (and values and goals) instead. To encourage this critical distance, to enable us to make such choices, is the purpose of this book.

The "us" I refer to, the "we" whose language is the book's subject, is normal adult users of standard American English today: the people to whom television news is addressed would be one way of putting it. Probably users of English in other countries are also included in most of what I say about "us," but I'm not familiar enough with the popular culture of countries other than my own to be sure of how far the particulars of my analysis apply to them. My general comments, though, about how "we" use (and are used by) our language do apply not only to English speakers in all countries but to speakers of other modern Western languages as well, and sometimes also to "we" in Western culture since the Greeks or even to "we" humans as thinking beings in all times and places. I've tried to make it clear when I extend "we" or "us" in any of these ways.

Usually though, as I said, the "we" whose language the book studies is Americans today who watch television and films, who listen to radio, who read newspapers and magazines and books, who go to meetings and workshops, who talk to each other in the normal ways: all, that is, who come into contact with the main communication networks of our time. This includes those who produce the television shows and films, who talk on radio, who own or write for the newspapers and magazines, who publish the books, who run the meetings and workshops. These people who control the communication networks in the socio-economic sense don't, it turns out, necessarily have any more control over how they use and are used by their language than anyone else does. The power of critical detachment required to free ourselves from the control of our language doesn't come from economic power or political power or even intellectual power as it's usually exercised. One of the book's points is that the common words running through scientific papers and business reports and political speeches and news broadcasts are pulling along not only the consumers of such lines but their supposed producers as well.

There are, of course, many more common words with a strong pull on us today than the few words examined in this book. I should explain, then, why I've chosen to examine these four sets of terms: *self–feelings–inner, growth–development–evolve–fulfill-ment–potential, relative–opinion–consensus,* and *relationship–whole–system–community–environment.*

One reason that I've selected these particular words is that they are dominant words in one of the dominant ideologies of our time: humanism. In fact, it's because they are leading words of a leading ideology that they play a leading role in our lives. But this doesn't mean that the ideology comes first, suddenly appearing in our midst as a monolithic structure, like the huge slab in the film *2001*, and laying its language on us in a block. An ideology, any system of thought, is a fluid structure (that's how, as we'll see, it influences us). It is always in the process of being shaped by its language; and its language is always in the process of running into and out of other systems of thought and various areas of activity, shaping and being shaped by them as it goes. This process of ongoing mutual influence among language, thought, and activity is fascinatingly complex and intricate — so much so that we'll need the whole book to see how it works, even with respect to just the few words under consideration.

And these words by no means exhaust the vocabulary of humanism, or even its dominant vocabulary. Other powerful humanist-related words could just as well have been selected for examination but were excluded for various practical reasons. One such group of words, the rationalist set including *reason–consciousness–awareness–control*, is given only passing attention here because the nature of its power over us has recently been examined in depth by David Ehrenfeld in *The Arrogance of Humanism* (1978). Although Ehrenfeld's focus is not directly on the words themselves but on the concepts and beliefs associated with them, his analysis is close enough to the one I would have done that a lengthy examination of my own would have been merely repetitive. Another large area of leading language connected with humanism, the language of technology, has also been avoided here except where attention to it is necessary for understanding the power of the words under consideration. The reason for otherwise excluding technology-related terms is just that they would need a book of their own in order to be adequately examined.

The selection of *self, growth, relative, relationship,* and their associated words as the focus of the book's attention has been determined by another factor as well. These are words that have come to play an especially powerful role in the area of our lives that I find myself now most concerned about: the private and domestic realm. Every book on words (except, of course, unabridged dictionaries) makes some such selection based on its main area of concern, no matter how general the title of the book sounds. C. S. Lewis's *Studies in Words* (1960) and William Empson's *The Structure of Complex Words* (1967), though both exploring the general workings of language, are particularly concerned with how language works in literature; so they select for examination words like *nature, sense,* and *wit.* Similarly, Stuart Chase's once very influential *The Tyranny of Words* (1938) and Raymond Williams's recent *Keywords* (1976), while also exploring how language operates in general, are especially concerned about the operations of language in the socio-political area of our public lives; they therefore focus on words like *democracy, capitalism, equality,* and *masses.* Even I. A. Richards's *How To Read a Page* (1942) and S. I. Hayakawa's *Language in Thought and Action* (1939–78), both of which are concerned with an extremely broad area of language use, still have a central focus that determines which words they give most attention to; the focus for Richards is on how words affect our private thought, for Hayakawa on how they affect our public communication. My central concern with how we live our private lives has led me to pay particular attention to the words we live with, and in a sense live by, in our everyday comings and goings. I've noticed that we rarely, any of us, go through a day without at least the passing company of a *relationship* or an *opinion* or a *development* or a *self* or one of their associates; and I've wanted to know what difference it makes that these words are so much with us.

But though these particular four sets of words have been selected because of their power in the private and domestic area of our lives, the book's examination of them is not at all confined to this area. In fact, what I've come to see in the course of looking into the way these words lead us is that — and this is one of the book's themes — their attraction in any one area of our lives is intricately connected with their attraction in other areas. Going words tend to go all over the place, and to come from all over the place as well. The attraction of these particular words comes to a large extent, as we'll see, from their associations with certain prestigious fields of academic research, especially psychology, sociology, biology, and physics; and so to understand how these words operate in the area of our private lives, we have to look into their operations in these fields, as well as in other areas (like business, government, religion) where these words play a leading part.

The subject matter of the book has had to be, that is, interdisciplinary. And the book's approach and methodology are interdisciplinary, or nondisciplinary, as well. A great many current disciplines — including psychology, neurology, anthropology, philosophy, literary criticism, linguistics, semiotics, semantics, and communications — are engaged in the study of language. Their particular methodologies and specialized vocabularies often allow them to see deeply into the workings of language covered by their particular field; but these specialized vocabularies can also keep them from seeing how what they're studying connects with the studies of other fields. Since the operations of language that we'll examine here run through a variety of fields, I've drawn gratefully on the findings of many disciplines, but have drawn away from the specialized vocabularies of all of them.

Instead, I've drawn my methodological vocabulary as much as possible from ordinary language. This approach has the additional advantage of allowing me to speak directly to the audience I primarily have in mind: the general reader. While certain sections of the book, which examine what a particular discipline has done with a set of leading words, will, I hope, be of use to members of that discipline, the book as a whole is addressed not to the members of any particular discipline but to anyone who can read and who likes to think about "what it all means."

Rochester, N.Y.   P.R.
September 1983

Acknowledgments

One of the pleasures of writing a book about common words, words that move into and out of many different areas of thought and practice, is following the words into each of these areas and finding there people who really know what they're talking about. I've seized on such people, have interrogated them intrusively about what the words I was following were doing in their particular area, and have always received the most perceptive and good-natured of replies. I'd especially like to thank, for their professional advice on specific matters, Betsy Haigh, Dr. Christopher Hodgman, Holly and Michael Kane, Michael Nill, and Dr. Kenneth Zierler. For generously giving careful critical readings of whole chapters on their areas of expertise I'd like to thank Ronald Levao, Margaret Poloma, Stephen Rosenthal, Susan Wolfson, and Gerald Zuriff. Ellen Kuiper also read portions of the manuscript and offered illustrations which I've gratefully made use of.

The extensive library facilities in my adopted hometown of Rochester, New York, made research for this book a delight to do. The Rochester Public Library's impressive resources provided me with most of the materials I needed; and they were always provided quickly and easily thanks to the well-informed, helpful staff and to administrative policies designed with a sensitive concern for library patrons. Specialized historical and technical materials that a public library couldn't be expected to have were graciously made available to me, by successive Heads of Circulation, at the University of Rochester Library. Herb Leventer, whose Park Avenue Book Store has become a sort of personal research center for Rochester's many writers and avid readers, enthusiastically acted as my emergency research consultant, finding on his shelves exactly what I'd run in for or immediately ordering for me what he didn't have in stock.

I'd like to thank two people who helped bring this book into existence without their being aware of it. Richard Poirier, who was head of the graduate program in English at Rutgers University when I was a student there in the late 1960s, encouraged us all to apply what we'd learned about reading literature to our reading of nonliterary language, especially the language of popular culture. His 1967 essay on the Beatles in *Partisan Review* was an inspiration for us. Richard Ohmann, who was editor of *College English* when I sent a couple of articles there in the early 1970s, encouraged me to think and write about the way language shapes and is shaped by social movements and institutions. Through his warm, supportive replies to my occasional letters over the years and through his own published writings, he has guided my thinking so strongly that it's hard for me to believe I've never met him.

For the practical business of getting the book written and prepared for publication, generous support has come from many directions. Curtis Church and Kim Lewis, at Oxford University Press, have worked on the manuscript with an intelligent attention that puts me in awe of their editorial talents. Andrea Walter and Alan Fischler, my department heads at Rochester Institute of Technology, have cheerfully readjusted my teaching schedule from year to year so that I could concentrate on writing. Pat Schurr and my student intern, Mary Steiner, have provided a variety of indispensable support services at crucial times. So have Duane Litchfield and Michael More, brilliant friends who have also given hours to poring over portions of the manuscript with me to help me figure things out.

Three other special friends, who have supported this project from the beginning in so many ways that they're practically collaborators, deserve separate thanks: Robert Atwan, who got it started one night at dinner five years ago when he responded with a rousing "yes!" to my hesitant question "do you think I should write a book about the words that drive us wild?" and who then kept it going by supplying me with source suggestions and esoteric old usages culled from his voluminous reading, by acting as my informal agent, and by sending back stimulating comments on the earliest drafts of the manuscript; my editor, John Wright, whom I first met over the phone when he called to say, after seeing Part One, "I like it, let me see more," who waited for more with the patience and good humor and wise guidance that have made me value his friendship as one of the greatest rewards of having written the book, and who nobly waged a losing battle against my tendency to turn out too-long sentences like this one; and my husband, George Dardess, the extent of whose loving support is beyond words.

P.R.

Contents

PART THREE
It's All Relative — or Is It?

PART FOUR
Relationships

ONE

The Attractions of *Self*

Introduction

If the word *self* were a stone and the sentences we hear or read or say were pathways, we'd probably be unable to get through an ordinary day without stumbling across all the stones in our way. The lines of best-sellers, popular magazines, and television talk shows are strewn with *self:* we're urged to fulfill ourselves, realize ourselves, know ourselves, be aware of (but not beware of) ourselves, love ourselves, create ourselves, feel good about ourselves, actualize ourselves, express ourselves, improve ourselves. Self-fulfillment therapy and self-improvement courses are booming businesses, run by alchemists who know how to turn the stones of *self* into gold. There is even in the city where I live an organization called The Self Center: a perfect title for our times, in which the self stands firmly in the center of our path, worshipped as our rock and our redeemer.

If we turn from the main roads of popular public discourse (and by discourse I mean all uses of verbal language, both written and spoken) into the areas of special-interest groups, we still stumble upon *self* almost wherever we go. "Women's self-knowledge," "self-fulfillment," and "self-identification" are proclaimed as goals of the Women's Movement. "Energy self-sufficiency" is our nation's goal, and "Palestinian self-determination" a goal for many in the Middle East.

Even on the narrower roads of academic disciplines, the ground remains familiar. We find *self* all over the place in the writings of philosophy: no surprise, since the self has been one of philosophy's prime subjects of study ever since the Renaissance. Recent philosophical books like *The Nature of the Self,* then, follow a time-honored tradition. But in the profession of literary criticism the hundreds of recent articles and books taking *self* as their subject ("Saul Bellow's Idea of Self," "The Divided Self in the Fiction of Henry James," "The Flexibility of the Self in Renaissance Literature," *Imagining a Self*) are a relatively new development, and an unexpected one unless we realize that literary criticism is much more in touch with popular concerns than is usually granted.

When we come to psychology, *self* is no longer just a stone that we trip over, or pass by, or stoop to examine, on our way; it has swollen into a huge rock, even a cave, which we have to enter, explore, probe the depths of as we go through the discourse of the profession. And as we go through, we find ourselves coming full circle to where we began, since the cave of psychology opens onto the main road of popular discourse — even, we could say, spills onto it, considering the amount of best-seller material (*Games People Play; I'm OK, You're OK; Passages; Pulling Your Own Strings; Living, Loving, and Learning* is just some of it) that is the direct product of psychology.

Once we notice how often *self* turns up in our current public discourse, both popular and specialized, we can easily see why *self* is a main term in our private discourse as well, and even in our private thoughts. The going terms of an age tend to be, naturally, the ones we think with, talk to our family and friends with, figure out things with. So it's no surprise that we often think these days in terms of *self,* seeing *myself* as the unquestioned justification for almost any action and as the goal toward which everything else must lead. Adolescents choosing a career are counseled, for example, to study themselves and know themselves fully in order to figure out which career will be best (meaning most self-fulfilling). We don't question whether, in laying our heavily weighted *self* on people who are already at the most self-absorbed stage of life, we might be burdening them unfairly, even preventing them from moving at all. Nor do we question our own or our friends' divorces when they're justified, as they often are, in terms of *self* (self-fulfillment, self-realization, etc.); there's no doubt that without the word *self*, and the values and concepts it currently brings with it, the divorce rate would be considerably lower than it is.

But what are, exactly, the values and concepts that *self* brings with it? From the examples given so far, we can see that *self* has a clearly positive value — doubly positive, in fact. Repeated use of and attention to any word gives it a certain positive value, the value of being treated as worthy of our attention. *Self* undoubtedly has this sort of attraction for us. But we can be attracted to a word, in the sense of making great use of it and paying attention to it and to what it stands for, without finding it attractive in the sense of desiring or respecting or approving of what it stands for. *Cancer*, for example, or *inflation* or *immature* or *victimized:* these words are attractive in the first sense but not the second; we use the words repeatedly but find their referents repellent. *Self*, however, attracts us in both ways: it carries the positive value of being a much-used word and also the positive value of referring to something we like.

All of the words examined in this book carry the first sort of positive value; they're words that we use a lot today. Little more will be said, then, about this sort of value. When I refer to a word's "value," I mean, except in a few places that will be clearly specified, value of the other sort: the value a word gets from our attitude toward what it stands for. Such value can be positive or negative, and it can be so much a part of a word's meaning that whenever we use the word we practically see a plus or minus sign over it: the sign of our approval or longing or some other positive attitude, or else of some negative attitude like our disapproval or maybe our fear. Not all words carry such vivid values, of course.

The many words that we don't feel strongly about either way carry neither a plus nor a minus sign. But these neutral words won't concern us much in the book, since our subject is words that have a strong pull on us in one direction or the other.

Though I don't want to get bogged down here in methodology, I have to make just one more distinction in order to be accurate about the way *self* pulls us: a distinction between the ways that a word's values, whether positive or negative, can be carried. Words lead complex lives and lead us along with them in complex ways; if we want to see how we're being led, rather than being led along blindly, we have to make an effort to follow our language with our eyes open to its subtle workings. What we see, then, when we look at how words carry their values, is that two different ways are possible. Some words carry their values inherently, in their very beings, so to speak: these are words whose referent *is* a certain value, words like *good, pleasure, comfortable,* or, on the other side, *disgraceful, worthless, evil.* Many more words, though, carry their values not as inherent parts of themselves but *ad*herently, like labels stuck on their heads or behind their backs, or like little flags sticking up from them and bearing the imprint of a plus or a minus. These are words whose referent is not itself a value and which take on whatever attitude we have toward the referent at the time. Adherent values can therefore change over the years, as our attitudes do. For example, *sex* for the Victorians carried, at least on the surface of public discourse, a minus of untouchability, as if the word itself carried VD; whereas for us *sex* has become a bearer of all the good things of life, a word universally proclaimed from the rooftops by faces beaming with pleasure. Or *simple,* which once carried the positive sense of "guileless" or "sincere" when applied to a person, now tends to carry the negative scornful implication of "simple-minded" or "simpleton." Adherent values can vary not only over time but for different speakers at the same time: *car* spoken by the president of General Motors carries a proud plus, but in the mouth and mind of an environmentalist fighting air pollution, or of an energy conservationist, it carries a menacing minus, the sign of the skull and crossbones.

Self's positive value today is of the adherent and almost universal kind, like that of *sex*. Though critics of our self-concern have started speaking out in the past few years and so have begun to move *self* into the ambivalent category of *car*, *self* is still generally seen as an unquestionably good thing. But what's so good about it? What is there in *self* that we find so attractive? This is a question, really, about what *self* means to us. And it's a hard question to answer, not only because *self* has a variety of meanings, but also because *meaning* itself (and here another dual distinction is necessary) means at least two things. By *meaning* we mean the definition of a word: *jogging,* for example, means running at a slow, regular pace. But by *meaning* we also mean the concept or concepts carried by — or, as we usually say, "behind" — a word: *jogging* now carries the concept of good health, physical well-being, and even for some people mental well-being and peace of mind. Note that along with this concept of jogging as well-being (physical or mental) comes a positive value; the mere definition of jogging is neutral. Concepts often, as in this case, imply values: the attractiveness of jogging today seems to lie in the concepts behind it.

Whether or not this is also the case for *self* we can't say until we've sorted out its various definitions and concepts. This can be done most clearly, I think, by means of a brief historical sketch of the word. Words tend to collect and drop meanings (both definitions and concepts) over time, and generally to do more collecting than dropping; so by following *self*'s history we can start to see where our current sense of *self* comes from. We can also note along the way whether *self* has always been, as it is for us now, doubly attractive, drawing both our attention and our praise.

1

From "God sylfa"
to "I celebrate myself"

The *self* is a common noun today, but it hasn't always been. *Self* began life, in English, with no substantive existence, but merely as a means by which to emphasize or reflect back on or indicate identity with something else. Today the emphatic and reflexive functions, as grammarians call them, are usually performed by the compounds *myself, yourself, itself,* etc. We say "I myself wouldn't do a thing like that" or "the debate itself could go on for hours." Old and Middle English would have said, though with different spellings, "I self" and "debate self." Actual examples given by the *Oxford English Dictionary** go from 900 ("Nu is rodera Weard, God sylfa [self] mid us": "Now is the guardian of the heavens, God himself, with us") through the 1500s ("Thys is the thing selfe that is in debate"). A related use of *self* during its early life was to emphasize possession, the way we now do with the adjective *own:* in *Beowulf,* Hildeburh committed "hire selfre suna" (her own son) to the flames of Hnaef's funeral pyre. This use lasted into the seventeenth century, as in "They gormandize at their selfe pleasures."

---

*Hereafter called by its familiar name, the *OED,* the *Oxford English Dictionary* is the source for all my etymologies and all quotations for which no other citation is given.

During this same period, the tenth through the sixteenth centuries, *self* was also used in the way that I've just used "same": to indicate identity with something else. A man in the sixteenth century was said to be "of this selfe opinion with Plato"; another "was requited with the selfe treachery that he offered before." (An extension of this meaning of *self* as "same" is still found, though rarely, in descriptions of implements when we want to say that one part is of the same material as the rest: an *OED* 1888 example is "a solid tool with a self-handle.") Note that in its emphatic, reflexive, and identifying functions, *self* carried no value marker, no sign that emphasis, reflexiveness, or identity were either good or bad. This neutrality of *self* seems appropriate, since in itself *self* had no content, no substance. It just pointed elsewhere.

Self first became a substantive by accident — by a spelling accident. In the Old English genitive *his selfes, selfes* was a pronominal adjective modifying *his;* but since the spelling was the same as if *selfes* were a genitive noun modified by *his, selfes* came to be seen in this case as a noun. And once seen on its own in this (genitive) case, substantive *self* spread to other cases, so that by 1300 it made independent appearances in expressions like "my own self" or "your two selves." But even though the noun *self* came into being by accident, it wouldn't have lasted unless there had been a need for it. As the *OED* says, "Although the substantive use of the pronoun thus appears to have originated in morphological processes, it came to supply a need of expression which has been felt and variously supplied in other languages." The need seems to have been for the concept of reflexiveness to be given independent existence: that is, for reflexiveness to be seen in its own right.

Once on its own, however, *self* seems almost immediately to have been rejected: "Oure own self we sal deny, And folow oure lord god al-myghty" is a 1400 instance quoted by the *OED*. Standing now for reflexiveness, *self* gets judged as reflexiveness gets judged. And since reflexiveness, as reference to oneself, can take on the negative implications of exclusive or excessive reference to oneself, or reference to oneself at the expense of some other more desirable referent, *self* can take on a minus sign and be set in opposition to a corresponding plus. In the quotation above, negative *self* is opposed to positive *God,* a common opposition which we'll see more of later. Notice, though, that the opposition "negative *self* / positive *God*" implies the opposition "positive *self* / negative *God*" as well. That is, if "oure own self" hadn't had some positive pull, the 1400 writer wouldn't have had to pull away from it and deny it. Early reflexive *self,* then, while proclaimed as negative, must also have had some positive attraction.

Reflexive *self* doesn't have to carry either value sign, however. It can be simply neutral, as in "If the discussion were confined to your two selves" (Jowett's 1875 translation of Plato). Many early instances of substantive reflexive *self* are of this neutral sort, especially those where *self* is a noun possessed by another noun: "For that thei abused the kynges selfes" (1542); "And Wisdoms self Oft seeks to sweet retired Solitude" (Milton, 1634). A similar later (1816) instance is:

> Though dark his brain
> It has, thou seest, an heavenly visitor
> That comfort brings when reason's self is gone.

In cases like these, *self* seems to be more than just emphatic — more than *itself* alone would imply. Something closer to "being" or "essence" or "real identity" seems to be suggested here by *self,* though not with the specific philosophical implications that *self* could take on, as we'll see, after the Renaissance. But if we can't be sure about *self*'s definition in cases like those just quoted, we can be sure about its value, which is clearly neutral: the king, wisdom, and reason are being neither praised nor condemned for having a self.

In its early life as a noun, then, *self* stood for the concept of reflexiveness, and reflexiveness tended either to be a neutral concept or to take on negative implications. *Self* didn't at first, in other words, have much positive attraction: it drew little attention and little praise. But all this changed dramatically in the Renaissance. From its modest place near the wings, where it quietly pointed elsewhere or turned away with bowed head, submitting humbly to rejection, *self* suddenly leapt onto center stage to the accompaniment of trumpets, cymbals, and loud adoring cheers. Or, to be more precise, we should say that *self* split into several roles: it kept performing (though more and more rarely) its original modest functions, as we've seen from some of the dates of those performances; but its major appearances were now in its new role at (even as) the center of attention, making a spectacle of itself.

One way of putting what happened in the Renaissance is to say that reflexiveness became a subject: a subject of investigation, of celebration, of controversy. The concept of reflexiveness had been around, as we've seen, for centuries: but only in the Renaissance did it become a dominant concept — one of the concepts, that is, that significantly shaped the behavior and thinking of the time. The reasons self-reflection became a major activity in the Renaissance — an activity engaging the energy, skill, inventiveness, and devotion of the best educated minds — have been covered by innumerable scholarly studies beginning with Jakob Burckhardt's *Civilization of the Renaissance in Italy*. What we should note here, for our purpose of tracing the history of the word *self,* is the role that *self* played in this explosion of what Burckhardt called "unbridled subjectivity."

I've said that *self,* in the Renaissance, leapt onto center stage and made a spectacle of itself. It didn't leap out there alone, though; generally it held some other term by the hand — or by the hyphen. Though there had been a few *self* compounds in Old English, most disappeared in Middle English, and, according to the *OED,* "self first appears as a living formative element about the middle of the sixteenth century." Then we find, making rapid entrances one after another, such couplings as *self-praise* (1549), *self-love* (1563), *self-pride* (1586), *self-contained* (1591), and *self-regard* (1595). Similar pairs kept entering the scene through the seventeenth century: *self-knowledge* (1613), *self-preservation* (1614), *self-made* (1615), *self-pity* (1621), *self-denial* (1642), *self-interest* (1649), *self-confi-*

dence (1653), *self-created* (1677), *self-consciousness* (1690), and so on. Note that these couplings have remained in our linguistic repertoire to this day. Note too that, for the most part, they carry plus signs with them: they signal, that is, a positive attitude toward the self. Of the compounds just listed, only *self-denial* implies that the self should be definitely denied rather than preserved, pitied, known, loved, created, etc. *Self-pride* and *self-interest* also tended at first to reflect negatively on the self (though that tendency has been reversed today, for reasons we'll see later): *self-pride* at first meant excessive or unjustified satisfaction in one's achievements; and *self-interest* meant something like *selfishness,* a word which made its first appearance at about the same time (1643). These negative *self* compounds were, though, as I've said, in the minority; most of the terms newly compounded with *self* shook *self*'s hand with delight, honor, enthusiasm, and praise.

All these new compounds for talking about the self wouldn't have rushed into the language if the self hadn't suddenly been much talked about in the Renaissance. And yet there's an inaccuracy in putting it just this way. What was talked about was indeed what we now call the self, or the concept of the self; but to refer to this concept, the word *self* itself was rarely, if ever, used. We're so accustomed to hearing about the Renaissance "concept of the self," a phrase which appears in almost every twentieth-century discussion of the subject, that it's strange to discover that this is not in fact a Renaissance phrase. Not that the concept of the self didn't, as we're told, first come on the scene in the Renaissance; it did. But it came in clothes not exactly like those we're now used to seeing it wear. When the Queen in *Richard II,* for example, says "my inward soul with nothing trembles," we tend to see trembling her "inner self." And when later in the play Richard laments that "[I] know not now what name to call myself," we write in the margin that he's having an "identity crisis" or that he "has a weak sense of self." And when contemporary Renaissance scholars quote, as they love to do, God's speech to Adam from Pico della Mirandola's *Oration on the Dignity of Man* —

> We have made thee neither of heaven nor of earth, neither mortal nor immortal, so that with freedom of choice and with honor, as though the maker and molder of thyself, thou mayest fashion thyself in whatever shape thou shalt prefer. Thou shalt have the power, out of thy soul's judgment, to be reborn into the higher forms, which are divine

— when they quote this and then comment on it, they tend in their commentary to translate Pico's combination of *soul, shaping* metaphors and reflexive forms into more familiar terms: "I suppose [says one commentator] there has never been . . . a more extravagant assertion of human freedom, particularly of the freedom to select one's destiny, to mold and transform the self."

Where we today would refer to *the self,* then, Renaissance writers were likely to say *soul* or *man,* or to use a reflexive pronoun or a *self* compound. Yet by these terms they were indeed referring to what we call a concept of the self. For the Renaissance this concept was already — immediately — a multiple one. As the examples quoted suggest, it included what we would call concepts of identity and of self-creation. It also included, as we saw in connection with the new *self* compounds, the concept of reflexiveness, but expanded and elevated to become what we could call the concept of subjectivity. Subjectivity — man's awareness of himself as a subject — in turn involved concepts of individuality (Italy began "to swarm with individuality," says Burckhardt), of personality, and of the powers of reason. "Involved" is a vague term with which to indicate connections, yet it's about as precise a term as we have in English for talking about concepts that developed together in intense interrelation. We can be more precise, though, about the value carried by these interrelated concepts that we group together as "the concept of self." The concept of self marched into the Renaissance loaded with pluses: though a few spear-like minuses were poked at it in terms like *self-interest,* they barely penetrated the multiple-layered regal robes of self-glorification and were generally pushed back anyway by the always-present surrounding crowds worshipping this new concept — worshipping, that is, themselves.

It wasn't long before the concept of self, with all its positive attractions, attracted the noun *self* as well; but by then the concept of self was itself changing. As man studied himself (and it was indeed man, not woman, who engaged in this self-scrutiny), searching intensely and devotedly for his true nature and definition, he discovered in himself various apparently essential qualities, each of which tended to get attached to the word *self*. And so as the noun *self* came into its own in the seventeenth and eighteenth centuries as a major term in definitions of man, it actually came into three different and sometimes conflicting "owns." One of these, *self* as "one's personal welfare and interests as an object of concern, chiefly in bad sense" (OED), seems to have been a negative reaction to all the positive attention that man was giving himself. The earliest OED example of this new definition of *self* as selfishness — "Self is the great Anti-Christ and Anti-God in the World" (1680) — reminds us, as it must have been intended to remind its readers, that primary concern with one's personal welfare is opposed to primary concern with God. This is the same "negative *self* / positive *God*" opposition that we saw when *self* first became a noun, standing for reflexiveness. Here, almost three hundred years later, the opposition remains, but the negated *self* side is loaded with a much more densely complex content — loaded, that is, with everything that had been stuffed into the Renaissance concept of self.

But while *self* as selfishness reflected negatively on *self,* the other two new definitions of *self* were neutral or possibly even, in a sense, positive. One of these was a definition invented by seventeenth-century philosophy to serve a particular function: seeing man as primarily a conscious, thinking being, philosophers like Locke used the term *self* to denote the permanent subject of that consciousness. Locke also used *person* for almost the same purpose, a sign of how problematic this definition of *self* was — and would have to be. Since concepts of man's true nature can only be speculative, the terms that stand for these concepts are necessarily surrounded by question marks; and so what philosophy now calls "the problem of the self" was contained in this new definition of *self* from the beginning.

Compounding the problem, if not for philosophy then for the language generally, was another usage of *self* that developed at the same time as the philosophical definition and that to some extent conflicted with it. In this third usage, *self* was "what one is at a particular time" (such as "my former self" or "my later self") or "what one is in part" (such as "my better self" or "natural self" or "spiritual self," as in "Every man may, yea, ought to love himself: not his sinful self, but his natural self: especially his spiritual self, the new nature in him" — 1703). This third definition of *self* — we can call it, for convenience, the partial *self* — conflicted with the *self* of philosophy in two ways. While philosophical *self* was permanent (the permanent subject of consciousness), partial *self* was changing, for example from a former to a later self; and while philosophical *self* was unified (the single subject of consciousness), partial *self* was divided, or was the product of division, one part of us set potentially *against* other parts.

These three new definitions of *self* that took shape in the seventeenth and eighteenth centuries — *self* as self-interest, *self* as a principle of unified identity, and *self* as an element of divided identity (one of our many selves) — are familiar to us because they're still our basic definitions of *self* today. New concepts have been added to these definitions over the years, as we'll soon see, but no new basic definitions have arisen; so in these three definitions we can start to get a picture of our current sense of *self*. But the picture we get is a confusing one. *Self* as a permanent unity certainly looks very different from *self* as a changing part. And *self* as self-interest seems drawn from another area of meaning altogether: it seems designed to pass judgment at least as much as to identify. Further, the judgment it passes tends to contradict the judgment mutely implied by the other two *self*s. While *self* as self-interest scowls at us (at least in these early years), condemning our self-concern as selfishness, the other two *self*s sit expressionless, neither openly smiling nor frowning; but they're more ready to smile than to frown, to smile at all the attention they're getting as they become key terms of modern discourse. They carry, then, the faint markings of an emerging plus sign, the sign that shows them worthy of our attention; while the other *self* (dare we say their other self?) boldly condemns if not exactly this attention to one's *self*, then at least attention to oneself.

To fill out the picture of our current sense of *self*, we now have to trace the nineteenth- and twentieth-century developments that added their lines and color to the picture. Chief among these in the nineteenth century was the Romantic movement, which didn't add new lines so much as extend certain lines and highlight certain areas drawn in the Renaissance. The area of *feelings*, for example, had been part of the Renaissance concept of self: Burckhardt praises Dante because "with unflinching frankness and sincerity he lays bare every shade of his joy and his sorrow." But while feelings were only a small part of the Renaissance self, in Romanticism they swelled to become almost the whole, and the expression and celebration of one's personal passion came close to seeming the entire purpose of one's existence. This Romantic self, swollen with its passions, swelled, in turn, to include the whole world in its compass, a world which it then — as at the end of Wagner's *Ring* — could destroy along with itself when its passion swelled to bursting, or could re-create in its own image, as Whitman comically and exuberantly imagines in "Song of Myself."

Renaissance poets also had seen themselves as creating new worlds in their work, and they had puzzled about the obviously blasphemous implications of man's taking over God's creative function. The puzzle had been there, as the Renaissance knew, from (almost) the beginning: when God created man in His own image, did He therefore create man a creator like Himself? And Christianity had only added to the mystery when it saw God come into man through Christ: if the divine was *in* man, did this mean that an external force (divinity) entered man and lent him its powers, while also remaining outside him; or that man himself contained *all* of divinity in himself? The Renaissance hedged and squirmed over this puzzle but tended to go with the first possibility, while Romanticism, with its two extra centuries of man-centered experience, leaned toward the second.

But puzzles remained even in this choice. If man contains all of divinity in himself, if man is the locus of God, is man divine by God's gift or in his own right as man? The puzzle lies in a slippage in the word *divine*: originally attached to God, divinity moves into man when God does; and after long residence there, it starts to look as if it belongs to man. The slippage isn't apparent as long as God and one's self are in harmony: for example, when Emerson refers in "Self-Reliance" to "that divine idea which each of us represents," we don't know whether the divine idea is ours or God's, but we don't really need to know. It's when a conflict arises between oneself and traditional godliness that we see how divinity can slip, for Romanticism, from God to man. Emerson recalls in "Self-Reliance":

> I remember an answer which when quite young I was prompted to make to a valued adviser who was wont to importune me with the dear old doctrines of the church. On my saying "What have I to do with the sacredness of traditions, if I live wholly from within?" my friend suggested — "But these impulses may be from below, not from above." I replied, "They do not seem to me to be such; but if I am the Devil's child, I will live then from the Devil." No law can be sacred to me but that of my nature.

A Renaissance character might have made such a blasphemous self-assertion, setting his own sacredness above all else (including, implicitly, God's); but he would have been punished, like Macbeth, for this claim. But Romanticism reveled in its flirtations with blasphemy; "Nothing, not God, is greater to one than one's-self is," Whitman exults. To the Renaissance picture of the divine creative force in the poet, Romanticism added its own raging color, splashing such divine brilliance over the individual self that God nearly got painted out of the picture altogether (as He in fact was, and still is, in some later versions of Romanticism). Romanticism also enlarged the area of individual creativity to include not just the poet, as in the Renaissance, but all people. Whitman's song of *my*self is sung to everyone's self: "It is you talking just as much as myself . . . I act as the tongue of you."

Filling each self with divinity, Romanticism set this divine self against society. This *self / society* opposition, formulated most influentially by Rousseau, places all natural goodness in the self and all evil in society, which is evil precisely because it threatens what is good (passion, creativity, individuality, freedom) in the self. Note that with this opposition of positive *self* to negative *society,* the minus sign attached to *self* as self-interest disappears. Self-interest, attention to one's personal welfare, can in this construction be only good; so while in 1680 we were told that "Self is the great Anti-Christ and Anti-God in the World," in 1870 — with *self* now on the plus side with *God* — we can be assured that "respect to self and its ultimate good pertains to the very nobility of man's nature" (*OED*).

This is a change not in the definition of *self,* but in the value carried by it. The Romantic *self,* and all that comes with it, is wholly positive. What comes with it — passion, divinity, creativity, individuality, freedom — all these attach to all three definitions of *self.* But they attach even more to words like *individual, man,* and the personal pronouns *I* and *you;* these are the words that Romanticism used most frequently to refer to what we today call the self. As with the Renaissance, we have to make a distinction for Romanticism between its concept of the self and its use of the word *self.* Though Romanticism says *self* much more than the Renaissance did, it still doesn't say it nearly as much as does twentieth-century commentary on Romanticism (including my own in these paragraphs). Romanticism did its great work on the concept of self without making any more use of *self* than of related words like *individual* or *I;* it was modern (post-Freudian) psychology that took special hold of the word *self* and made it central to the concept — and to millions of people's daily lives.

2

Psychology's *Self*

Psychology's Slippery Sense of *Self*

In 1956, a psychologist began his book with the statement: "Concern for the self with all its contributing attributes and potentials is rapidly becoming a central focus of contemporary psychological inquiry." Today we might smile at the obviousness of such a statement, but our smile should be one not of scorn at its naiveté but of admiration at the astuteness of its prediction. *Self* and its compounds have indeed come to take up much of psychology's attention — so much that they fill, for example, fourteen columns of titles in the January–June 1982 *Psychological Abstracts* Subject Index (with *"Self Concept," "Self Esteem,"* and *"Self Perception"* the longest entries) and seven inches of the Psychiatric Card Catalog at the University of Rochester Medical School (including titles like "On the Beginnings of a Cohesive Self," "The Finding and Becoming of Self," and "On the Development of the Experience of Mental Self, the Bodily Self, and Self Consciousness"). These statistics, though admittedly crude, confirm the sense of probably anyone who comes in contact with psychology (and is there anyone who doesn't?) that contemporary psychology is inseparable from *self.*

The "contemporary psychology" I refer to includes, as my reference to the Psychiatric Card Catalog indicates, psychiatry and psychoanalysis and some of the psychotherapies as well. This inclusion is sure to rankle some members of these various disciplines who insist on the distinctness of their fields. But in the use they make of *self*, these fields are far from distinct. In fact, they seem to have developed their sense of *self* on common ground: ground initially laid by Freud (who, however, made no significant use of the term) and then sown and cultivated by workers with professional concerns and styles as varied as those of Jung, William James, Karen Horney, Carl Rogers, and Rollo May. The *self* produced by this crossbreeding has then spread into general public discourse from all the psychology-related fields except behaviorism, which has worked hard to hold back the spread. One field in particular, though, has been most strongly behind the push of *self* into popular discourse: the field known as "humanistic psychology" or "personal growth psychology" or "the human potential movement." Since my ultimate concern in this part of the book is with our popular sense of *self*, the psychology I have in mind when I talk about "psychology's *self*" is primarily this personal growth psychology. Primarily but not exclusively — because, as I've said, no *self* of any field of psychology is cut off from the *self* of the others.

What exactly *self* means for all these areas of psychology that make so much of it is surprisingly difficult to discover. Soon after the above-quoted psychologist began his book by noting psychology's central "concern for the self," another psychologist began hers by noting that "in psychological discussions the word 'self' has been used in many different ways." And sixteen years later, those differences hadn't yet been resolved: a 1977 article in *Psychology in the Schools* complains that "currently scores of theories and definitions of 'self' are found in the literature." In trying to find out what *self* means for psychology, then, we can't hope simply to open a dictionary of psychology and find there a comprehensive definition. Nor, it turns out, can we go to the literature itself to find clear statements of those scores of meanings: even though the self is one of psychology's central concerns, *the self* rarely gets directly defined by those concerned with it.

By "direct definition" I mean statements in the form "the self is. . . ." Occasionally in the literature we find such a statement: for example, "The self is . . . the center from which one sees and is aware of . . . different 'sides' of himself." More frequent, however, are indirect definitions of various kinds: definition by apposition ("it indicates that the person, the self, is generous"), by *or* ("the archetype of wholeness or of the self"), by *as* ("I speak now of the real self as that central inner force"), or by a combination of these ("conceiving ego or self as a constellation of interrelated attitudes"). Writers using grammatical forms such as these don't usually think of themselves as defining; yet these forms act as definitions, and in the absence of direct definitions we often have to rely on them to discover what writers mean by the words they use. Another, even more indirect, way of learning what is meant by psychology's *self* is by noticing the metaphors that *self* gets used in, or the terms that surround it. Even the terms that *self* gets opposed to will give us a clue about its definition: when we read, for example, that often a client "discovers that he exists only in response to the demands of others, that he seems to have no self of his own," we know that *self* is *not* exclusive responsiveness to others' demands and is some sort of opposition to those demands.

Reading through the writings of psychology, both technical and popular, with these various methods of definition as a guide, we can begin to sort out what psychologists have in mind by *self*. One thing they often seem to have in mind is that *self* is a goal of some kind. But the kind varies. It can be the goal of what sounds like a treasure hunt (the familiar "finding of one's self"), a trip ("the long journey to achieve selfhood"), a vegetable ("the maturation of the self"), or a vaguely Aristotelian process ("self-actualization is actualization of a self"). Sometimes, though, *self* seems not to be a goal but to have goals of its own: "the [mature] self now expresses . . . its intentions and goals."

In these various uses of *self* in relation to goals, the nature of the self's presence is unclear: on the way to finding, or achieving, or actualizing the self, is the self wholly absent before it's reached? or is it partly there all along? This problem about the presence of the self is solved when *self* is seen, as it is, for example, by Willard Gaylin in *Feelings: Our Vital Signs,* as a sort of balloon that expands and contracts with our moods: there's "that enlargement of self that goes into feeling good," whereas "in despair we have a reduced sense of self." In Gaylin's usage, the self is always fully present, but subject to extreme changes in size.

But while Gaylin's usage clarifies one aspect of *self,* it confuses another. In the passages just quoted, *self* and *sense of self* seem interchangeable: "enlargement of self" corresponds to "reduced sense of self." *Self,* then, seems to be equal to, or to mean, "sense of self." But how can this be? Can the sense, or awareness, of something be equal to the thing itself? Often in psychology (not only in Gaylin) this seems to be the case: *self* seems to mean "self-awareness" — awareness, knowledge, or perception of oneself. "The self is not the sum of the roles you play, but your capacity to know that you are the one playing these roles," writes Rollo May, defining *self* directly as the "capacity to know." Carl Rogers, too, seems to see *self* as a knowing or perceiving agent when he defines *self* as "an organized, fluid, but consistent conceptual pattern of perceptions." If *self* were consistently defined by psychology as a perceiving agent, we could infer that psychology uses *self* as a shorthand for *sense of self* or *awareness of self.* But such an inference becomes impossible to make when we find, elsewhere in psychology, *self* being treated not as the perceiving subject but as what is perceived: the *International Encyclopedia of Psychiatry, Psychology, Psychoanalysis, and Neurology* begins its entry on *self,* for example, with "The self is defined as the object of an individual's own perception." The confusion between subject and object reaches a limit (one hopes) when *self* appears as both the considering agent and the object of consideration in the same sentence:

> . . . when the self is free from any threat of attack . . . then it is possible for the self to consider these hitherto rejected perceptions, to make new differentiations, and to reintegrate the self in such a way as to include them.

Not only is *self* here both the considering agent and the object of that agent, it also is a "reintegrating" force. This usage of *self*, as an integrating or unifying force or function, is another common one in psychology — as common as *self* as goal (or possessor of goals) and *self* as awareness (or object of awareness). For Horney, for example, "the real self" is "that central inner force, common to all human beings and yet unique in each, which is the deep source of growth"; for Rollo May, "the self is the organizing function within the individual"; for social psychology, as presented in the encyclopedic *Psychology: A Study of a Science*, "ego or *self* is a developmental formation in the psychological makeup of the individual, ... a constellation of interrelated attitudes." (This synonymous use of *ego* and *self* is appropriate here, since Freud, who didn't use the term *self*, defined *ego* as "a psychical organization.") "Central inner force," "organizing function," "developmental formation," "constellation": these definitions of *self*, while having different shades of meaning ("force," for example, implies a pressure absent from "function"), share a common dual concept — of *self* as both pattern (organization) and oneness (unification). Heinz Kohut's notion of the "cohesion" of the self and Jung's definition of *self* as "the archetype of wholeness" also share this dual concept. Jung, in fact, chose the term *self* because he felt it was capable of expressing not only this duality but also certain paradoxes that he saw inherent in the archetype of wholeness: *self* was, he felt, "a term on the one hand definite enough to convey the essence of human wholeness and on the other hand indefinite enough to express the indescribable and indeterminable nature of this wholeness." (Jung's awareness and appreciation of the complexities of the term *self*, and his careful direct definitions and usage of it, stand out among the less than careful treatments that *self* usually gets in psychology.)

Along with the various technical and occasionally conflicting definitions of *self* that we've seen so far — *self* as goal (or as possessor of goals), as awareness (or as an object of awareness), and as unifying force or function — psychology sometimes uses *self* simply to mean "person," in our everyday sense of the word. This meaning is obviously intended in an appositive definition like Gaylin's ". . . the person, the self, is generous in the sharing of that self." And it's implied in a formulation like "the self now expresses . . . the purposes and values of its life," since what else besides a person can have "life"? *Self* as *person* is an equation that Rogers, too, often makes: as when his title "What It Means To Become a Person" is restated in the chapter as what it means to "get in touch with this real self." But for Rogers, *person* no longer has its everyday meaning: in everyday usage, "becoming" a person makes no sense; each of us already is a person.

Self as *person* gets complicated elsewhere in other ways. Rollo May, like Rogers, seems to equate "experiencing one's self as a self" with "becoming a person"; but he goes on to equate "becoming a person" with "the experience of one's identity as a being of worth and dignity." Though the inherent vagueness of the term *experience* makes it hard to pin down meanings connected with it, *self* apparently becomes here an attitude toward oneself: the attitude of respect for one's worth. *Self,* in other words, means "self-worth." But *self* can also apparently mean, elsewhere, "self-concern" or "self-interest." For Erich Fromm, one's "real self" is defined as one's true "self-interest," and his worry is "not that people are too much concerned with their self-interest, but that they are not concerned enough with the interest of their real self."

Self as self-interest brings us back to the *OED* because this is one of the three definitions of *self* that the *OED* gives as still current. Since the *OED* was written before the development of modern psychology, it doesn't include psychology's uses of *self* in its definitions. But we should be able, now, to include them ourselves, after our survey of what *self* means for psychology. Besides *self* as self-interest — which, we should note in passing, always carries a plus sign for psychology — the other current *OED* definitions were *self* as a principle of unified identity (*self* as a whole) and *self* as an element of divided identity (*self* as one of many selves, or as a part). Which of these definitions do psychology's uses of *self* fit into? Is *self* for psychology a whole or a part?

We have to conclude that it's both. When *self* is seen as a unifying force, as a "totality," as a "cohesive" principle, then it's being seen as a whole, as a principle of unified identity. When it's seen as a "real self," or (as by Laing) as a "false self" or a "true self," or as a "glorified self" or an "actual self" or a "despised self" (as in "From the position of the glorified self, the actual self with its human limitations is experienced as the despised self"), it's being seen as a part of a larger unity. Psychology's use of *self* as both whole and part originated, according to the *International Encyclopedia of Psychiatry, Psychology, Psychoanalysis, and Neurology,* with Freud:

> Freud's use of the word *Ich* (*I* or *ego*) encompasses a variety of meanings, such as the totality of one's own person as well as parts thereof like one's personality; in a more restricted sense it gradually came to represent also the system ego, one of the three structures (agencies) that make up the psychic apparatus. Freud's usage thus included the concept *self,* and in its lack of a precise definition did justice to the subtlety and compexity of psychoanalytic data and theory.
>
> The concept of the self as distinct from the ego began to emerge in post-Freudian psychoanalysis. . . .

Whether or not Freud's lack of a precise definition of *self* and *ego* did justice to the subtlety and complexity of psychoanalytic data and theory, I'm not qualified to say. But the practice of post-Freudian writing on psychology has hardly done justice to the subtlety of Freud's apparently deliberately imprecise definition of *ego,* or to Jung's sense of the necessarily paradoxical meaning of *self.* Great thinkers, like Freud and Jung, seem to be those capable of grasping and working productively within paradox — that is, within the contradictions that seem inherent in the key terms of our thought. For the rest of us with less capacious and comprehensive minds, the delicate balance of unified contradiction crumbles into petty scraps, and the clear paradox muddies as we stare at it. No wonder, then, that the followers of Freud and Jung have been unable to sustain the precise imprecision, or the imprecise precision, of Freud's definition of *ego* and Jung's of *self.* No wonder that today psychology has, instead of a clearly articulated if

complex working definition of *self*, a scattering of unclear, confused usages working at odds with one another.

Self's Companions in Psychology:
Inner–Individual–Feelings

How psychologists manage to work at all under such circumstances, when one of their key terms is unclear even to themselves,
is a fascinating and disturbing question. But it's a question I can't
pursue at this point, since my focus here is on psychology's use of
self not primarily as a term in a professional discourse, but as an
influence on our popular sense of *self*. And to understand that
influence, we have to look not just at how psychology defines (or
doesn't define) *self*, but also at the terms and values associated
with *self* in psychology. Definition, remember, is only part of a
word's meaning; the concepts carried by a word also add to its
meaning. And while concepts can get carried, for a word, by its
definition (the definition of *self* as a "constellation of interrelated
attitudes" carries, for example, the concept of organization), they
most often get carried by other terms that tag along after the word
wherever it goes. Words are in this way like people: we can learn
something about their characteristics and values by noticing who
they hang around with, what sets they travel in. What, then, are
the associates of psychology's *self*? In what company do we usually find it?

We've already noted psychology's *self* in frequent company with
the *growth–becoming–development* set, and in Part Two we'll look
more closely at the characteristics of that set of terms. For now,
then, we can focus on some of *self*'s other connections, as we find
them in the pages of modern psychology.

"Self-actualization is actualization of a self, and no two selves
are altogether alike," Abraham Maslow tells us. And in telling us
that no two selves are altogether alike, he's affirming a connection
between uniqueness and the self that is one of the basic connections of psychology. We've seen it affirmed already in Horney's
view of "the real self as that central inner force, common to all
human beings and yet unique in each." *Unique* is such a treasured

post-Renaissance, and especially Romantic, plus word (who in Western society dares not assume, and celebrate, the uniqueness of each of us?) that in our pleasure at receiving the special favor it bestows we tend not to notice the questionable nature of that favor. The question lying beneath *unique*'s gilded surface is this: if, as one psychologist puts it, "a man's self may be defined in terms of his unique manner of playing his roles," does this mean that a man automatically and always plays his roles uniquely, or is a "unique manner" the goal he's aiming for? Is uniqueness, in other words, a given or a goal? The question is lying in Maslow's formulation as well: are selves always not alike, or are they not alike only when they've become actualized?

A closely related question lies in the word *individual*, a frequent companion of *self* that often goes along with, or takes the place of, *unique*. We're often told by psychology, in effect, that "the individual must become an individual" or that "the individual fulfills himself by becoming a true individual." Such formulations — which I've presented in a cruder form than they usually appear, so that their structure stands out — pass on a slippage in *individual* that is part of our Renaissance–Romantic heritage: the notion of each individual (each one of us) as individual (unique). Since *unique,* as we've just seen, contains some slippage of its own (between uniqueness as a given and as a goal), this *individual–unique* connection slides unavoidably into the given-vs.-goal problem. And this whole problematic complex then slides into psychology's *person* when, as we saw earlier, psychology urges each person (each one of us, as given) to "become a person" (reach a certain goal, usually defined as "individuality"). We shouldn't be surprised to find the terms of the *unique–individual–person* set slipping into each other, and into each other's confusions, this way: associated terms, rather than settling each other down, tend to take on each other's problems. Nor should we be surprised to find this set slipping around in psychology just as it has in Western thought for hundreds of years. Psychology has neither created — nor resolved — the problem in the *unique–individual–person* set; it has just taken the whole slippery set and hooked it up to *self.*

Another *self*-associated set of terms that psychology has taken

over from Romanticism is the *inner–internal* set. For most psychologists who depend on *self*, *inside* is where the action is. Not
only where *their* action is (Horney, May, Rogers, Maslow all
proudly claim man's "inner" nature as their subject of study), but
also where *our* most important action is: "The struggle to become
a person takes place within the person himself." This struggle, this
inner action, is (we're told) of the greatest — even ultimate — importance. "The only question that matters," Rogers tells his clients
and his readers, "is: Am I living in a way which is deeply satisfying to me, and which truly expresses me?"

This question puts the ultimate reference of value (what in the
end matters) in the inner person, in "me" and my "deep satisfaction." *Inner–self*-oriented psychologists go even further, too, and
put inside the person the source of value (what tells us what matters) as well. As Rollo May puts it, "unless the individual himself
can affirm the value; unless his own inner motives, his own ethical
awareness, are made the starting place, no discussion of values
will make much real difference." The "personal values" that we
hear so much of (and so much praise of) from psychology are,
then, doubly personal and doubly internal: both their source and
their standard of reference are in the person alone. Everything that
matters, as well as everything that tells us what should matter, is
inside.

Putting their plus sign on what's "inside," these psychologists
go along with the rest of the Romantic opposition of positive *self*
to negative *society* and place a minus on what's seen as "outside."
In what sounds like Rousseau sifted through a filter of psychological terminology, the theories of Gordon Allport, Fromm, Horney,
May, Rogers, and Maslow get collectively summarized by the *International Encyclopedia of Psychiatry, Psychology, Psychoanalysis, and Neurology* along strict *self / society, inner / outer* lines:

> . . . man is basically constructive, accepting, creative, sponta-
> neous, open to experience, self-aware, and self-realizing. It is pa-
> rental, societal, and cultural controls, through manipulation of
> rewards and threats of punishment, which inhibit the otherwise
> natural development of self-expression and self-actualization.

Not all psychologists go along, though, with this *self* / *society* split and its congruence with *inside* / *outside*. Behaviorists refuse even to recognize *self* as a valid, independent term; and social psychologists, while liking the term *self*, refuse to cut it off from *society*. Following William James's expansion of the self "to include one's clothes, one's home, one's society," they see the self as, by definition, a social construct, the product of our interrelations with others. But in their battle to tear down the Romantic wall between *self* and *society*, they're fighting a still-strong tradition. As one social psychologist admits, "traditionally" experience "is subdivided into self (emotions, thoughts, memories, desires) vs. not self."

The parenthetical inclusion, here, of *emotions* as part of *self* brings us to one of psychology's favorite *self* associations: *feelings*. If *self* is there, we might ask rhetorically of psychology, can *feelings* be far behind? Actually, *feelings* have never been far behind *self*, and in a sense have been right next to it from the start. We could even say from before the start, since before there was a word for self in Western culture, Greek ψυχη covered both *feelings* and *self* (along with *life, soul, spirit,* and *personality*) in its large range of meaning. As the concept of self developed in the Renaissance, feelings went along with it, as we've seen, and played a part in that development. The part was small, though, compared to the grand role that feelings came to play in the Romantic self. Psychology has continued the time-honored connection between self and feelings, while bringing *self* and *feelings*, the words, into prominence in this connection.

Exactly what connection psychology sees between *self* and *feelings* is, however, not clear. In the formulation of the *International Encyclopedia of Psychiatry, Psychology, Psychoanalysis, and Neurology* that "the more real selfness one has, the greater is one's spontaneity of feelings," the connection seems loosely proportional. A tighter, and possibly different, connection seems to be made in Rogers's equation that the "experiencing of feeling . . . is really the discovery of unknown elements of self." Here the connection is of part to whole: *feeling* is grammatically parallel (and hence in a sense equal) to certain "elements of" self, and so pre-

sumably not to the whole self. But the part-to-whole connection
gets confused when Rogers also equates feelings with what he calls
one's "organic being": "when [the client] fully experiences the
feelings which at an organic level he *is* . . . , then he feels an
assurance that he is being a part of his real self." If feelings are a
"part" of the real self, and feelings are also what one at an organic
level "is," then when one fully "is" at an organic level, he is still
only "part" of his real self. What the rest of his real self consists
of, Rogers doesn't say.

Nor does he say how *feelings* as organic being, and / or as part
of the real self, connect with other definitions of *feelings* that he
gives elsewhere. In, for example, the statement "all of these diverse
attitudes are feelings," *feelings* are directly equated to *attitudes*.
But *feelings* then become *perceptions* in "I have found it enriching
to open channels whereby others can communicate their feelings,
their private perceptual worlds, to me." The apposition here makes
feelings apparently the same as *perceptions;* but right afterward
the two words are split by *and,* and thus presented as two separate
things (the therapist accepts the client "as having these perceptions
and feelings"). *Feelings* and *attitudes,* too, which we saw above as
one, can also appear as two: "the individual becomes more openly
aware of his own feelings and attitudes." Feelings then, for Rogers, appear to be, and not to be, both attitudes and perceptions
(neither of which is defined — nor is the relation between them);
feelings also have some sort of partial relation to real self and full
relation to "being" at an "organic" level; the connection, in turn,
between attitudes and / or perceptions and organic being is impossible to untangle. In fact, the entire web formed by the terms
feelings–self–organic–experience–attitude–perceptions appears in
Rogers's work with no perceivable pattern but rather as a knot
that has gotten hopelessly tangled on the loom of thought.

I'm paying particular attention to Rogers's work because of the
great influence that his treatment of feelings has had, both within
and outside of professional psychology. While his treatment of
feelings has certainly increased our sensitivity to and tenderness
toward each other, his treatment of *feelings* (the word) has, just

as certainly, decreased our sensitivity to language and our capacity for intellectual rigor. I question, further, whether feelings can be treated well when *feeling* is treated so shoddily. Rogers's therapy depends on words; its medium is talk. What sense can this talk make when both therapist and client have so little sense of one of its main terms?

An example of what Rogers considers model talk between himself and a client shows not only the extent to which they rely on *feel* and *feeling*, but also the sort of positive value that *feel(ing)* can carry despite its lack of precise definition:

> CLIENT: Really, I don't think I've had that feeling before. I've —uh, well, this really feels like I'm saying something that, uh, *is* a part of me really. (*Pause*) Or, uh, (*quite perplexed*) it feels like I sort of have, uh, I don't know. I have a feeling of *strength,* and yet, I have a feeling of — realizing it's so sort of fearful, of fright.

> THERAPIST: That is, do you mean that saying something of that sort gives you at the same time a feeling of, of strength in saying it, and yet at the same time a frightened feeling of *what* you have said, is that it?

> CLIENT: M-hm. I am feeling that.

The sort of positive value carried by *feel(ing)* here is the value a word gets just from repeated use. By using a word extensively, we demonstrate our need for it, and hence its (positive) value for us. *Feeling* carries this value not only for Rogers but for all of psychology except behaviorism — which vehemently insists that psychology should *not* make such extensive use of the term.

For those who give the word *feeling* this value of assumed usefulness, feelings (whatever they are) carry another sort of positive value as well. They are proclaimed as worthy of our best attention; and increased attention to them is seen as the most desired of our activities, even as the goal of our existence. Attention to our feelings thus takes on a particular kind of value, which we can call a "teleological plus": the positive value carried by a desired end. A client who is moving in a positive direction, toward "that self which he most truly is," "is increasingly listening to the deepest recesses of his physiological and emotional being," Rogers tells us enthusiastically. And Rollo May rhapsodizes that "the mature person [*mature* is another teleological plus, which will be examined in Part Two] becomes able to differentiate feelings into as many nuances . . . as in the different passages of music in a symphony." May defines this supersensitivity to feelings as "health" (another teleological plus: who aims to be sick?). In *Feelings: Our Vital Signs* — both in the title and throughout the book — Gaylin makes a slightly different connection between health and attention to feelings: our vital signs, in medical terminology, are those (like pulse rate) that indicate our physical condition; attention to feelings is thus for Gaylin not equal to health but a way of determining the state of our health. The ideal image projected by Gaylin, though, is the same as May's and Rogers's: their ideal person, he whom we should strive to emulate, walks through life with his ear bent to his heart, his hand over the other ear to block out any sounds that might interfere with his sensitive taking of his emotional pulse.

For psychology, not only does attention to feelings carry a teleological plus; the feelings themselves carry an additional plus sign, as themselves a good. These two pluses need not go together. We can see as good paying attention to something that is not itself seen as good: poison ivy, for example. But feelings are seen by psychology as good in both ways: it's good to pay attention to them and they are themselves good.

They're even doubly good, according to Gaylin. "Feelings are internal directives essential for human life. In addition, and not just in passing, they are their own rewards. They are the means and the ends." Feelings thus encompass an entire teleology. And as Gaylin goes on in this passage, feelings are seen to encompass not only a single teleological system but our entire moral sense: "All goodness and pleasure must be ultimately perceived in the realm of feelings. It is in the balance of small passions of daily existence that we measure and value our lives."

This is a daring moral statement. To perceive "all goodness" in the realm of feelings, and to "measure and value our lives" in "the balance of small passions of daily existence," is to deny the operation of any moral realm apart from the emotional realm. The term *good*, which traditionally is a key term of moral reference as well as an indicator of standard in a variety of nonmoral contexts (a good steak, a good outdoor paint, a good investment, a good Republican), loses here its independent moral reference. Moral *good* is completely absorbed by emotional *good*, as when Gaylin proudly proclaims what sounds like a hedonistic imperative: "That sense of good feeling, whether exploited for other purposes or enjoyed directly, is the sole support of the value of living in this world. It is, at any rate, good to 'feel good.' "

Gaylin may be the only member of the psychology professions to devote a whole book explicitly to the promotion of feelings, but he is far from the only one to articulate this feelings-centered morality. Rogers, for example, asserts with confidence that "when an activity *feels* as though it is valuable or worth doing, it *is* worth doing" — the italicized emphases being, significantly, his own. Even Romanticism would not have made such a claim as this, or as those of Gaylin quoted above. For Romanticism, feelings were indeed of ultimate value, but only some feelings, only the grand passions. The rest of life (which is, in fact, most of it, since we experience the grand passions only rarely) presumably had to be valued in other ways. But with psychology's democratization of feelings to include all the "small passions of daily existence," and with its absorption of our moral vocabulary into the realm of feelings, there remains no other way to value.

Trying to describe what "feeling good" is like (and Gaylin is often excellent at describing the mechanisms of the small feelings that do, in fact, operate in our daily lives), Gaylin evokes "that enlargement of self which goes into feeling good." We are thus reminded that *self* and *feelings* "go into" each other — and that, like the love and marriage of the song, you can't have one without the other. At least you can't in psychology. Nor, as we've seen, can you have psychology's *self* without taking the *unique* set and the *inner* set along too. These sets had long been associated with self, but with the concept of self much more than with the word. What psychology did, we can now say in summary, was to link the word *self* to these terms and to the concepts behind them; to give *self* and its associates scientific status by making them part of a technical vocabulary (without, however, developing for them clear or agreed-on definitions); and to link them all with teleologically weighted terms like *goal, growth,* and *health* — thus offering us this extended network of terms, bright with the golden glow of scientific validity, as the ideal pattern for us to follow in our talk, our thinking, and our shaping of our lives.

3

The Power of a Positive *Self*

Our Best-selling and God-given *Self*

Have we accepted this *self* that psychology offers us? How much of our sense of *self*, as we ordinarily use the word, comes from psychology? All, we might be tempted to say — especially when we notice how many of our best-sellers (those prime providers of terms for public, and private, discourse) either are written by psychologists or are, like *Passages*, popularizations of psychology. *Passages*, in fact, has itself become a passage: a conduit through which the terms of self-oriented psychology have poured into the main stream of general discourse.

While *self* is not a frequent term in *Passages*, the self as conceived by psychology is the book's subject, and all the familiar *self* associations of psychology are there. The "inner realm" is for Sheehy where the action is; her study — like Freud's, Jung's, Maslow's, Gaylin's — is of our "internal life system." And her proudly positive *inner* is, in the best Rogersian fashion, set against an *outer* conceived as restrictive and artificial: when you move into midlife, "you are moving out of roles and into the self." This inner self — like May's, Maslow's, Rogers's — is the source (the only "authentic" source) of values: the move into the self is a move "away

35

from external validations and accreditations, in search of an inner validation"; and "one of the great rewards of moving through the disassembling period to renewal [another positively loaded term] is coming to approve of oneself ethically and morally and quite independent of other people's standards and agenda."

"Coming to approve of oneself ethically and morally" turns out, in the book — as in Gaylin and Rogers — to be inseparable from feeling good about oneself. Sheehy, as we would expect from our familiarity with *self*'s associates in psychology, makes much of *feeling*, both as a main subject and as a main term in her vocabulary. "How do we *feel* about our way of living in the world at any given time?" she asks as one of the book's central questions, letting her italics show where her emphasis lies.

But, of course, this emphasis on feelings is not only Sheehy's. It has become — through *Passages* and all the other mass media productions through which psychology's terms come to us — the emphasis almost everywhere we go. When, for example, we go to meetings on the job, we find that once-objective business (a company's marketing changes, a college's curriculum changes) has been sucked inside and comes out of speakers' mouths as "how I feel about these changes." If we go to church, we're likely to hear sermons on the importance of feeling good about ourselves and having a "positive self-image." And if we happen to go to medical school, we're likely to find the anatomy professor concentrating on how to "help the students deal with possible emotional tensions arising from the experience of the dissecting lab." The dissecting lab is no longer a classroom but an "experience"; an experience must be "felt"; and Sheehy's question "How do we *feel* about our way of living in the world at any given time?" seems to be asked now at every given time.

While we're asked constantly about our feelings, we're assured constantly about our individual uniqueness. From Mister Rogers's assurance, to the four-year-old in each of us, that "you're a very special person" to Dr. Wayne Dyer's best-selling line that "you are unique in all the world" to Dr. Joyce Brothers's sales pitch that each of us should have "a unique and personal program" for success, psychology's line about the value of the individual seems to have spread everywhere. Or, more accurately (since the line isn't only psychology's), what has spread is psychology's version of a general humanist line: as *The Humanist* magazine reminds us, "the preciousness and dignity of the individual person is a central humanist value."

As pop psychology spreads the positive *unique–individual* line through our culture, it necessarily spreads also the confusions and ambiguity that we saw running through psychology's use of the line. When, for example, Sheehy offers "each of us . . . the opportunity to emerge reborn, authentically unique, with an enlarged capacity to love ourselves and embrace others," she's offering us, along with that uniqueness, the ambiguity between given and goal that psychology leaves unresolved in *unique*. For if we have to "emerge" unique, we're presumably not unique already; yet our given uniqueness is one of the working assumptions that Sheehy takes over from developmental-personality psychology. To qualify the aimed-for uniqueness with *authentically* (and thus apparently to distinguish it from ordinary or inauthentic uniqueness) is to make no real qualification at all. *Authentic* is what we could call an "empty plus": it carries positive value but is void of content ("says nothing," as we often put it).

All my talk about the "spread" of psychology's *self*, via the popular media into our common language, makes psychology sound like a creeping vine or like a virus spreading through the population or like a guerrilla force acting underground to take us over town by town (or term by term). These implications of my metaphor are, of course, inaccurate and unfair to psychology: psychology has no conspiracy against us, and it's not an alien force. It's part of us, part of our culture: the part, we could say, that studies for us what we want (even long) to know about our individual selves. If psychology gives us its *self*, this is because we ask for it.

So while we can truly say that we get psychology's *self* through the mass media, we can't say that we get it against our will. Nor can we say, despite the dominant impression given by popular lit-

erature and by this analysis of it so far, that the *self* we get is
entirely psychology's. Obviously, to a large extent it is — so obviously, maybe, that this examination of how the mass media re-
peat psychology's lines has been, for many readers, simply repeti-
tious. But if we now look more closely into these best-selling lines,
we can see something more in them than what psychology alone
has put there. In, for example, that promise of Sheehy's of "the
opportunity to emerge reborn" there's a touch of evangelicalism
that we can't say comes from psychology. Or, if it does — and
there is, certainly, something of the promise of a new life in Maslow's and Rogers's goal of a new or renewed or higher self — it
comes into both professional and pop psychology from elsewhere:
from, originally, Christianity. There are other places, too, where
Christianity enters into our sense of *self;* and we should look briefly
at one of them in order to correct the impression that the *self* we
get through the mass media, and hence our common sense of *self,*
is entirely and simply psychology's.

In our common (both widespread and frequent) assertion of the
value of each individual, we're indeed expressing what *The Humanist* called a "central humanist value." But before "the preciousness and dignity of the individual person" was a central humanist value, it was a central Christian value. By moving the locus
of spiritual activity from external rites and laws into the individual, Christianity brought God's infinite value into each person.
Individual and *internal* have thus always carried pluses for Christianity: the plus signs of God's presence in the individual. "Are
you not aware that you are the temple of God, and that the Spirit
of God dwells in you?" St. Paul asks rhetorically. One way of
looking at what has happened to the positive term *individual* over
the past two thousand years is to see the plus sign remaining over
individual while the source of the word's plus, the Spirit of God,
is gradually removed by the secular Renaissance–Romantic–psychology tradition. To St. Paul's question, psychology (speaking for
secular humanism generally) answers no. And yet this answer
doesn't decrease the value placed by us on the individual. In fact,
it reinforces it.

This reinforcement works because we hear or see words but not the concepts behind them. Behind (or in) the Christian *individual* is the concept of God; behind (or in) the secular humanist *individual* is the concept of man alone. But while these concepts are far (infinitely far) apart, the words expressing them can be identical. Assertions of "our individual uniqueness" or "the preciousness of the individual" can sound exactly the same no matter who makes them. When Billy Graham asserts, for example, that "the central theme of the universe is the purpose and destiny of every individual," he sounds just like *The Humanist* (even though he means something different). And because Christian and secular voices can sound the same, each "sounds better" because we've heard the same line from the other; each, that is, lends its particular authority to the line. When Graham, then, tells us that each conversion process is "very personal" ("God looks at each of us differently, because each of us is different), this sounds right because we've heard Mister Rogers telling us, since we were four, that each of us is special and different; and when Dr. Wayne Dyer assures each of us that "you are unique in all the world," we tend to believe it even more because we've heard it in church.

We've heard it even if we don't go to church — heard, that is, the Christian lines asserting the value of the individual. We tend to pride ourselves on living in a secular culture; yet a culture in which a major television network considers it profitable to broadcast Billy Graham during prime time, and in which the *New York Times* regularly (religiously!) prints the Pope's addresses, is hardly simply secular. Even those of us who grow up without opening the Bible cannot have avoided contact with Christian lines. Where those lines contradict the lines of a secular authority like psychology, of course we have to choose which to follow. But where the lines overlap, as in assertions of the worth of the individual, we can easily nod our approval to both. The fact that Christianity places positive value on the individual just reinforces our sense of that value, and thus adds to the positive sense of *self* that we get from secular sources.

What Good Is the *Self*?

If we return now to the original question of this chapter — the question of how much of our sense of *self* comes from psychology — we find that the answer has to be a bit complicated. In the area of *self* covered by *individual,* our sense of positive value seems to come at least as much from Christianity as from psychology, though the amount is hard to measure since in most praise of the individual we can't tell where that praise is coming from. As for the rest of the extensive area covered by *self* and its associated terms, we've seen that while our common *self* is to a large extent psychology's, psychology's *self* is to a large extent not its own but that of four hundred years of Western culture. The Renaissance's positive valuing of subjectivity, individuality, and creativity; seventeenth-century philosophy's positive valuing of self-consciousness and identity; Romanticism's positive valuing of all these along with internalness, freedom, and feelings — all this is carried on in psychology's *self*.

This is quite a lot of good (or goods) to be carried by a single word! And yet there's still more. Because besides Christianity and psychology (and through it the Renaissance–Romantic tradition), other powerful traditions and ideologies come into play in *self* and add their weight to the word.

We've seen, for example, that *freedom* is one of the plus terms associated with *self* in the Romantic tradition carried on by psychology; but *freedom,* along with terms like *independence* and *self-determination,* has also been a plus word in every expression of democratic political ideals since the French Revolution. Furthermore, terms like *self-sufficiency* and *control,* which operate in close connection with the *freedom* set in both psychology and democratic political discourse, are plus terms also in the ideology of modern technology. These terms, of course, have different applications in each of these places. For technology, *self-sufficiency* and *control* are terms applied primarily to machines and ideal mechanical functioning; for democracy, these terms apply to governments and to people as political units; for psychology, they apply to individual personality. Yet the application in each case is to something valued positively by the ideology or discipline concerned.

These terms then carry along with them, in all of their uses, the positive values of all the ideologies and disciplines and activities and traditions of thought in which they operate. I don't mean that they necessarily carry along the particular applications from these various places; nor do I mean that we're aware of all these sources adding their weight to a word we use. What I mean is that our sense of a word's positive value is increased, usually without our awareness, when that word carries positive value in ideologies and activities and so on other than the one we're consciously using it in — especially when those other sources of its value are themselves highly prized by our culture.

Take, for example, the call for independence in "Your Declaration of Independence," a 1977 *Harper's Bazaar* article: "Independence, simply, is the freedom to choose what is pertinent to your needs at any given time. It is a feeling of freedom that comes from within." Because of the neat overlap of political and psychological terms here, the positive political values of *independence* and *freedom* are brought to bear on the positive psychological values of *independence, needs, feeling,* and *within.* For the authors of this "Declaration," as well as for readers who respond positively to it, *independence* is attractive because it carries some of our most cherished political and psychological values; and it has this double attraction whether or not the authors and readers are aware of the sources of this attraction. Similarly, in the calls we've heard so often in recent years to "pull our own strings"—whether in ads like *Ms* magazine's picture of a female marionette with text urging women to cut the strings that control them from outside, or in best-sellers like *Pulling Your Own Strings* — what is being appealed to is our generally and overwhelmingly positive sense of *self-sufficiency* and *control of our lives,* a sense which derives from the combined positive appeal of these terms in psychology, democracy, and technology. Because of the multiple strength of this appeal, then, we tend to go along unquestioningly with our sense that *self-sufficiency* is a good thing — pulled less by our own strings than by those of the powerful networks of meaning and value operating on the word from behind the scenes.

It's odd, maybe, to think of words working like this, apart from our awareness or our conscious intentions: we're so used to assuming our control of everything (we're so attracted by the idea of pulling our own strings) that we assume that, where our language is concerned, we can simply "say what we mean" as long as we just take a minute to choose our words carefully. That words can mean things apart from what we intend for them, that words say what *they* mean more than what *we* mean, is indeed disconcerting. Yet when we look at how our common language actually operates — when we look, for example, at why certain words attract us — we have to admit that it operates to a large extent outside of our conscious intentions. We can indeed increase the extent of our consciousness of its operations, as we're doing here, and thereby give ourselves more control over our language than we usually have. But unless we make this deliberate effort to watch how our words are working, we'll be worked on by them and manipulated by their meanings unawares.

One thing we've seen so far about the way words operate is that they act as receptacles into which different disciplines and ideologies and traditions of thought pour their particular meanings, their favorite value-laden concepts. The word *self*, we can now say, is the container of heavily weighted meaning from some of our culture's most influential sources; it's a loaded term. This is the case even though *self* has no precise definition, either in any of the places where its value comes from or in our everyday use. If you ask someone who speaks in terms of his self — who talks about fulfilling himself or having a negative self-image or knowing his true self — what exactly he means by his *self*, he's unlikely to be able to tell you. How could he have a precise definition when the sources of his sense of *self* don't give him one? What they give him instead of a definition is, as we've seen, a complex of positively valued concepts — an overwhelmingly good (yes) feeling. And it might be that if *self* had a tighter definition, it couldn't carry such a variety of concepts. A definition is (by definition) a boundary, an assumption of finiteness. A tightly defined word has definite boundaries and therefore limited room for concepts to fit into it. But a loosely defined word like *self* is flexible, stretchy; its sides can move out easily to accommodate all the concepts that come into it from the various places where it operates. And the more concepts it has room for, the more it then tends to draw in other terms associated with these concepts — and thus the more likely it is to operate, by itself or through its associates, in our everyday thought.

Our practically undefined *self,* then, brings with it an array of concepts: mainly from the Renaissance, Romanticism, and psychology, but also from Christianity, democracy, and technology (and from evolutionary theory too, as we'll see in Part Two). And these concepts carry almost unanimously positive value. No wonder we're so filled with self: because *self* is filled with the prize concerns of centuries of our culture.

All the positive concepts converging in the word *self* are enough to explain its great attraction for us. Yet there's another sort of attraction, too, that I think self has: what we might call a natural attraction. In a study like this one, which focuses intensively on words, it's easy to lose sight of other forces that operate in our lives besides (or, probably, along with) language. We have to step back occasionally, therefore, so as to keep our study of language in proper perspective. And if we step back from the word *self* and from the intellectual constructs that are our concepts of self, we can see still another force pulling us toward self, the force of what appears to be natural self-interest or self-concern. I use the word "natural" uneasily, since the debate on what constitutes our true human nature is far from settled. Yet from what we can observe, and from what people have observed throughout history, self-concern does seem to be a fact, a given of our natures. That is, we tend naturally to look out for our own interest (however that interest is perceived).

If self-concern is clearly a given, how to take it is not so clear. The given may be a fact. But the taking is a question of values. During the course of Western culture, our self-concern has been taken, valued, in a variety of ways ranging from Rousseau's embracing of self-love as the prime natural good to Jesus's command that we utterly deny our natural self and follow him instead. Usually, though, at any one time there have been voices on either side, such as we heard in the sixteenth-century battle between Renaissance positive *self-interest* and Christian negative *self-interest*. Sometimes voices on either side can even come from a single source: the meaning of self-love for both Rousseau and Jesus, for example, was extremely complex and included valuings of self-concern opposite to those of their main injunctions.

What has happened today is that *self,* the word, has added its voice to the positive side. And its voice is a loud one, swelled by the praise attached to *self* in all the many places in which the word is heard. Our current language, then, is pulling us in the same direction that we naturally tend to go in anyway. With our language — our words and the concepts behind them — adding its considerable force to an already natural attraction, we're entirely sucked into self. (Or almost entirely. What few forces remain to pull us away will be examined in the final chapters of the book.) As for the sort of behavior our *self*-absorption leads us into, that can best be seen in conjunction with a look at another set of terms with which *self* is often joined: the *growth and development* set.

TWO

Growth and *Development*
To *Realize* Your *Potential*

4

The Growth and Development
of *Growth* and *Development*

Early *Growth*

Growth is nothing new. The word *grow* is as old as our language (Old English *grówan*) and even older, going back to the Old Teutonic root *gró-*, from which also come *green* and *grass*. What originally *grew*, naturally enough, were plants. But by Middle English the compelling image of increase by natural process had been transferred from vegetative life to both human life ("the child growide," 1382) and immaterial things ("error groweth," 1390).

By the sixteenth century, figurative (nonvegetable) *growth* had taken on the additional sense of increase toward a goal. *Growth*, that is, had become in some of its usages growth with a specified direction and toward a specified end. The direction and end were specified by various prepositions and their objects: "For ever may my knees grow to the earth" (1593); "I grow in hope day by day" (1576). This association of *grow* with completion, and *grow*'s original connection with plants, made it appropriate that when, during the Renaissance, *mature* entered the language (via French) from Latin *maturus:* "ripe," "timely," it immediately became associated with *growth*. "Mature fruit" and "mature judgment" both implied, around 1600, growth to completion; and in Shakespeare's "This bastard graff shall never come to growth," the graff (graft) was condemned never to mature.

Develop came into English about the same time as *mature* did. It came, like *mature*, via French from Latin: from *voloper* ("to wrap up") plus *dis-* (indicating reversal). *To develop* is thus literally to unwrap or unfold. Since "unwrapping" or "unfolding" makes sense only if there's something inside to be unfolded, *develop* carries in its etymology the idea of latency, of an inner something to be brought out in the process of development. The idea of "inner potential" therefore became associated early (by 1750) with *develop,* and it was this association that made *develop* attractive as a technical term for various newly discovered scientific processes that seemed to bring forth what had previously existed in a latent or potential form. The most famous of these processes is, of course, photography, which began to talk in terms of *developing* pictures in 1845, even before it had learned much about how to develop them.

Develop as used by photography is, we should note, a transitive verb, as was *develop* in all its early (sixteenth- to mid-nineteenth-century) usages. If an object is to be brought forth from a latent condition, the transitive form implies, there must be an agent bringing it forth. For the rare cases when agent and object might be the same — when something might be seen as bringing itself forth — a reflexive use of *develop* (*develop* plus *itself*) appeared in 1793 ("this prominent part of their character began to develope itself"). The reflexive form was never very popular though; before long, an intransitive *develop* was usually substituting for *develop itself.* And, not at all accidentally, at the same time that this substitution was taking place, *develop* was becoming closely connected with *growth.*

The association of *grow* and *develop* was, in a double sense, a natural one. *Develop* had come to mean "bring forth what is potentially contained in" or "bring forth from a latent condition"; and the growth of a plant from a seed is a natural occurrence of a bringing forth from a latent condition. Nature itself thus provided, in the organic process of plant growth, the image for a natural (i.e. logical) connection between *grow* and *develop*.

This image of organic growth that connected *grow* and *develop* was a very attractive one to the early-nineteenth-century mind. Drawn in general to nature as a source of inspiration and of images, Romantic writers were drawn particularly to the organic metaphor as a way of picturing all processes of life. Since the process they wanted most to picture was that of their own creative geniuses, theories of "vegetable genius," as one scholar has called them, abounded in Romantic aesthetic thought from its German beginnings. These theories, as versions of the organic metaphor, were characteristically expressed in terms of *growth* and *development:*

> Organic form [in a work of art] is innate; it unfolds itself from within, and reaches its determination simultaneously with the fullest development of the seed.

These terms are Schlegel's, but they could be those of Coleridge — who took them over almost word for word and was primarily responsible for their English promotion. (Coleridge was also responsible, we should note, for introducing *actualize* and *actualization* into English: he made the distinction, in 1825, of "being from existence — or potential being . . . from being actualized." Since *actualize* and *potential* are today familiar associates in certain popular expressions of the development concept, it seems appropriate that they were first linked by the same person who did so much to bring us *grow* and *develop*.)

By the mid-nineteenth century, *grow* and *develop* had become so closely associated in the organic metaphor that when the new intransitive form of *develop* appeared around 1843, it appeared as a synonym for *grow*. At the same time, though, another concept was being linked with that of growth in the meaning of intransitive *develop*. According to the *OED*, the meaning of the new intransitive *develop* was "to unfold itself, grow from a germ or rudimentary condition; to grow into a fuller, higher, or maturer condition." This growth "into a fuller, higher, or maturer condition," seen as the natural process not only of single organisms but of whole species and of the entire organic universe, was a central image of what was rapidly coming to be the new concept of evolution.

Evolutionary *Development*

Actually, to call it "the new concept of evolution" isn't quite accurate. There were many such concepts taking shape in the first three-quarters of the nineteenth century; and most of them were seen as concepts not of *evolution* but of *development*. *Development*, that is, was the general term for what we now call evolution before *evolution* was. As in the case of *self*, our current concept (of evolution) was to a large extent formed without the word we've come to label it by.

Etymologically, *develop* and *evolve* are almost identical, and *evolve* had been in the language (meaning "unroll," usually figuratively) as long as *develop* had; so the preference for *develop* among the pre-Darwinian evolutionists, as we now call them, had to be due not to the definitions or legitimacy of the two words, but to their previous associations. Though the vernacular *evolution* had long been associated with the idea of progressive change, in biology the word had taken on an almost opposite association: the eighteenth-century preformationists Albrecht von Haller and Charles Bonnet had used *evolution* as the name for their static view that all forms of life were preformed by God at the creation and are preformed individually in each embryo, merely "unrolling" in time. *Develop*'s associations, on the other hand, were just what the pre-Darwinian evolutionists wanted for their vision of a changing, transforming natural universe: associations, from the organic metaphor, of growth according to natural laws and toward a higher state.

The terms of organic *development* were thus the ones in which pre-Darwinian evolutionary ideas found expression. And the reflexive-intransitive form of *develop*, with its meaning of self-unfolding of a natural process, was especially suited for the radical extension of these ideas into a vision of the organic universe not only changing but changing on its own, transforming itself by its own natural laws and without the need of an outside Subject. This vision became common only after Darwin; but we can still fairly say that God began to disappear from our view of the universe with the appearance of reflexive-intransitive *develop*.

Evolution didn't become linked to this *develop–growth–change–maturity* set until Herbert Spencer announced the term as the label for his bold all-encompassing theory of universal change, in his *First Principles* (1862) and *Principles of Biology* (1866). He chose *evolution*, he says, because he wanted a term that would be "coextensive" with his previously favored term "Progress," and yet would go beyond *progress*'s human and social implications; and because *evolution* — this is amusing to us today — had no confusing "pre-established associations." (Preformationism had evidently declined so much in reputation that its quite opposite associations with *evolution* had been lost.) The associations that Spencer then proclaimed for *evolution* were those of *development, organic growth,* and *progress;* in explicating his universal "law of Evolution," by which everything moves toward greater complexity and integration, he used *development* and *evolution* interchangeably and called the result of both an *advance:*

> . . . this law of organic evolution is the law of all evolution. Whether it be in the development of the Earth, in the development of Life upon its surface, in the development of Society, of Government, of Manufactures, of Commerce, of Language, Literature, Science, Art, this same advance from the simple to the complex, through successive differentiations, holds uniformly. (*First Principles*)

Since Spencer then went on, in *Principles of Biology,* to embrace Darwin's theory of natural selection in the expansive arms of *evolution,* the terms of the *progress–development–evolution* set were soon connected not only with Spencer's large-scale vision but with Darwin's minute and careful observations as well.

Darwin himself, curiously enough, had made no such connection. It's fascinating to read through the *Origin of Species* today and find in the first (1859) edition no *evolution,* a single *evolved* (used, in a nontechnical sense, as the final word of the book), just a bit more *develop* and *development,* and a very hesitatingly mentioned *progress.* In Darwin's mind (and language), his theory was one not of "evolution" but of "the descent and modification of species by means of natural selection." The main terms with which he presented his theory were *species, natural selection,* and the now infamous *survival of the fittest,* which he borrowed from Spencer and which brought with it *struggle, compete,* and *advantage.* These war-like terms were the ones Darwin chose to represent his central view of nature as a battlefield on which competing forms struggle for life. Such a view is hardly compatible with the organic metaphor's images — of peaceful growth to maturity and inevitable unfolding of inner potential — associated at that time with *development;* so it's not surprising that Darwin, who always chose his words with painstaking care, tended not to choose *develop* very often.

When he did, he used it not in association with the terms of the organic metaphor (*growth, mature,* and *potential* rarely appear in Darwin's writing) but as a synonym for *produce.* Darwin used *produce, develop, form,* and *evolve* all synonymously to describe the action of natural selection ("natural selection produces" varieties, species, structures, etc.), but his favorite of these verbs was *produce.* And his favorite form of *produce* and its synonyms was the passive voice of the transitive. Species, that is, "are produced"; "organic beings have been formed"; a part of an organism "is developed"; "endless forms" of nature (in the closing words of the book) "have been, and are being evolved." Darwin's preference for the passive voice of these verbs was probably due to his extreme caution. Though he was certain that natural selection was the material producer of species, he was less than certain about the role of a higher Producer and, unlike Spencer, uncomfortable speculating about such nonscientific (as he saw them) questions. The passive voice allowed him to present species as indeed the passive productions of a force working on them and yet to avoid having to continually name this force as something other than God.

Despite Darwin's reluctance to label his theory in terms of either *development* or *evolution,* these were the labels that were, in turn, affixed to it. *Development* was the first to be applied: the earliest reviews of the *Origin* referred to natural selection as a "theory of development." Then during the 1870s, as Spencer's and Darwin's writings rapidly gained in popularity and in association with each other, Spencer's *evolution* began to replace *development* as the general label for what Darwin had discovered. By the end of the 1870s, Darwin's theory had become in the public mind a "theory of evolution"; by the end of the century, with its scientific validity generally recognized, it had become *"the* theory of evolution."

The attachment of Spencer's language to Darwin's discoveries was of the greatest significance in the history of *develop*. Darwin's theory was being acclaimed as scientific truth at the same time that it was becoming known as a theory of *development* and of *evolution. Develop, evolve,* and all of their associates thus received from Darwin (even though he rarely used any of them!) the positive value of scientific truth. With this value — in fact, because of this value (though Spencer's forceful rhetoric gave them an extra push) — they then quickly spread from biology into other areas of thought. By the end of the nineteenth century, *evolution, development, growth, progress* had become the leading terms of the day.

Whatever area of thought a society invests with the power of discovering truth is the area from which it takes much of its leading language. This is reasonable: we want our words "to tell the truth," and the persistent hope is that if certain words tell the truth in one place, they'll continue to tell it in another. For the past few hundred years in Western society, and especially the past one hundred, science has been seen as the place where truth is found and told. Terms that come from science therefore seem to come with a special validity, a sort of truth-value. We saw this in the case of *self,* which owes much of its attraction today to the scientific validity granted to it by psychology. In the nineteenth century, even well before Darwin, biology was seen as the science that was discovering the most exciting truths. Other disciplines therefore reached to biology for language to apply in their own investigations. With Darwin's great discovery, the reaching became a grabbing, a universal almost instant appropriation — so great was the force of truth perceived in *evolution.*

Though the immediate impetus behind the spread of *evolution* and *development* in the late nineteenth century came from Darwinian evolution, *development* had also for some time been getting a push from another direction as well. A half-century before Darwin made known his evolutionary view of natural history, Hegel had envisioned all of human history and thought as a process of progressive development: of thought unfolding out of itself in ascending "stages" and according to its own inner laws, and of human history unfolding out of thought. Marx then reversed the vision — turned it on its head, the (Engelsian) saying goes — and saw history unfolding out of itself, producing thought along the way. The reversal didn't change the central role of *development:* the concept of development, if not the word itself (Marx used the word, *Entwicklung,* more than Hegel), was essential to the Hegelian–Marxian vision, whichever way you looked at it — or through it. This German *development* was indistinguishable, too, from *evolution:* German had just the single word *Entwicklung* to cover both English terms — which were, as we've seen, being treated almost indistinguishably in English anyway.

By the late nineteenth century, then, *develop* carried the concepts of Hegelian history and of Darwinian evolution,* both of which drew on the organic metaphor and its *growth–organic–maturity* language; both of which carried the positive value of *sci-*

---

* Poor Spencer. He had a greater immediate influence than Darwin in converting the English-speaking public to biological evolution, and a greater immediate influence than Hegel in converting them to progressive historical development. Yet we refer today (and I will in the remainder of this book) to "Darwinian evolution" and "Hegelian development." Probably we do this, and I think justifiably, because Darwin and Hegel were much closer to the truth of their respective subjects than Spencer, whose thinking was flamboyant and chronically sloppy and disrespectful of detail.

ence and of scientific *law;* and both of which assumed (though Darwin himself hadn't) that with development inevitably came *progress.* This complex of terms and concepts carried by *develop* was carried by it wherever it went. And it seemed to be going everywhere. Titles appearing in English between 1875 and 1900 include *The Development of the Athenian Constitution, The Development of the English Novel, The Development of Transportation Systems in the U.S., The Development of Marriage and Kinship; The Growth of Capital, The Growth of the Oral Method of Instructing the Deaf, The Growth of a Century; The Evolution of the Thermometer, The Evolution of the Massachusetts Public School System, The Evolution of English Lexicography, The Evolution of the Constitution of the U.S., The Evolution of Morality, The Evolution of the Idea of God.*

Though these studies vary in the amount of use they actually make of the terms of the *development* set, and in their awareness of the concepts behind these terms, all tend to use *evolution* and *development* synonymously and to use *develop* more than any other term of the set. (Even books titled *The Evolution of* . . . use *develop,* rather than *evolve,* as the main operative term within the text.) Viewing their subject — whatever it is — in terms of *development,* these studies tend to see it *developing* (or, less often, *growing* or *evolving*) according to *laws.* These laws are sometimes those of Darwinian or Spencerian *adaptation,* sometimes those of Hegelian *stages* and *synthesis,* sometimes a more or less well-integrated combination of both. But almost always the *law* of *development* is one of *progress,* and the latest form of the subject — whether lexicography, the Massachusetts public school system, or religion — is seen excitedly as its "supreme development."

The excitement about *development* has continued unabated throughout the twentieth century, leading not only to an ongoing supply of books but also, in the first quarter of the century, to such diverse productions as the *Oxford English Dictionary* (hardly a mere "book"), the discipline of anthropology, and the Russian Revolution. As for what *development* leads to today, before we

can see that, we have to take note of some additional associations — especially those with humanism and with psychology —
that *develop* has picked up on its way through our century.

Humanistic *Developments*

One of the reasons that Darwinian evolution initially caused such
a fuss was that it seemed to dethrone man from his high place
near the top of creation (just a little lower than the angels) and
thrust him down to the level of a mere animal. But man's apparently innate positive self-image didn't allow him to remain in this
lowly position for long; soon evolution was seen not as lowering
man but as elevating him to the highest position yet reached by
the developing organic universe. As biologist Julian Huxley put it
in the popular *Evolution in Action* in 1953, "the human species
. . . represents the furthest step yet taken in evolutionary progress." Evolutionary theory therefore caused the usually positive
term *man* to suffer the negative implications of lowered status only
temporarily; within a century after Darwin, *man*'s positive value
had been restored and even increased by the evolutionary vision
itself.

This post-Darwinian association of positively valued *man* with
evolutionary *development* has taken on the label "humanism."
Though the label itself, and its elevation of man and especially his
reason, dates from the Renaissance, the merging of the positive
man–reason line with evolutionary thought produced what Huxley elsewhere calls a "new pattern of thinking." What's new about
our twentieth-century humanism is that it is indeed, as Huxley
says, "evolution-centred." To call it "Evolutionary Humanism,"
as Huxley sometimes does, is thus redundant: humanism today
assumes evolution as its very premise. (To call it "secular humanism," as it's now called by both sides in the much-publicized battle
between the fundamentalist religious Moral Majority and the Secular Humanists, is also redundant: both sides add the "secular"
for rhetorical emphasis, but the added term adds no new meaning

to twentieth-century humanism, which is already secular in its assumptions.)

In this evolution-centered humanism of ours, man is doubly plussed. Not only is he the highest product of biological evolution, but he is the producer of future evolution: "the sole agent for the future evolution of this planet." The "climax of all the eons, the epochs, and the years," exults Time-Life's popularized *Evolution* (1962), is that "as man reshapes his world and replaces the relentless but cleansing action of natural selection with a new, cultural evolution and inheritance, he is taking control of the future." "We have virtually conquered the planet," echoes the 1973 "Humanist Manifesto II"; and we can now "control our environment, conquer poverty," and "alter the course of human evolution and cultural development." The breathless Superman rhetoric — "who can change the course of mighty rivers" — recalls, with its exultant talk of *conquering* and *control,* the old battle language of the (presumably now discredited) theory of the struggle for existence.

What has given man his great power in the evolutionary struggle is, according to humanism, his mind. "It is only through possessing a mind that [man] has become the dominant portion of this planet and the agent responsible for its future evolution," Huxley tells us. And it is by becoming conscious of his own agency, of the unique role of his mind in "the cosmic process of evolution," that man is now taking full control of that process. "Today, in twentieth-century man," Huxley exclaims in a vision of Hegelian bliss, "the evolutionary process is at last becoming conscious of itself and is beginning to study itself with a view to directing its future course." Humanism's proud worship of mind follows (reasonably!) from this vision. The "chief commitment" of humanism, asserts former *Humanist* magazine editor Paul Kurtz, is "to the ethic of the free mind. For the freethinker . . . the only authority is the authority of intelligence, the only master is reason."

The authority of reason (*mind, intelligence*) in turn implies, for humanism, the authority of *science.* Science, that is, is both the method and the product of human reason working at its best. Science then gets further valued in the form of *technology*, that "vital key to human progress and development" ("Humanist Manifesto II"). The relation between the plus words *man* and *science* in humanism is thus one of reciprocal back-patting. Science (as biology) praises man as the pinnacle of creation; man, in turn, praises science (as technology) as the instrument by which he will lead the future to new heights.

A common term with which this mutual positive stroking of *man* and *science* is done is *progress*. (Man represents the furthest stage in evolutionary progress; science is the means to man's future progress.) Though Darwin was very doubtful about the propriety of calling evolutionary movement "progress," his humanistic followers have had no such doubts; and "human progress and development" is repeatedly evoked, as in the quotation in the previous paragraph, as if *progress* and *development* were obviously synonyms — even as if the whole phrase constituted a single, inseparable word.

Also inseparable from *human progress and development* in the network of humanist plus words is *fulfillment*. *Fulfillment* even has a privileged status in the network: "fulfillment," Huxley writes in *Evolution in Action,* "seems to describe better than any other single word the positive side of human development and human evolution — the realization of inherent capacities by the individual and of new possibilities by the race." *Fulfillment* (or sometimes *satisfaction*) is thus the master plus over not only *human development* and *human evolution* but also *realization, inherent capacities,* and *possibilities* (or, more often, *potential*). Note that *human,* as the locus of *fulfillment,* refers to both single and collective man: both the individual and the race are to be fulfilled. Thus "Humanist Manifesto II" can put side by side on a single page the assertion that "the ultimate goal should be the fulfillment of the potential for growth in each human personality" and the assertion that the central concern of humanism is "the question of the survival and fulfillment of the human race."

We should note that these quotations bring in — as humanist

statements about fulfillment inevitably tend to do — *potential, growth,* and *survival. Survival* is, of course, a holdover from the "survival of the fittest," though the attempt is made, somewhat awkwardly, to hold it apart from its Darwinian battlefield implications. ("The struggle for existence has been largely superseded, as an operative force, by the struggle for fulfillment" is Huxley's cut-and-paste way of separating *struggle* and *survival* from the now negative Darwinian *competition* and joining them to positive *fulfillment.*) *Growth* comes down to humanism from the organic metaphor; *potential* from the early meaning of *development. Growth* and *development,* in turn, get connected to each other in other expressions of humanism — so closely connected, in fact, that "growth and development" has become another of those phrases that act in humanism as one word, even as one key on the typewriter.

In a sense, all the plus terms of humanism act almost as one key on the typewriter. That is, when humanism says one of them, it automatically says them all. It might not say them all at once; but with each plus term it tends to say at least one other, and a different one at different times, so that eventually all the terms get connected in a web of positive pairings. *Development and evolution, progress and development, scientific progress, progress through control, control through reason, reason and intelligence, potential intelligence, potential for growth, realization of potential, fulfillment of potential, survival and fulfillment, satisfying survival, satisfaction and fulfillment, development and fulfillment, growth and development* — these pairs (and others) interconnect to form a network that is the basic language of humanist thought.

This humanist language, in turn, is woven into the fabric of most of our contemporary institutions, ideas, and activities. Our entire technological establishment, for example — as David Ehrenfeld has shown in *The Arrogance of Humanism* — is designed on the assumptions carried by *science, control,* and *progress* as positive terms. In our economic thought, *growth* and *development* are still central threads, represented, for example, by President Reagan's line before the 1981 Cancun economic summit conference that "in its ultimate form, development is human fulfillment — an ability by men and women to realize their potential." The assumption of *control through reason* runs through all our political institutions; it's noteworthy that Julian Huxley was the founding director of UNESCO. Each of these areas into which humanistic *development* moves then adds its own associations, prestige, and reinforcement to the *development* network. One area in particular, though, has added so much that it has in effect made over *development* in its own image: the area of psychology. Before we can see, then, where our current sense of *development* takes us, we need to look at where psychology has taken *development*.

Personal *Growth*

Most simply put, psychology takes *development* into the self. The main result — the area of overlap between psychology and humanism — has come to be called, appropriately, "humanistic psychology" or the "human potential movement." The movement's catchphrases neatly catch the nature of this overlap: "self-realization," "self-actualization," "self-fulfillment," "personal growth." As these phrases indicate, humanistic psychology operates within the individual sense, rather than the collective sense, of humanism's *man;* and into this individual (the area, as we saw in Part One, of psychology's *self*) it brings the *fulfillment–satisfaction–potential* segment of the *development* network.

Other senses of *development* are, we should note in passing, brought into play in other areas of psychology besides the human potential movement. In what is specifically called "developmental psychology," for example, the biological (especially embryological) concept of *development* — which we'll have occasion to examine in Chapter 5 — is applied to the study of both human and animal behavior. Also derived from biology's *development* is Piaget's theory of cognitive development; Piaget, originally a biologist himself, deliberately modeled his theory on Darwinian concepts, seeing intelligence as a "biological adaptation" and the mind as a living structure that, in the words of a textbook paraphrase, "grows, changes, and adapts to its world." The title of the text-book from which this paraphrase comes, *Human Development,* indicates how extensive *development* is in psychology: the book aims at covering impartially all the fields of current psychology, and *development* was considered a term general enough to cover them all. If we were to undertake an exhaustive study of today's *development,* we would have to look into all of these fields. But since we're tracing here only the main lines that our popular sense of *development* draws on, and not every detail that comes into it, we'll follow *development* only into the widely popularized area of humanistic psychology.

When humanistic psychology looks at the *self* in terms of *development,* or at *development* in terms of the *self,* it's bringing evolutionary significance into the process of change of individual personality. Often *evolution* is explicitly named, as either the cause or the nature of the process. Erik Erikson, one of the prime movers of the human potential movement, links each of his "stages" of the life cycle to an "essential strength which evolution has built both into the ground plan of the life stages and into that of man's institutions." Daniel Levinson, modeling the "developmental periods" of his *Seasons of a Man's Life* on Erikson's "stages," equates *development* with *evolution* ("when I speak of adult development, I mean the evolution of the life structure during the adult years") and claims that "evolution, and not the attainment of any particular final state, is of the essence of adult development." But even when *evolution* isn't literally present in the prose of humanistic psychology, it's there in spirit; all the various developmental stages, schedules, and ladders that have been set up for us to advance through life on seem inspired by Huxley's "evolutionary vision" that when the individual develops his own personality, then "in his own person he is realizing an important quantum of evolutionary possibility."

There's probably something of the Hegelian "Spirit," as well, in the construction of all these developmental steps and stages. At least, when the resolution of conflicts or contradictions is seen as the motivating force behind advancement up the ladder — as it is in both Erikson and Levinson — Hegel's *Geist* developing *in sich selbst* through contradiction-resolved-at-a-higher-level seems to be at work behind the scenes. Reinforcing this Hegelian "Idea" is Jung's *individuation* process, which also sees opposition as a positive force in personality development. And Hegel's and Jung's joint promotion of *integration* as the goal of development — along with Spencer's, way back at the beginning of evolutionary *development* — certainly adds to the value of *integration* and *wholeness* as the prize held out to us if we do our developmental tasks well.

In addition to, or instead of, "resolution of contradiction," many ladder-building psychologists talk about "adaptation" as the way to climb from step to step. Erikson talks about both: while his "psychosocial development" proceeds by "critical steps" requiring the resolution of contradiction at each step, it's also at each step a process of "adaptation" of self to world, or of individual to society. For the Grant Study team of Harvard psychologists who traced the "climb to maturity" of forty selected men, *adaptation* is also a key term; and for them the adaptation is "to life." Conceiving of "adaptation" as "the evolution of mature defenses," they seem to be drawing both on Darwin's war-like picture of adaptation and also, in the very un-Darwinian idea of "maturity," on the organic metaphor.

The organic metaphor lies in fact (or in image) behind much of the thinking of the human potential movement. Carl Rogers repeatedly calls on images of *growth* and *maturity* to represent what he sees as the "basically positive direction" of personal development: a "moving toward self-actualization, growing toward maturity, growing toward socialization." And Abraham Maslow's theory of self-actualization — claimed by some as the conceptual foundation of the human potential movement — is inconceivable without the organic metaphor. His "quite meaningful and researchable concept" of "mature, fully-human, self-actualizing people in whom the human potentialities have been realized and actualized," which he abbreviates as the concept of "good-growth-toward-self-actualization," seems to get its meaning entirely by stringing out the terms associated with organic *development*. (What exactly this meaning is, we'll examine in Chapter 5.) Maslow's basic Romanticism is easy to see if we just alter the grammatical subjects of his sentences. For example, substitute "the poem" and "full poetic development" for "man" and "full health and normal and desirable development" in the following statement of Maslow, and we could be reading Coleridge:

> Man has an essential nature of his own. . . . Full health and normal and desirable development consist in actualizing this nature, in fulfilling these potentialities, and in developing into maturity along the lines that this hidden, covert, dimly seen essential nature dictates, growing from within rather than being shaped from without.

We might recall here, from Part One, that the explicit linkage Maslow makes between *actualization* and *self* is that "self-actualization is actualization of a self." He thus seems to equate the self with the seed of the organic process: the self is what grows, develops, is actualized. We might also recall that Karen Horney, who her biographer claims introduced the concept of self-realization (and who thus, we could say, planted the first seeds of the human potential movement, as Erikson designed its first stages), makes a different equation. For her, the self (or the "real self") isn't what grows; it's what causes growth: she speaks in *Neurosis and Human Growth* "of the real self as that central inner force . . . which is the deep source of growth." Since in the introduction to this book, called "A Morality of Evolution," she suggests that "inherent in man are evolutionary constructive forces, which urge him to realize his given potentialities," she seems to be imagining the self *as* the force of evolution in man.

Horney and Maslow have different concepts of self-fulfillment because they have different concepts of the self. And, generally, psychology can make various connections between *self* and *development* because — as we saw in Part One — it has various *self*s to connect with. It also has available, we've now seen, various *development*s; and humanistic psychology has availed itself of all of them at one time or another. Or at the same time. We've noted Erikson talking in terms of both adaptation and stages; to these

Darwinian and Hegelian concepts of *development* he can also add, in the same breath, the fruit of the organic metaphor ("only in him who . . . has adapted himself to the triumphs and disappointments adherent to being . . . may gradually ripen the fruit of these seven stages." All these *development*s brought into the self by humanistic psychology bring with them, furthermore, the grand concept of evolution, since humanistic psychology is an extension of humanism and humanism an extension of evolutionary thought. In the "personal growth" of humanistic psychology, then, we see the attachment of evolution to the individual, whose personal development thus takes on all the significance of Huxley's "cosmic process."

We've now seen something of how *development* has come down (or up) to us: through the organic metaphor, evolution, Hegelianism, humanism, and psychology — gathering on its way a web of associates including *growth–potential–mature–adapt–survival–integration – stages – fulfillment – control – reason – individual–self*. We've watched these associations being formed over time; we've traced the *development* network, that is, in its historical or temporal dimension. Now, in Chapter 5, we'll shift our focus and look at the entire current network in its semantic dimension: look at the meaning "behind" or "underneath" the surface connections of this set of words. Then in Chapter 6, shifting our focus once again, we'll bring ourselves into the picture and look at how the *development* set attaches itself to us, and at what happens to us in our attachment to *development*.

5

The End of *Growth*

The terms of the *development* set are "leading" language in three senses. They're obviously dominant, powerful terms today, with extensive connections in a great many areas of thought and behavior. As leading (dominant) terms, they in turn lead (direct) us to think and act in certain ways, which we'll look at in Chapter 6. All leading language leads in these two senses (of dominating and directing). But *development* and its associates lead in a third way as well. Their meanings — particularly those of *evolve, develop, fulfillment, growth,* and *maturity* — have reference to change, and yet are more specific than general *change.* They each specify (though with varying degrees of specificity) a direction of change and / or a goal of change. Their meanings have, that is, a teleological (goal-directed) content; these terms actually mean "leading in a certain direction and / or to a certain end."

I say "and / or" because, while a term can refer to a particular point or phase of the teleological continuum (*maturity,* for example, refers to a goal), the entire vocabulary of teleology, like the vocabulary of any concept, is an intertwined complex of terms; so that ultimately we can't disentangle "direction" from "goal," or either of them from "end" or from "purpose." We interchangeably say, for example, "he has no sense of direction," "no sense of purpose," "no goal." Or, for another example, "end" can mean (among other things) either "final point" or "purpose"; and these geometrical and teleological definitions often slip into each other in actual usage — as in "reaching the end of a trip," at which point we've both reached the final point and accomplished our purpose. (Notice that "point," too, shares in this geometrical–teleological ambiguity: was the point of the trip to reach the end point?)

Given the inherent slipperiness of teleological language, we'll try in this chapter to pin down as much as possible the teleological meaning of development. We'll try to find out where, exactly, the terms of the *development* set "lead" in this third (teleological) sense. For each major term of the set we'll ask what teleological content it carries — that is, what direction, purpose, goal, or end the meaning of the word indicates (either implicitly or explicitly). We should also ask, where appropriate, whether the term specifies how the indicated goal can be reached: that is, whether the term gives "directions" in the sense of "guidelines" for reaching the desired end.

Evolution

Since all the terms of the *development* set are linked (it's their linkage, in fact, that makes them a set), our examination of the teleological content of each will eventually take us into all the others; so it makes no great difference where we start. Having to start somewhere, though, we might as well begin with *evolution,* since — as we've seen in tracing the history of *develop* and its associates — the concept of evolution has been the main force drawing these terms into connection with each other, and into prominence in our lives.

Evolution is, of course, primarily a biological concept and has been for the past one hundred years; so in looking for its teleological implications, we should ask first how biologists see them. This is easier asked than answered, however, for biologists see them in a variety of ways, while claiming for the most part to see none at all.

Most biologists disclaim any teleological significance to evolution because they associate teleology with purpose, and purpose with conscious intention, and conscious intention with the Intending Being who is beyond the empirical limits of proper scientific explanation. "Purpose," then, is ruled out of evolutionary vocabulary. "I do not feel that we should use the word purpose save where we know that a conscious aim is involved," proposes Julian Huxley in a move to keep teleology out of evolutionary considerations. Other eminent biologists second the motion with declarations of "no purpose": adaptation shows "no sign of purpose" (George Gaylord Simpson); adaptation has no "reference to any purpose" (Ernst Mayr); "evolution does not strive to accomplish any particular purpose" (Theodosius Dobzhansky); "Darwin argues that evolution has no purpose" (Stephen Jay Gould, identifying himself as a Darwinian).

Yet in cutting "purpose" out of their discussions of evolution, biologists have by no means cut out teleology altogether. Looking at the evolutionary process, almost all see it as having a direction; they've thus cut out one aspect of the teleological concept while retaining another. Agreeing for the most part that there's direction in evolution, they don't, however, agree on what that direction is. For Mayr, evolution seems to move in the direction of increased diversity; for Simpson, Huxley, and G. Ledyard Stebbins, the direction is toward increased complexity of organization and also, for Huxley, toward greater control over and independence from the environment; for J. Z. Young, picking up the geneticists' new cybernetic vocabulary, the direction is toward "increase of information" transmitted between generations.

As for whether or not these various directions lead to man as the end (result, if not purpose) of the evolutionary process, and whether or not evolutionary direction (whatever it is) should be labeled as progressive — this is a pair of teleological entanglements that biologists have tried to sort out in various ways. The simplest way is to see evolution as moving in a single ascending direction, with man as the high point so far, and to call this direction "advance" or "progress." This is Teilhard de Chardin's view: that, as Dobzhansky paraphrases it, "the evolution of the living world so far has been on the whole progressive" and that "the highest development of this progressive trend is man." Julian Huxley enthusiastically shares this view; but Dobzhansky himself, along with Simpson, is more cautious. They both object to this single-line view of evolution, insisting that evolution has moved in a variety of directions and that progress has many possible definitions. Yet after meticulous tracings of the various directions of evolution and careful qualifications of the anthropocentric implications of "progress," they still end up seeing evolution as progressive and man as, in Simpson's careful words, "on the whole but not in every single respect the pinnacle of evolutionary progress" — as if a teleological force in their own thinking were pulling the various threads of their argument to a single point where *evolution, man,* and *progress* inexorably meet.

Stephen Jay Gould will have none of this kind of thinking and is determined to cut the thread that draws evolutionary thought into humanistic arrogance (man at the top). Gould refuses to see man as a special product of evolution or to see evolution in terms of ascending lines and higher levels; he insists that " 'progress' of this sort plays no part in modern evolutionary theory." It's fascinating, then, that *progress* of some sort still plays a part in Gould's own writing. Not of the anthropocentric arrogant sort: when Gould refers, for example, to our size "as a controlling factor of our evolutionary progress," he doesn't mean that we're superior to other species; all he intends by *progress* here is something like "how we got where we are." Yet even the best intentions can't rid *progress* of its inherent plus; and Gould probably does intend to give the impression that we're biologically better off now than at an earlier stage of our evolution. Intentions aside, the linkage of *evolution* and *progress* in a view of evolution so far from that of Teilhard is evidence of how strongly attached the two terms are in biology. Commonly, in fact, *progressive* is treated as an essential attribute of evolution, as in a title like *The Basis of Progressive*

Evolution; and, whether as "evolutionary progress" or "progressive evolution," the two terms move through biology as inseparably (and at times as quarrelsomely) as lovers.

While biologists differ, then, in the direction they see evolution moving in, they still tend to label this direction as progressive, and most associate man with the high point (end) of this progressive process. As *evolution* moves from biology into the larger world of ordinary language, it therefore carries *progress* with it. Current dictionary definitions of our ordinary sense of *evolution* generally imply movement in a direction seen as good. The "central" definition of *evolution* in the *American Heritage Dictionary* is typical: "a gradual process in which something changes into a significantly different, especially more complex or more sophisticated, form." *Webster's Third* even explicitly labels evolutionary direction as "progress," giving its most general definition of *evolution* as "a process of continuous change from a lower, simpler, or worse condition to a higher, more complex or better: progressive development: *growth, progress.*"

Note that *evolution* is given here not only as "progress" but also as a kind of development. This connection shouldn't surprise us: we've seen that *evolve* and *develop* have been used interchangeably ever since *evolution* took over as the label for "development of species," and in fact every current dictionary I've seen includes *development* as part of its definition of *evolution*. To understand the full meaning of *evolution*, then, we must turn to *development*.

Development

Like evolution, development is a "fundamentally biological" concept; such at least is the judgment of the editor of an interdisciplinary collection of essays called *The Concept of Development*. And not only is the concept of development fundamentally biological; it is a fundamental concept *in* biology. Yet despite the central role played by *development* in biological investigation, the scientists contributing to *The Concept of Development* admit — with varying degrees of chagrin, irritation, or resignation — that *development* has no well-defined or consistent meaning in biology. One contributor, tracing the meanings given to *development* by biologists during much of this century, finds that *development* has been defined sometimes as "growth plus differentiation," sometimes as equivalent to "differentiation" alone, sometimes as equivalent to "growth" alone, sometimes as equivalent to "maturation" in distinction from "growth." *Growth* and *maturation,* in turn, have been defined, and used, vaguely and inconsistently. The concept of development, concurs the editor of the volume, is as "slippery" as Proteus "and of limited usefulness"; yet it continues to be used, along with its attendant vocabulary of *development–growth–maturation,* in all fields of biology. Like *self* in the language and thought of psychology, *development* plays a major role in shaping scientific research while having no definite shape of its own.

We frequently hear complaints about the vagueness of much popular language, and this vagueness is usually blamed on the undisciplined nature of popular thought. So it might be a bit shocking to discover that the language of presumably disciplined thought — the thought of professional disciplines — can be just as vague. Science, especially, we've come to regard as the place where precise thinking gets done and precise definitions are made. New disciplines trying to justify their validity tend to do so by proclaiming themselves sciences and by offering, as evidence in support of their scientific claims, a string of allegedly well-defined terms. Yet when we follow a term from popular discourse back to a scientific area where it plays a major role, hoping to find there a precise definition to sharpen our understanding of it, our hopes are often disappointed — so often that we have to wonder whether imprecision might not for some reason be necessary for the proper operation of scientific language. What that reason might be, scientists themselves would be most qualified to investigate. Meanwhile, all that seems clear is that the clarity of scientific language cannot be simply assumed: we can't, that is, assume that a word has a precise definition just because it comes to us from science.

After finding that biology has no agreed-on definition of *devel-*

opment and that science generally often cannot agree on the meanings of even its major terms, we shouldn't be surprised to find that the teleological implications of *development*'s meaning are a matter for considerable debate among biologists. And for considerable uneasiness and anxiety, too, it turns out. In listing some of the "essential" ideas commonly included in biological discussions of development, such as the ideas of "movement over time toward complexity of organization," of "hierarchization," and of "an end-state of organization," the editor of *The Concept of Development* concludes that "these last ideas inevitably bring us to the troublesome issue of 'purpose.'" "Purpose" and other teleological notions are troublesome for biologists because, as we saw in looking at the teleology of biological *evolution*, "purpose" seems to imply a Purposer, and the strictly empiricist scientific method has to operate entirely apart from a nonobservable directing force. Yet certain biological processes, including ontogenetic (individual) development, obviously do have direction — a dilemma which led the noted biologist John Haldane to quip that "teleology is like a mistress to a biologist: he cannot live without her but he's unwilling to be seen with her in public."

Biologist Ernst Mayr has recently offered a way to legitimize the relationship between biology and teleology. While still insisting that "it is illegitimate to describe evolutionary processes or trends as goal directed (teleological)," he asserts that "goal-directed processes involving only a single individual are of an entirely different nature from evolutionary change," and that "to apply 'teleological' to a goal-directed behavior or process" such as ontogenetic development "would seem quite legitimate." To facilitate general acceptance of this legitimacy, he proposes the term "teleonomic" as a substitute for the metaphysical-sounding "teleological" and proposes the language of information theory, especially "program" and "code," as a respectably mechanistic purpose-oriented vocabulary with which to describe biological goal-directed processes. Mayr's sober, rigorous reasoning and his own professional respectability may encourage other biologists — most of whom have long seen the directedness of ontogenetic *development* but, nervous about the otherworldly sound of teleological language, have enclosed all mention of "direction" or "end" in squirm quotes — to remove the quotation marks and let these terms move openly through their discussions of *development*, now that (in Haldane's metaphor) biological teleology has been revealed as a good, solid, down-to-earth girl after all.

No such uneasiness about teleological implications has ever surrounded *development* in the other area from which our current sense of it primarily comes: Hegelian *development* embraced teleology openly and passionately from the start. The *Entwicklung* that Hegel saw as the central process of all history was a clearly directed, even determined "Becoming," which followed inner laws through a sequence of ever-higher stages and reached its desired end in the state of "full development." This teleology of historical *development* as "progressive" change directed by "laws" was then reinforced, in the English mind, by Spencer's "law of Evolution."

Until well into the twentieth century, historical thinking consciously and enthusiastically molded itself into the form of Hegelian *development;* and by historical thinking I mean the thinking not only of professional historians but of all who study changes in human society over time (anthropologists, economists, some sociologists, philologists, and so on). The mold was so firmly cast that even though most historians today claim to have broken out of it and repudiate the rigid determinism of Hegelian development, *stages* and *growth* and *develop(ment)* remain key terms of their vocabulary, carrying with them certain (often unconscious) assumptions: for instance that development proceeds by continuous yet discrete "stages," that later stages are "determined" by or "built on" earlier ones, and that later ones tend to be more desirable — that is, that change in time is likely to be change for the better.

This last assumption, that when change is *development*, it's change for the better, is carried into our current ordinary sense of *develop(ment)*, according to its most general dictionary definitions. The *American Heritage Dictionary*'s first ("central") meaning of transitive *develop*, for example, is "to expand or realize the

potentialities of; bring gradually to a fuller, greater, or better state."
The *Random House Dictionary*'s first ("most frequently encountered") meaning is almost the same: "to bring out the capabilities
or possibilities of; bring to a more advanced or effective state."

Both these definitions not only judge the end state of *development* positively (as "greater," "better," "more advanced"), but they
also specify how this desired end is reached in the process of development: by "bringing out possibilities" or "realizing potentialities." This specification is familiar to us: we've seen that "realization of potentialities" has been part of the meaning of
development since *develop* first joined the organic metaphor. That
it's now a central part is tribute to the widespread influence of
humanistic psychology, which has brought *fulfillment* and *potential* (as we've nicknamed "potentialities") to the forefront of the
concept of development. With "realizing potential" as central, then,
to our sense of *developing* — even, according to the dictionaries,
what we primarily mean by *developing* — we have to look into
the teleological implications of *realize–fulfill–potential* in order to
see all of *develop*'s teleology.

Fulfillment of *Potential*

As they're commonly used in connection with the concept of development, the words *potential, realize, actualize,* and *fulfillment*
work together to form a teleological continuum. *Potential* is the
beginning point: where development starts from (*potential* and
undeveloped act as synonyms). The end point, or goal, of development is variously called *fulfillment, realization,* or *actualization.*
The process of reaching this goal, of moving from *potential* to
fulfillment, goes by the same names as the goal itself: the process
of *fulfillment,* or of *realization* or *actualization* of potential (all of
which can also appear as verbs: *fulfill, realize, actualize*). The chain
potential–realize–actualize–fulfillment thus refers to a self-enclosed
teleological (goal-directed) process. But does it refer to anything
else as well? Do these terms, that is, refer to anything other than
to their relation to each other along this teleological continuum?

Potential does not. The word *potential* has no meaning apart from its opposite, "actual." *Potential* just means "having potency or power"; it refers to a state of being — specifically, the state of being not yet actual but capable of becoming actual.

Actualizing, in turn, has no meaning apart from *potential:* it just refers to the process of moving from potential to actual. Similarly, *realizing* just means "making real or actual"; as used in connection with *potential,* it is synonymous with *actualizing.*

Fulfillment, like *potential,* refers to a state of being. Literally, *fulfill* means "to fill full"; it's the opposite, therefore, of "empty." In its early usages this material sense was primary: "all the land thereof shall be fulfilled with desert" (1483); bones "to fulfil the hollow places" (1548). Since filling something full is a kind of completion, *fulfill* has also been used for a variety of nonmaterial completions: the fulfilling of prophecies, commands, or obligations. *Fulfillment,* then, can be used in connection with a variety of subjects and processes. By itself, though, it gives no indication of which subject or process it is connected with; it just indicates the completion of the process, its end.

The chain of terms *potential–realize–actualize–fulfillment,* then, refers to a process but does not tell us anything about how the process works. All we know from these terms is that the process begins with *potential* and has *fulfillment* as its goal. As for how this goal is reached, the verbs *realize, actualize,* and *fulfill* tell us nothing except that the goal (of realization, actualization, or fulfillment) is being reached for. If we try, using these terms, to picture how to reach this goal, we can't. We have to supply for ourselves an object going through the process and a way of proceeding. There is thus an essential emptiness to the string of terms leading to *fulfillment:* they contain no images, metaphors, or referents other than each other. (*Fulfill* has long since been emptied of its original metaphor of "filling full.") Their combined meaning is entirely that of two points, labeled "start" and "end," with a directional arrow between them.

In their current usage, though, these terms are treated as if they have more meaning than they do. Meaning "direction" in the sense of pointing, they're treated as if they give directions in the sense of guidance; and yet, as we've seen, they give us no directions in this sense — no specifications of how to get where they say we should go, or even how to know when we've gotten there. Empty of the concrete meaning that we pretend they have, they at the same time are full of positive value. They are thus what I think of as empty pluses: terms that march through our prose and our lives surrounded by a halo which we'd find — if we took the trouble to look through it — to be shining forth from nothing.

We hear go by, for example, an immensely popular line like "the goal of every person is to fulfill his potential." It sounds so glorious; we cheer enthusiastically. (Crowds at Dr. Leo Buscaglia's "The Art of Being Fully Human" sessions actually applaud when he sends forth this line.) In our excitement we run after it; yet, trying to follow it, we immediately stumble, stop, not knowing which way to go. To *fulfillment*, yes; but where is that?

As we stand there scratching our heads, along comes the promise of an answer: the goal goes by again, now parading as Maslow's "mature, fully-human, self-actualizing people in whom the human potentialities have been realized and actualized." This certainly sounds as if it's giving us plenty to grab and follow. We reach first for the tail end(s) of "realized and actualized," but they slip from our grasp; they're end points, therefore ungraspable from our as yet unrealized position. "Human potentialities"? Yes, we can hold onto that as a label for where we are now, but it doesn't get us anywhere. "Self-actualizing"? That just means that we do it (whatever it is) by ourselves; we still don't know what to do. "Fully-human"? Another end ("fullness"), with no clue about how to get there. "Mature"? Another completion, the desired end put in terms of the organic metaphor but still — as we'll see in the next section — giving no directions for how to achieve it. And so this long string of *fulfillment* terms goes by, and we're left empty-handed (though not, as we'll see in Chapter 6, unmoved).

Growth and *Maturity*

What the *fulfillment* chain tells us about the teleology of *development*, then, is only that development is indeed a highly (even essentially) teleological process. As for what that process consists of, the specification of *develop* as "realizing the potentialities of" tells us nothing. *Develop* has another connection, though, with a more specific process: growth. The connection between *growth* and *development* is so close, in fact, that *grow* is the primary definition given by current dictionaries for intransitive *develop*.

Since we've found, in looking to current dictionaries for the meanings of the terms of the *development* set, that each is defined in terms of the others (*evolution* is defined as *development, development* as *fulfillment* and as *growth, growth* as *maturity* and as *evolution,* etc.), a comment on the circularity of dictionary definitions seems in order. This circularity is often ridiculed, but it is entirely appropriate. Words do get their meanings from their associations with each other (and also from the situations and values associated with each of them, currently and in the past). Dictionary circularity is nothing but a tracing of these associations. We can therefore use a dictionary to get a quick sketch of the primary network of associations of a word — by looking up each word of the definition, and then each word in each of those definitions, and so on. The words repeated most often in the definitions will be the main terms of the network (the inner circle or inner set, to use the language of social politics); definitions appearing just once or occasionally will be extensions of the set, which, if followed, would lead into other networks of meaning. Theoretically, this procedure would take us eventually through every word in the dictionary, and many times through most of them, giving us finally a complete picture of all the interconnected networks of meaning which our language forms and through which it runs — though such a picture, of the entire metanetwork of our language, would be too extensive and complex for the imagination to grasp.

Returning, then, to the small segment of the metanetwork with which we're presently concerned — the connection between *grow* and *develop* — we can look to the meaning of *growth* in order to try to specify what is involved in the process of *development*. *Growth* does refer to a specific, well-understood process, at least in regard to plants. We know what we mean by "seed," "germination," "fruit," "ripeness," "maturity," and the other terms that specify stages of growth or products of particular stages. These stages are visibly verifiable and are measurable: we can easily see whether a plant has bloomed or has fully grown; we can measure its height or number of leaves or the size of its fruit and can compare these measurements to the norms of growth for this species or variety.

A difficulty comes, however, when *growth* leaves its reference to plants and becomes a metaphor; it then brings with it the terms of organicism (especially, along with *grow, unfolding* and *mature*) while leaving behind any clear sense of what exactly these terms refer to. This is the fundamental difficulty in, for example, the "personal growth" metaphor of humanism and humanistic psychology. "The ultimate goal," says "Humanist Manifesto II," "should be the fulfillment of the potential for growth in each human personality." But do we know what "growth" in the "human personality" consists of? Human personality is an imaginative construct; it has no physical existence. Though it seems to have some relation to our physical natures, what that relation is remains (despite the best efforts of scientists in many fields to discover it) a mystery. When psychologists claim, then, to describe stages of personality growth and to measure levels of maturity, they are describing what must be at least to some extent a personal vision and are trying to measure a fiction. Like all fictions, this one has some basis in fact: many of us (at least those of us from the literate, white, upper-middle class, from which the subjects of "growth studies" are overwhelmingly drawn) do seem (at least in late-twentieth-century America) to go through some similar changes, corresponding roughly to our physical age. But to label this process *growth* — or even *a* process, which already implies a singularity and uniformity — is to appear to know more about it than we do.

The appearance of knowledge, of giving answers to our questions, is one of the primary intellectual attractions of metaphors and analogies generally. It is also the cause of a recurrent intellectual error: the mistake of taking our metaphors literally. In our eagerness to know, we seize on terms as answers when they're valid only as questions; we see a likeness and press it into an identity. Psychologists seem to identify personality with plants — to draw, that is, on the organic metaphor — when they see individual development as the positively directed unfolding of inner laws and want, reasonably enough, to know how these laws work. For example, Karen Horney, looking for a way to describe what she saw (in reaction to Freud's negativism) as the "constructive forces in man," was convinced that the organic metaphor gave her the answer:

> You need not, in fact cannot, teach an acorn to grow into an oak tree, but when given a chance, its intrinsic potentialities will develop. Similarly the human individual, given a chance, tends to develop his particular human potentialities. He will develop then the unique alive forces of his real self. . . . In short, he will grow, substantially undiverted, toward self-realization.

For Horney and other *growth* psychologists like Maslow and Rogers, the attraction of the organic metaphor as an explanatory device, an instrument of understanding, is probably reinforced by a strong attraction that the organic has for all of us: the attraction of nature, of naturalness. ("All people feel that growth is good," Mary McCarthy has said.) Around the organic metaphor, and all its attendant language of *growth* and *maturity* and *unfolding* and *ripeness,* hovers a warm glowing sense of sun-ripened natural goodness. Our attraction to this language seems to be part of a basic human longing for identification with nature, maybe for a return to the Garden of Eden. Psychologists eager to learn about our "basic needs" might learn more if — instead of elaborating tables, stages, surveys, and measurements — they examined their own need for certain metaphors.

The *growth* of the organic metaphor comes close, then, to being an empty plus. In its literal meaning, in reference to a plant, *growth* is neither empty nor much of a plus: it is full of particular concrete referents and is generally merely descriptive, neutral (with perhaps the slight plus that it's better for a plant to grow than to die). In becoming a metaphor, *growth* drops its concrete referents and picks up an enormous plus: it fills with good feeling, with positive emotive content, but otherwise is emptied of meaning. It fills also with certain logical difficulties which we should now take note of, especially as they appear in the place where they're likely today to cause us the most problems: the *growth and development* of humanistic psychology.

One difficulty in the organic metaphor is its deterministic implications. A plant grows according to its inherent laws of development; it simply follows these laws; it has no choice in the matter. The organic metaphor is thus a poor choice (!) when we want to assert human freedom: any assertion of free choice in terms of the organic metaphor has to simply assert that these (organic) terms have stopped. This is how, as critic M. H. Abrams points out, Coleridge bluntly handled the difficulty. Wanting to liken the artistic creative process to the spontaneous self-evolving growth of a plant, but also wanting to acknowledge the artist's conscious control over the process, Coleridge just asserted that the organic analogy should stop where free will starts: "what the plant is by an act not its own and unconsciously, that must thou *make* thyself to become." Abrams's comment — that "in Coleridge's aesthetics, no less than in his ethics and theology, the justification of free-will is a crux" — applies as well to all other attempts (of which there are many in humanistic psychology) to glorify *growth* and *freedom* at the same time.

Another difficulty in the organic metaphor, which Abrams also finds in Romanticism's organic aesthetics, is a confusion about whether to glorify *growth* as a process or as an end. The noun itself can refer to either: the first meaning of *growth* given by the *American Heritage Dictionary* includes both "the process of growing" and "full development; maturity." *Growth* can't, however, mean both at the same time. Nor can one of the meanings be celebrated without diminishing or even denying the value of the other, nor without raising additional logical and sometimes moral problems.

When the *process* of growth is celebrated, *growth* is seen, in Abrams's words, as "an open-ended process, nurturing a sense of

the promise of the incomplete, and the glory of the imperfect."
We hear this promise today in popularizations like "there is no
limit to our capacity to grow." The promise of unlimited growth
is an attractive one (at least, many are attracted to it); yet it carries
with it certain moral and logical difficulties. It can easily lead to
what Abrams calls "the Faustian ideal of insatiability": the greed
for more and more growth, which involves (since organic growth
is a process of assimilation and expansion) assimilating more and
more of the world into oneself for the sake of one's own expansion. This cannibalistic and proprietary view of growth is the one
recommended by the Harvard Grant Study team in *Psychology
Today:*

> To reach full maturity, we must first rediscover our parents so
> that, now internalized and immortal, they become a source of
> fresh strength. Second, we must acquire new people to care for
> faster than they die or move away. In other words, to incorpo-
> rate is to grow.

Besides leading in this problematical moral direction, the promise of unlimited growth leads also to biological nonsense. Such a
promise simply can't, in strictly biological terms, be kept; biological growth always has an end. In biology, the end of growth is
designated as *maturity*. This is usually a neutral designation: the
name for the final ontogenetic stage ("a mature cell," "a mature
animal"). Outside biology, *mature* in its most general sense retains
this designation: the *American Heritage Dictionary* gives *mature*'s
first meaning as "complete and finished in natural growth or development."

As the point of completion of growth, *maturity* obviously does
not fit anywhere in the picture of *growth* as the promise of the
incomplete. Or, to look at it (the whole metaphor) from the other
end, if *maturity* is seen as the end (goal) of *growth*, *growth* cannot
be seen as an unending process. Focusing on *maturity* as the desired goal of the growth process thus avoids the moral and logical
difficulties of celebrating limitless *growth*. Yet celebrating *maturity* brings difficulties of its own.

One difficulty is that of deciding what exactly to designate as *maturity*. Since *growth* in the organic metaphor is just a metaphor, with — as we've noted — no clear concrete referents for its terms, the point to be labeled *maturity* is pretty much up for grabs. And what tends to be grabbed is whatever point (or condition or stage or product) we already consider valuable according to other criteria. T. S. Eliot's mature work will be seen, for instance, by Christian readers as *Four Quartets;* while agnostic or pessimistic readers will find *The Waste Land* representative of Eliot's mature vision and will see the *Quartets* as a falling off from *The Waste Land*'s rich, dense complexity into a poorer, thinner religious view. Similarly, when applied to individual human development, *maturity* can refer to a variety of points, and on a variety of scales: *maturity* can be a moral term, designating a type of desirable behavior (the ability, for example, to admit one's mistakes); or a chronological term (one reaches maturity at a certain age); or a term designating the ideal of personality development or even of general psychological health (Maslow's goal of the "mature, fully-human, self-actualizing" person). *Maturity* thus acts as a floating halo, coming to rest glowingly on whatever in human life we already value.

Another difficulty in celebrating *maturity* as the end of growth is that, as B. F. Skinner has said, "it emphasizes a terminal state which does not have a function." Nor, we should add, does it have a future. As the final good, the desired end, of growth, *maturity* can have nothing good (or as good) beyond it. When seen as the goal of human development, as it often is in psychology, *maturity* therefore leaves us with the problem of how to see the rest of life, the post-maturity years, in positive terms.

This problem could be resolved if *maturity* were imagined as a state of completion that, once reached, remained (was in fact a state, static). But such a view, of unchanged continuousness of a single (even if ultimate) state, directly contradicts the view of growth as a continuous process. We're thus brought back to the uncomfortable fact of an unresolvable contradiction within the teleology of the organic metaphor. As a teleological model, the organic metaphor gives conflicting directions: toward *maturity* as the end of the growth process and toward *growth* as an end in itself.

Conclusion

The conflict between the ends of *maturity* and *growth* occurs elsewhere in the *development* set as well, as we can see if we look back over the teleological implications of the set's various terms. On the teleological continuum formed by the set as a whole, *fulfillment* represents the same (final) point as *maturity*, while *develop* and *evolve* cover the same unidirectional process as *grow*. (*Potential* and *undeveloped* are interchangeable markers for the starting point.) Since the process finds its end (goal, purpose) in *fulfillment*, any valuing of the process for its own sake, as an end in itself, will conflict with the end of *fulfillment*. Yet the process is commonly valued in just this way, not only in celebrations of *development* but also in most contemporary references to *change*.

All development is, of course, change; but not all change is development(al). Or it didn't use to be. But with *development* coming to be seen during the past century and a half as almost the universal way of the world, the way of so much that happens that almost anything that happens is now called a development (the "Evening News" reports "the day's developments") — and with every *development*, whether organic or evolutionary or historical or all of the above, seen as progressive — our sense of *change* has altered. While far from covering all that we mean by *change*, development is seen so commonly as the assumed mode of change that *develop*'s plus sign has adhered to *change* itself. We noted earlier in this chapter that when change is *development*, it's change for the better; we should also note that, unless specified as "change for the worse" (as it rarely is, except in reference to sickness or the economy), *change* itself is now generally assumed to be for the better. *Change* is assumed, that is, to be a positive term.

When *change* turns from a neutral into a positive term, any opposition to it is seen as negative (*fixity, permanence, final state, even state* itself). This structure of values opposing positive *change* to negative *fixity* is the common structure underlying contemporary expressions as otherwise different as Stephen Toulmin's celebration of "intellectual flux" in his massive philosophical work *Human Understanding,* and Carl Rogers's gushings that "life, at its best, is a flowing, changing process in which nothing is fixed." This currently common *change / fixity* value structure, with its positive value all on the side of change, has been produced largely by *development;* yet it conflicts, as we've seen, with *development*'s own professed end of *fulfillment.*

Another conflict within the teleology of *development* is between its two dominant metaphors of plant and ladder. Organic *development* lends itself to cyclical images ("the life cycle is an organic whole," says Levinson in defense of his title *The Seasons of a Man's Life*); Hegelian *development* encourages hierarchical images of stages, steps, and levels (like the developmental ladders pictured by Levinson and other Adult Developmentalists). Since the organic life cycle pictures us going round and round on a course recurring like the seasons and the ladder pictures us moving upward through a series of unique nonrepeatable stages, it's hard to picture both at once. Yet developmentalists draw on both anyway, even in a single phrase like "The Climb to Maturity" of the Harvard Grant Study.

If we try, then, to look at the teleology of *growth and development* as a whole, we have to conclude that it doesn't look like much of "a whole" (certainly not an organic whole). The teleological picture presented by the *growth and development* set is one of confusion and conflict: the central metaphors of plant and ladder offer irreconcilable images; directions are given to conflicting goals of endless, always progressive change (*development, evolution, growth*) and of satisfying finality (*fulfillment, maturity, actualization*); or directions are given with huge gaps left in them, empty directions that specify highly desirable goals (like *fulfillment* or *maturity*) without specifying how to reach them.

Such is the confusion of directions in which *development* language, in its semantic dimension, leads. We should now look at why, despite this confusion, we try our best to follow *development*'s directions — and at what sort of behavior we're led into as a result.

6

"You Must Develop"

"For nature must be right"

A friend of mine told me the following true "growth" story, about a married couple of her acquaintance. After twenty years of marriage the husband, in his forties, began an affair with a younger woman. It followed the usual course for such affairs: betrayal, self-justification, guilt, agonized confession, heart-broken efforts at understanding by the hurt wife, unsuccessful attempts at hiding the ongoing tension from the children, months of tears alternating with knotted stomachs and forced smiles, decisions to break up the marriage alternating with decisions to patch up the marriage, well-intentioned vows on both sides broken in helpless confusion — all in all what my friend summed up as "a turbulent destructive affair." When it was over, the husband and wife, reconciled, reported enthusiastically to my friend that they both had "grown so much from the experience."

Our culture's plus terms are always available to justify our actions. We can find a plus term to cover anything we do, so that it will appear (even to ourselves) well done. Political murders are masked, and have been throughout history, as *liberation;* industrial capitalism is notorious for masking self-interest as *free enter-*

prise; and, closer to home, we tear ourselves and each other apart, then drape a lush green cover of *growth* over ourselves and look in the mirror and see only good.

But besides masking our behavior, *growth* — along with *development* and their associated terms — can also mold it. *Growth* and *development* act as a mold because they've become a must; we live under a developmental imperative. This imperative ("you must develop") shapes our personal and family lives, our collective social enterprises and institutions, our intellectual pursuits.

To understand how exactly the developmental imperative operates on us in these particular areas, we need to be aware first of how it operates generally. Below (Sample 1) is an analysis of its operations offered a century ago in response to one of the earliest voicings of an imperative to develop: the call thundered out in Spencer's universal "law of Evolution." The other quotations below are a chronological sampling of developmental musts heard since then. Samples 2–4 will be examined in the present section, to determine generally how the developmental imperative works: where it comes from, why we obey it, and what happens when we do. Sample 5, and recent extensions of it, will be examined in the next section, where we'll look at a particular developmental imperative that affects us today with special force: that of the psychology of Adult Development. Then in the final section of the chapter we'll glance at some other areas of our individual and collective lives that are currently shaped by the imperative to develop.

1. To Mr. Spencer . . . the doctrine of evolution seems to supply the end of conduct. He conceives of morality as essentially an observance of the laws of life. . . . It is easy to look upon the natural process as a tendency towards an end, and to conceive of our conscious actions as being bound by this tendency, so that the highest end of our existence must be to co-operate with the natural forces.

JAMES SULLY, "Evolution in Philosophy,"
Encyclopaedia Britannica, 1878

2. Since it is the order of nature that the new organism should pass through certain developmental stages, it behooves us to study nature's plan and seek rather to aid than to thwart it. For nature must be right; there is no higher criterion.

C. GUILLET, education theorist, 1900

3. [History develops according to] natural laws, which we must accept whether we want to or not, whose workings we cannot obviate, however much we may thwart them, to our own failure and disadvantage.

EDWARD CHEYNEY, Presidential Address
to American Historical Association, 1923

4. Religions must evolve if they are not to become extinct.

JULIAN HUXLEY, ed., *The Humanist Frame*, 1961

5. Each individual, to become a mature adult, must to a sufficient degree develop all the ego qualities mentioned.

ERIK ERIKSON, *Childhood and Society*, 1950, 1963

James Sully already saw, in 1878, where the imperative of evolutionary development comes from: from a view that nature develops according to "laws" which we, in turn, are bound by. The evolutionist, looking at the direction of nature's development, projects what he sees onto us as an imperative. The direction observed (seen) in nature, that is, gets projected onto us as the direction we "must" observe (follow, obey).

The imperative comes in because, as Sully recognized, our actions are "conscious." Nonconscious nature doesn't have to be encouraged or ordered to follow natural laws; it follows them by necessity, "by nature." Our own nature, though, involves consciousness, and consciousness involves choice. Presumably we can choose *not* to *co*-operate with (work along with) natural forces; otherwise we wouldn't have to be ordered (directed, told) that we "must" do so.

In ordering us to follow a direction that it claims we are bound by, the developmental imperative is obviously caught in a logical difficulty. This is the same difficulty that we saw in the teleology of the organic metaphor: if our human development is just the unfolding of natural laws, then choice can play no part in it, so to urge us to follow these laws makes no sense. Put another way, in terms of the traditional necessity / free-choice dichotomy, the difficulty is this: as soon as an element of choice (even the tiniest act of free consciousness) is brought into the operation of necessity, necessity is no longer operating exactly the same way; it's no longer entirely necessity. As soon, then, as laws of necessity are applied to matters involving choice, they cease being laws of necessity. Therefore the laws of nonconscious development (necessity, nature) cannot, logically, be applied to consciousness.

In applying them, the developmental imperative is committing a logical fallacy, but this very fallacy is what gives the developmental imperative its force. The force is that of a threat: nature will by necessity follow her own laws; if we choose not to go along with her, if we "thwart" her (Samples 2 and 3), we are choosing to resist necessity, a choice which is doomed to failure. This failure is imagined in a variety of ways, from Cheyney's mild "disadvantage" to Huxley's violent "extinction." We had better, then, not only "accept" (Sample 3) but also "aid" (Sample 2) nature's laws, the threat goes — *or else.*

This is a very powerful threat, and it accounts for much of the developmental imperative's effectiveness in directing our behavior. The entire process of American elementary education was redesigned at the beginning of this century to Guillet's order because he presented it (and really saw it himself) as "the order of nature," which we thwart at the peril of damaging our children's natural development. And Marx convinced thousands of workers throughout Europe not only to accept (as Cheyney advises) but to actively aid the natural laws of historical development because history was bound to follow these laws anyway, and in the inevitable revolution to come, those not forcing their way to the top would inevitably be dragged under.

When the developmental imperative isn't scaring us into following its orders, it directs us by appealing to our moral sense, our sense of right. We get this sense, it believes, from nature: as Guillet puts it, "nature must be right." If nature is right, we'd be wrong (the reasoning goes) not to follow it. This assumption of a moral value in nature's direction can be extended, and has been ever since Spencer, into a whole system of ethics. "Evolutionary ethics," as it is sometimes called, conceives of morality, with Spencer, "as essentially an observance of the laws of life." To be right, to do our moral duty and achieve our highest end, we have only to observe (look at and follow) nature's own direction.

Such observance, however, can be very difficult in practice. The developmental imperative calls upon us, with the force of both a moral appeal and a threat, to look to nature's direction as a model on which to pattern our lives; yet we see a variety of directions in nature when we look. The universal law of evolution has appeared on closer observation as a variety of possible particular laws, each of which is proclaimed for a time as *the* law and then usually, at a later time, disclaimed. Meanwhile though, during the time that it is seen as the law of the land (and of all dwellers in the land), countless human enterprises, individual and collective, redirect themselves in order to follow it. The Law of the Survival of the Fittest, the most infamous of evolution's once-universal laws, drew social legislation, economic theory and practice, personal and professional behavior (a justification of competitiveness), and much more in its direction before it came to be seen as a misdirected view of nature (at least of human nature) after all. And Stephen Jay Gould has shown in *Ontogeny and Phylogeny* how a number of large human enterprises — including Freudian psychology and criminal law, as well as the educational program modeled by Guillet on "nature's plan" — redesigned themselves at the beginning of this century in order to follow the developmental guidelines of the evolutionary Law of Recapitulation. When this law was repealed, erased from the biology books, these enterprises were left having modeled themselves on a mistake.

The legalistic metaphor is appropriate here because, as a contemporary historian has written in direct reply to Sample 3, "the seeker after historical laws [and, we can add, all other laws of nonphysiological human development] is prone to become a legislator, who will make the laws after his own heart, his emotions, or preconceived ideas." This isn't to say that such a seeker *wants* to be a mere legislator, that he *wants* to make up his own laws rather than discovering those of nature. We can earnestly desire to know the truth, can stare at our object of investigation with the greatest attention, probe it with the most carefully designed instruments, measure it with the most elaborate scales; yet if we are staring at, probing, measuring an area of life that doesn't, in fact, operate according to laws of necessity (and all areas of human life involving choice are, as we noted above, free from strict necessity), any laws that we see there will be not pure fact but to some extent fiction — projections of an order formed, at least in part, in our minds.

One reason for our not noticing when we've projected our own order onto the world is that there's a slippage in the meaning of the word *order* itself. *Order* can have either a descriptive or a prescriptive meaning: *order* as "pattern" describes, maps, tells what is (the order of grades a child passes through in school); *order* as "command" prescribes, molds, tells what ought to be (an order given by the teacher to students). This same slippage is inherent in the meanings of many of the key terms connected with *order: law, direction, must.* A *law* can be a description of nature (the law of relativity) or a prescription for human conduct (a law prohibiting or permitting abortions). A *direction* can describe spatial relations (the direction of the Cape Horn Current is from west to east), or it can prescribe a pattern to follow (the directions in a cookbook). *Must*, similarly, can describe necessary relations as if on a map (to get from Manhattan to Staten Island, you must cross water), or it can prescribe, mold, behavior according to some view of right conduct (you must not steal).

It's impossible to know for sure why these key terms for talking about our human existence contain this slippage in their meanings; but I think maybe the reason is that our existence itself is, essentially, slippery. We are both bound and not bound; we both follow laws and make them; we are to some extent controlled by material forces and to some extent not. And no one knows where to draw the line. Wherever we try to draw it, it slips somewhere else — even if just the tiniest bit. The key terms with which we try to draw a line (write a line) both represent this slipperiness of our existence and allow for it.

Because of this slippage inherent in the terms *law, order, direction*, etc., we can legislate, order, and direct without intending to do so. We can refer to nature's direction in what we intend as a descriptive sense, yet be heard and understood as if we were giving a direction prescribed by nature. Our best intentions cannot remove the imperative overtones of these words. Huxley may have intended, in writing that "religions must evolve if they are not to become extinct" (Sample 4), merely to describe what he saw as a natural direction; the line sounds, however, like a threat to religions that they'd better follow this direction or else. Any line that "you must develop according to nature's laws" will be free of imperative overtones only as long as it refers to matters of strict necessity, over which we have no choice; as soon as it refers to a matter of choice it becomes — in effect, even if not in intention — a command and a threat.

"We must be willing to change chairs if we want to grow"

Today the imperative to develop threatens and commands our personal and family lives most forcefully as it comes to us from the popularized psychology of Adult Development. The best-selling language of Adult Development is indeed leading language: it dominates our lives and it directs them. We should look carefully, then, at how it manages to lead us and at what sort of behavior it leads us into — or, more accurately (given the imperative nature of developmental language), pushes or forces us into.

Below are some samples of the popular language of Adult Development (numbered in continuation of the samples of the developmental imperative given in the preceding section):

> 5. Each individual, to become a mature adult, must to a sufficient degree develop all the ego qualities mentioned.
> ERIK ERIKSON, *Childhood and Society*, 1950, 1963

6. [In each of us there is] the necessity to change and move on
to a new footing in the next stage of development. . . . We
must be willing to change chairs if we want to grow. . . .
Times of crisis, of disruption or constructive change, are not
only predictable but desirable. They mean growth. If we pretend the crises of development don't exist, not only will they
rise up later and hit with a greater wallop but in the mean-
time we don't grow. We're captives.

GAIL SHEEHY, *Passages*, 1974

7. For a man in period three, the path to further development
must cross four and five — there are no shortcuts or alternative routes. He can navigate a period in myriad ways, but
he cannot avoid it. In the present, if he is to find some satisfaction and create a basis for life in the next period, he must
deal with the current developmental tasks.

DANIEL LEVINSON, *The Seasons of a Man's Life*, 1978

The *must*s of Adult Development work the same way as the
general developmental imperative we examined in the previous
section. There's the same confusion between necessity and choice;
the same threatening tone; the same slippage between description
and prescription, between the *must*s of a map and of a mold.

The confusion between necessity and choice can be seen easily
in Samples 6 and 7. In both, change according to a given developmental pattern is presented as "necessity" ("the necessity to
change"), which we "cannot avoid." "We're captives" of it. Yet
at the same time as development is presented as a necessity, it's
also presented as a choice. To say "we must be willing to change"
(Sample 6) is to make change a matter of our will, a matter of
choice. Furthermore, the will to change is presented as conditional
on another choice: *if* we want to grow. If we choose the goal of
growth, this logic goes, the imperative to choose change follows.
But the conditional *if*-clause implies that we aren't forced to accept the condition: we don't *have* to choose growth.

This conditional-imperative construction — "if you want X, you
must do Y" — forms the basis of Samples 5 and 7 as well, and
even of the concept of Adult Development generally. The basic
structure of thought of Adult Development is this conditional-

imperative filled in as: "if you want to grow, you must develop according to the model or pattern given." The goal of *growth* can be offered explicitly (as it is three times by Sheehy in Sample 6); or it can be represented by a close associate like *maturity* (as in Erikson's goal of becoming "a mature adult"); or it can be supplemented by other of *growth and development*'s common ends (like Levinson's "satisfaction"). Always, though, the goal is presented as a choice: an option offered in an implied or stated *if*-clause.

This choice of goal is, however, taken away in the same breath with which it is (apparently) offered. We've already noted how the insistence on the "necessity" of the given developmental pattern makes a mockery — or at least a logical fallacy — of any offerings of choice in the matter. The element of effective choice is further reduced by the nature of what is being offered: *growth, maturity,* and *satisfaction* are such heavily loaded plus terms that we are hardly expected to choose against them. And if (*if*) we should be so inclined as to choose some other goal, no other goal is ever offered by Adult Development as a possible choice. The only ends that Adult Development ever mentions as worthy of our consideration are *growth, maturity, satisfaction,* and their associates; and the possibility of not considering these ends is never presented, except as part of a threat.

Sheehy, in Sample 6, puts the typical threat with striking directness: if we ignore the crises (stages) of development, they will "rise up later and hit with a greater wallop." This is the you'd-better-follow-nature-or-else threat that we saw giving force to the general developmental imperative; and it's a threat running throughout Adult Development — built even into the idea of developmental models.

Most psychologists recognize that their developmental models are hypothetical constructions: patterns designed to structure their further research, not to impose a structure or mold on people's lives. But the very word and concept of *model* suffers from the same slippage that we noted previously in *law, direction, order,* and *must:* the slippage between description and prescription, between map and mold. The researcher of Adult Development stares at the object of his research (individual personality change) and tries to make sense of what he sees. Drawing on the biological concepts and language of ontogenetic growth and development,* he sees in the individual personality a pattern of development, a direction as of the following of a law. Trying to follow this direction with his mind and his pen, trying to trace this pattern, he draws a model — usually a sketch that looks like a ladder — which he calls a developmental model.

Even if he is aware (as some, though by no means all, psychologists are) that this model can be an accurate representation of human development only to the extent that human development is bound by laws and is not free, and even if he intends (and explicitly states) that his model is to be seen as a hypothetical sketch of a possible direction followed by human development and not as a direction that he is advising us to follow, still that slippage in the word and picture and concept of *model* will have its imperative effect. The model drawn as a hypothesis, as a tentative tracing, acquires once drawn the appearance of permanence, solidity, and reality — so much so that even researchers who begin with an awareness of the hypothetical nature of their models often end by believing in their reality. Reinforced then by all the language of the developmental imperative, which — as we saw in the previous section — exerts its force on us whether or not its users intend to be forcing us, the Adult Development model presents itself as a model (guide, mold) for our conduct. When we hear from an authority like Erikson that "each individual, to become a mature adult, must to a sufficient degree develop all the ego qualities mentioned," we respond by trying our best to develop those qualities.

What exactly happens to us as a result? When we try to obey the imperatives of Adult Development, when we try to shape our lives according to its models, what shape do our lives take?

---

* In the takeover of biological *development* by psychology, there's another slippage: in *self*. From biology's meaning of "automatic" (self-development), *self-* slips into psychology's *self* of will and personal fulfillment.

A changing shape, certainly. The *change / fixity* structure in which the *development* set operates puts all its positive value, as we've seen, on the side of change. In Adult Development this value structure manifests itself as a strong encouragement, even pressure, for us to "change" our personal lives. For if we believe, with Adult Development, that our goal in life should be personal growth and that, as Sheehy puts it, "we must be willing to change chairs if we want to grow," we are likely to be not only willing to change but eager to. We are likely, that is, to become restless: to *seek* change, as both a means to and a sign of our growth.

Thus if I try to obey Sheehy's imperative that I must be willing to change chairs if I want to grow, I am likely to set about deliberately to change them. So I move into my husband's chair (go out and get a job); or I throw out the old chairs and buy new ones of a different style; or I try out a different man in my husband's chair (have an affair); or I move to a different apartment with chairs of my own; or I shift jobs (leave the counselor's chair for the teacher's chair) or go back to school (move into a library chair). If I stay put in the same chair year after year — sitting at my desk planning the sales operations for my company, or drinking coffee at the kitchen table while keeping a loving watchful eye on the children — the implication is that I'll end up stunted, deformed, incomplete, undeveloped. I won't grow.

In my eagerness to avoid such an undesirable, undeveloped end, I might even take an axe and chop up all the chairs in the house, leaving a pile of wreckage (and maybe also of debts), tearful children, and a bewildered husband; and nothing in Adult Development would tell me that this might be a bad way to change chairs. Adult Development has no way of seeing this, or any change, as bad. All its terms for change — *transition, passage,* even *crisis* and *disruption* — are treated as positive. "Times of crisis, of disruption or constructive change, are not only predictable but desirable. They mean growth" (Sample 6). Adult Development has us always "building the life structure," even when we seem, according to almost any other point of view, to be wrecking it. Presenting "disruption" as indistinguishable from, and equally desirable as, "construction," Adult Development gives us no standard by which to decide on one change rather than another.

Pressuring us to change and hence encouraging restlessness, but providing no standard by which we can decide what change exactly to make, Adult Development puts us in a chaos of commotion. And there it leaves us. Of course, it claims otherwise. It claims not to leave us in chaos but to lead us in a positive direction: toward the goal of *satisfaction* or *fulfillment*. But we saw, in examining the teleology of the *development* set in Chapter 5, that *fulfillment* is an empty goal: it marks the end point of development without telling us what to do to reach that end.

Particular means of reaching fulfillment can, of course, be named and often have been. Women's fulfillment, for example, was said in the 1950s to be motherhood, and in the 1970s to be career. Communism says the individual's fulfillment lies in joining the Party; Catholicism says it lies in joining the Church. These are all particular ways of filling in the empty plus of *fulfillment;* none of them is in itself fulfilling. Values from outside the *development* set are what label particular acts as fulfilling. The *development* set alone — unless joined with another set of values — directs us to no particular act when it directs us to *fulfillment*.

Nor does *fulfillment* always provide direction even when combined with another set of values. The most frequent combination in recent years, the combination of *fulfillment* with *self* in the much popularized goal of *self-fulfillment,* is far from the prize-winning (goal-winning) combination it at first appears to be. At first it certainly sounds like a winner, especially as trumpeted in the popular press: "finding the way to self-fulfillment," proclaims a *Parents Magazine* article of that title, is simply a matter of "getting up and doing what you want to do, every day." "Living is mostly a personal matter," chimes in *House & Garden* in an article called "The Dynamics of Personal Growth"; "it's up to you how you shape your life, what goes into it, what you get out of it, what you give."

Waking each day to this rousing call to self-fulfillment, sitting up in bed with a bright smile of eagerness to develop myself and with arms open to embrace the personal growth assured me that day if I only "do what I want to do," I'm likely to remain stuck in this expectant position. My outstretched arms start to feel heavy under their own weight, and my smile fades to a frown of puzzlement: how do I *know* what I want to do today? Consult your feelings, your self, urges the imperative of *self-fulfillment;* do whatever you feel like doing. But I know that my feelings change every day, and sometimes even every hour or minute, depending on the shiftiest of causes: the weather (air pressure, temperature), hormones (whether I'm getting my period), the dreams I've just had, who I happened to bump into yesterday and what mood that person was in. Surely I don't want my personal growth to be built on such a flimsy foundation as feelings. And if the *self* that I'm directed to build on has any firmer shape than my feelings, I'm unable to determine what that shape is — because psychology itself, which I look to for a definition of what my *self* is, has been unable to define it.

If I have only the directives of *self-fulfillment* to guide me, then, I'm likely to remain stuck in bed all day — unable to find, in the merely personal sources (self, feelings) to which I'm directed, any firm foundation on which to base a decision about what to do when I get up. But let's say I'm fortunate enough to have an obligation (a job to get to, children to pour orange juice for) that gives me a reason for getting out of bed. Once out, if I let the imperatives of Adult Development guide me through the day, I'm likely to become a dangerous person for others to be around. For while directing me to no particular actions, the model of Adult Development directs me and even commands me to a general attitude of self-absorption and self-indulgence. I'm directed to work at my developmental tasks with diligence; and threatened that if I don't, I'll "pay the price in a later developmental crisis or in a progressive withering of the self."

The great voices of humanistic psychology lend their authority to this threat, even augmenting its force with a moral imperative. "The way toward this goal" of self-realization, Karen Horney exhorts, "is an ever-increasing awareness and understanding of ourselves. . . . To work at ourselves becomes not only the prime moral obligation, but at the same time, in a very real sense, the prime moral privilege." With the stirring rhetoric of a call to self-sacrifice, Maslow takes up this call to self-absorption: "to be natural and spontaneous, to know what one is, and what one *really* wants, is a rare and high culmination that comes infrequently, and that usually takes long years of courage and hard work." (Those urging us to work at our personal development don't seem to hear the oddness of their calling for self-absorption in the traditional language of self-denial, nor to notice the contradiction of their insisting that we must consciously "work" at a developmental process that they claim to be inevitable, "natural," and "spontaneous.")

Spurred onward by these imperatives that I attend to my personal development, I concentrate all my attention on the developmental tasks to be done as I strive to work my way up the developmental ladder. And here is where I become dangerous to those nearby. Clinging to the developmental ladder for support, focusing my attention upward to the goal of self-fulfillment, I don't notice that my colleague next to me is overworked, or that my elderly neighbor needs a ride to the doctor, or that my children, playing on the steps, have been crushed beneath my feet as I triumphantly raise myself to the next rung.

And even as I step up onto it, the rung is likely to slip out from under me and leave me hanging. That step-like structure that looks so clear and firm on the book jacket (of whichever Adult Development book I'm looking at) tends to break into disconnected floating pieces when I try to place my own life on it. In the case studies in the book, every decision and action taken by an interviewee fits neatly onto a particular transitional step or represents clearly an act of reinforcement within a certain stable period. But in my own case, I can't tell where any particular action belongs, or even if it represents a transitional or a stabilizing step.

Say, for example, that I'm thirty-six years old and decide to accept a job promotion, from chairman of a high-school history department to vice-principal of another high school. Does this decision represent a "Settling Down" (Levinson's term) into my current life structure, a continued acceptance of my chosen career and its path of advancement; or does it represent a step into the "Mid-life Passage," a shake-up of my old life structure (built around a teaching career) and the first transitional step toward building a new (administratively based) structure of "Middle Adulthood"? Checking my age against the charts doesn't help me find out where I am. Age thirty-six can fit either into the transitional "Deadline Decade" of *Passages* (ages 35–45) or into the stabilizing "Settling Down" period of *Seasons* (ages 33–40). The authors advise me repeatedly, anyway, that the age ranges for each developmental period are highly variable ("do not take the ages too seriously," says *Passages*). Where my decision fits on the developmental ladder seems to depend mainly on how much fuss I make about it. If I make lots of fuss for myself and my family (which Adult Development, with its bias against stability and its positive valuing of *crisis*, encourages me to do), then it's a crisis and I'm in a transition. If I don't fuss, then I'm in equilibrium, stable. But even *crisis* is an uncertain criterion for discovering what developmental stage I'm in; maybe I'm just the fussy type, and call everything a crisis.

The developmental ladder is, then, a shaky guide to one's own life. Yet even though it's an uncertain guide to the meaning of any particular step we take, it still — as we've seen — can direct those steps. It directs us into self-absorption, self-indulgence, and continuous indiscriminate disruption of our lives and the lives of those around us.

If these developmental ladders, models, levels, etc. really represented, as their designers claim they do, natural laws which we are bound to obey, then we would have to obey them no matter how disastrous the consequences of this obedience. But we have no reason to believe that the professed laws of Adult Development, or any of psychology's other developmental laws, will prove to be any more natural, universal, and permanent than other laws of human development proclaimed as universal and natural in the past. Most such apparent laws, as we noted in the previous section, come to be seen before long as at least partially mistaken observations of nature's direction; and to the extent that they *are* mistaken, people who have tried to observe (follow) them, and who have guided their activities accordingly, turn out to have been misguided. To the extent that the models of Adult Development are in error, we will be misdirecting our lives to the extent that we follow these models. Like the educationists who redesigned primary education according to the direction proclaimed by the eventually disclaimed Law of Recapitulation, or like the Social Darwinists who, observing the Law of the Survival of the Fittest, saw the poor as unfit to survive and so left them to die, we are likely, by following the directions of Adult Development, to end up not in fulfillment but in error. Trying to shape our lives in the way we thought was right, we will again have gone wrong.

Research and Development

In the imperative of Adult Development, *develop* is conceived as a reflexive-intransitive verb: the order that "you must develop" is an order that "you must develop yourself." Outside psychology, the developmental imperative also exerts its force on us, but usually in a transitive manner: whatever we do, we are pressured "to develop it." We respond to this transitive developmental pressure in at least three ways: we tend to label whatever we do *development;* we tend to do it, whatever it is, differently because of this label; we judge what we (and others) have done by the standard of *development.*

There is hardly an area of our collective life that is free from the label *development.* We have urban development, land development, highway development, housing developments. Businesses engage in Research and Development and boast managerial development programs as well as program development. It's a poor organization in either the private or the public sector that doesn't have its Development Office. Schools and colleges offer Career Development counseling and Learning Development centers, while the instructors teach essay development and work on curriculum development. Science develops new theories; industry develops new technology; nations develop (or try to) their economies.

What effect does all this *development* have on us? Often an immediate and practical effect, just from the substitution of *devel-*

opment for some other name. A rose by any other name might smell as sweet, but a plan to tear down a block of houses doesn't sound nearly as good (and therefore probably won't get carried out) if called "neighborhood wreckage" rather than "urban development," and it's unlikely that we'd be pouring as many millions of dollars into the "developing nations" of the world if we still called them (as we used to) "backward."

We're more likely to give our support (our money, time, votes, etc.) to something that promises *development* because the very word itself promises good results. As we saw in examining its teleology, *development* carries the promise of progress, positive direction, movement to a good end; it guarantees that any changes made in its name will be changes for the better. Changes must, though, be made: by definition *development* involves change: you can't propose development and then do nothing. So the name encourages, even insists on, change — but without, as we saw in connection with Adult Development, specifying what sort of change it should be. Just as Adult Development tells us to change chairs if we want to grow but doesn't tell us how to change them, Urban Development tells us to change buildings if we want our city to grow but doesn't tell us whether to change from slums to new housing for the poor (confidently called *housing developments*) or to expensive restaurants and boutiques or to high-rise office buildings or to parks. All it specifies, as Jane Jacobs pointed out years ago, is that the area to be developed is not allowed to remain basically the same.

Development's promise that it will bring good in the end has another effect on us besides pressuring us to make changes; it draws our unquestioning support for things whose value we otherwise might have questioned. *Development* is such an enormous good that it spreads its good name over whatever is attached to it. "Highway development," for example, is assumed to be desirable because *development* is desirable; faced, in this phrase, with what looks like a necessary attachment between the two terms, we don't think to separate them and to ask whether highways (developed or not) are even desirable at all.

Not only do we act in response to the label *development*; we apply the label because we expect certain actions in response. For example, writers of grant proposals (who tend to work in Development offices) know that any project with *development* in its title becomes almost automatically entitled to funds. So they write proposals for Curriculum Development or a Job Development Bank or Resource Development or — especially — Program Development. *Program development* is doubly guaranteed funding because it doubly guarantees success: *development*'s promise of a good end is reinforced by the certainty of success carried by *program* (carried more than ever now because of *computer programs,* which by design automatically do whatever they are designed to do).

The general imperative that "you must develop whatever you do" pressures us, then, to act in the name of *development:* to name our actions *development* and to act accordingly. It pressures us also to judge accordingly: to judge what we and others do by the standard of *development.* According to this standard, the attributes *developing* and *developed* are of course good, *undeveloped* bad. A biographer or critic praises his subject's work by proclaiming it "the product of X's mature development"; he condemns it by calling it "undeveloped" or "immature." And he asserts confidently that "X never fully developed this idea" — as if we could recognize when an idea was "fully developed" (completed). Even Hegel had trouble picturing a completed, fully developed idea.

We use *development* to pass judgment on works in progress as well, and not just artistic works but public works and collective projects of all kinds. By referring to an enterprise as "in the early stages of development" or "approaching full maturity" or "experiencing rapid growth," we are judging it positively, declaring our assurance that it has a bright future (and thus assuring it of one). To proclaim videotaped course instruction, for example, as "in the early stages of development" is to proclaim it full of promise and on the way to producing good results; to say, on the other hand, that it has "outgrown its usefulness" or "hasn't fulfilled its promise" is, in effect (and in the same set of terms), to make an end of it. International economics, similarly, judges nations according to their stage of development and puts its money where its "early development" is. For example, W. W. Rostow's model in *The Stages of Economic Growth* considers countries at "Stage Four" ("the drive to maturity") to have already reached a level of development at which they can advance mainly on their own, without much aid, whereas countries at earlier "pre-take-off" stages need (and hence should get) outside aid to raise them to the higher self-developing levels.

Development acts as our standard in another way as well: as our standard of knowledge. We measure how much we know about something by how much we know about its development. The intellectual assumption behind this standard is one of the primary intellectual assumptions of our century: that, as Dobzhansky puts it in *Evolution, Genetics, and Man,* "living organisms" — including man in all his individual and collective aspects and activities — ". . . are products of their histories."

This assumption has become such a commonplace of contemporary thought that we tend not to notice what other possible assumptions it makes uncommon. In previous times, it was commonly thought that everything was produced by God; even if something had a history (as, for example, human society obviously did), that history was not its ultimate producer. To see God as the Ultimate Producer, the Maker of the world, is to admit that our knowledge of what is made must be limited. The ways of God are mysterious; they cannot be fully known by man. But as soon as God is no longer seen as Maker, and the world itself appears as making itself, the possibilities of our knowledge suddenly appear unlimited. The ways of the world *can,* the assumption goes, be fully known: they are entirely empirical ways, the operation of observable laws of cause and effect. If everything is a product of these laws, a product of its own history — and only of its history — we have only to study its history (that is, its development) to fully understand it. Great intellectual energy has thus been unleashed by the concept of development. For nearly a century now, propelled by the promise of knowledge, we have rushed to obey the developmental imperative that takes the form: "you must see your subject as developing."

We don't, today, see our subject (whatever it is) as developing exactly the way it was seen to at the turn of the century. The clear, bold pictures of Darwinian evolution and Hegelian *Entwicklung* have faded; we no longer see the fittest as inevitably surviving everywhere we look, nor an inexorable law of progress propelling every activity and institution toward its supreme development. Yet, though faded, the Darwinian and Hegelian visions have far from disappeared behind the vocabulary of *growth, evolution,* and (most frequently) *development* that dots the many recent books with these words in their titles. Though *Growth of . . .* studies are sometimes, especially in business and economics, merely statistical (measuring quantitative increase), they often — along with nearly all *Development of . . .* and *Evolution of . . .* studies — see their subject as undergoing continuous structural change "in response to its environment" and in accordance with "its own inner laws." Even when the picture behind the *development* vocabulary is so vague that *development* means only "what happened," some picture still remains: at the very least, of the *developing* subject as the always-changing product of a continuous series of causes that can be known.

Of course, it's possible to obey the imperative to "see your subject as developing" by obeying only its letter and not its spirit: it's possible, and very easy, to talk about one's subject in terms of *development–growth–evolution* without trying to picture anything behind one's terms at all. Textbook anthologies sometimes do this, as when they arrange their entries in chronological order, sprinkle their introductions with directional language like "increasingly showed," "later developed," and "went further," and then assume that they've expanded our knowledge about the subject. Since *develop* promises knowledge, it can be used as a show of knowledge, and thus as an excuse for a real search for knowledge. (This is generally how jargon works — or avoids working.) Any language can be used without paying attention to its meaning; how much, in that case, does it really mean?

7

But I Don't Mean All *That!*

The question that closes the preceding chapter is one that has perhaps been nagging at readers' minds throughout these pages — and justifiably so. We've seen the meanings of a few common words stretch out and multiply: we've watched the words *growth, development, evolution,* and *fulfillment* form inextricable associations with each other and with concepts of naturalness, of self-movement, and of progress; we've seen them take on the assumptions that the world changes continuously according to material causes and in a positive direction, that this direction is toward both individual and collective human satisfaction, that human reason is capable of comprehending all change up to the present and of controlling all change in the future; and we've noticed how these words, carrying these concepts and assumptions, carry us along with them — how they give direction to our lives, direction both as an imperative (what we must do) and as a sense of purpose (what our lives mean). After all this, a reader might justifiably object: "when I say that the industry is growing, or the program has evolved, or the plot develops, *I don't mean all that!*"

How much meaning is actually contained in any single usage of a word? And how much are we really led by any one usage? These are questions raised not just by *growth and development* but by the methodology of this book as a whole, so they should be confronted directly. The first step in answering them is to notice that their "how much" cannot be interpreted quantitatively: what these questions ask about is essentially immeasurable. We can't count amounts of meaning or graph how far a word leads us. Nor can we answer these questions by doing a survey of what people think they mean by a certain word and how much they're influenced by usages of it. Surveys can operate only on the level of consciousness, whereas the operations of language aren't confined to consciousness at all.

This distinction is unfortunately blurred by the word *mean(ing)* itself. When we say "I don't mean that, " *mean* is equivalent to "intend" (that is, to a conscious act); but *mean* and *meaning* have a much larger range of reference than mere "intention." Twentieth-century studies in anthropology, psychology, literary criticism, and semiotics have all shown us that while the world's networks of meaning (of signification) do pass through consciousness, they are far from restricted to it. We noted in Part One that our words can carry meanings apart from our conscious intentions; and we've seen in Part Two that they can carry us along whether or not we're conscious of where we're going, that they can lead us even when we don't intend to be following them.

As for how much we're led by any one usage of a word, I doubt that any single occurrence has much effect on us at all. And if it does, this is because of the meaning the word has already gathered for us from other occurrences and other associations. Language is a collective operation: words do their work not in isolation but in association — with each other, with particular concepts and values, and with the institutions and activities we use them in. This is why words are examined in this book in groups, and why two of the book's dominant metaphors for language are "sets" and "networks." The metaphor of "sets" helps to remind us of the collective nature of language, and it also carries the useful implication of a "social set": of words hanging around together and going places in a group, with some leading and some following.

The leading or dominant members of the group form a sort of "inner set" or "inner circle," so that the mathematical implications of "set" (a closed group with well-defined boundaries) are appropriate for one aspect of how language works. But members of a social set also have connections outside the set, and usually membership in a variety of loosely defined sets; and it is this extensive interconnectedness of language that the "network" metaphor helps us picture.

We've traced in Part Two some of the immense network of meaning — of interconnected concepts, values, assumptions, associations — that runs through the *growth and development* set. To particularize (and also to dequantify) the question about how much meaning a single usage of a word contains, we can ask: to what extent is this network brought into play in a single ordinary usage of one of its terms? That is, when we pick up a *grow* or a *develop* automatically, without paying attention to why we're choosing it, what meaning (for example, assumptions or values) — at the very least — does it carry? Answers to this question can only be tentative, speculative; we can't interview the words and ask "just what do you mean here?" (''just what are you doing here?'') any more than we can survey their users. We can, however, substitute an apparent synonym for the word in question and see if the sentence seems to make any different sense as a result. (The instances of ordinary *development*s offered below for speculation are all quoted or paraphrased from printed sources, but — with one exception — citations aren't given because they would be beside the point: the point is that these are common, probably unconscious usages — and so in a sense authorless.)

In ordinary transitive *developing*s like

- "you need to develop a new methodology to explore this question"
- "the committee will develop legislative priorities"
- "they are developing (or pursuing the development of) alternative energy strategies"

if we replace *develop* by, say, "devise" or "form," the sentences wouldn't lose much by the substitution. But it seems to me that they would lose at least something: a sense of our control (that we are able, without doubt, to bring into being the grammatical object of development); a sense that this object is desirable (that what we develop is for the good); and a sense that the activity of development is part of a larger human enterprise, that it is continuous with other human projects and activities.

In casual intransitive or passive *developing*s like

- "the program has evolved" (instead of: "has come about")
- "the industry is growing" (instead of: "getting bigger")
- "the plot evolves (or develops)" (instead of: "unfolds")
- "the evolution (or development) of Freud's ideas" (instead of: "formation")

the *development* terms seem to add a sense of continuity and of positive direction that is absent from, or weaker in, the alternative terms. In addition, *evolve* and *grow* (to a greater extent than *develop*) give a suggestion of naturalness: of the inevitability and inner determinism of a natural process.

In common historical intransitive *development*s like my own in Part One *—

- "another usage of *self* that developed at the same time"
- "we now have to trace the nineteenth- and twentieth-century developments . . ."
- "as the concept of self developed in the Renaissance"

— *developed* is almost synonymous with "came about." Almost, but not quite: because *develop* adds, at the very least, a sense that what has come about has done so according to a certain logic, a causative logic that can be known. The assumption of historical *development*s is that the world is a reasonable place and that our reason can comprehend it. A similar assumption seems to be carried by common intransitive *developing*s like

---

* In Part Two I've avoided terms from the *development* set in my operative vocabulary because I think it's inappropriate and confusing to use as one's operative terms words that are also one's subject; and I'm including my own previous usages of historical *development* as examples here in order to indicate where this book shares in the assumptions it's examining.

- "several things have developed since I last wrote you"
- "the day's developments" reported in the "Evening News."

Here, as with historical *developments*, *develop* means almost the same as "happen," but with just a bit more sense of sequence and order than a mere "happening" has.

In certain noun *developments* like

- "the development of the new science of genetics"
- "X's position in the development of anthropology"

it's impossible to tell whether *develop* is being conceived transitively or intransitively: that is, whether people are developing these disciplines (whether we're in control of our history) or whether the disciplines are developing on their own (as a result of historical forces). In either case, though, there is still the assumption — which all *developments*, even the most casual and apparently insignificant, seem to carry — of an unbroken continuity of events. There is also at least a trace of that smile of approval we've seen hovering over nearly all *developments*: the positive sense that what comes about by development (or growth or evolution) is for the good.

Development, then, always seems to make at least some difference in the meaning of sentences in which it appears. And this is probably as we would expect: I think we assume that the words we use make a difference, even if we don't often feel like figuring out what that difference is. (And no wonder: it has taken all these pages to figure out what difference just a handful of words makes.) Generally, the difference is that a different word brings a different set of assumptions, values, concepts, associations with it. So while we can justifiably say of the *growth and development* network, or any other network of meaning, "I don't mean (intend) all that when I use one of those words," the word can still mean (carry the assumptions, values, concepts, associations of) all that — or at least some of that — anyway.

There's another sort of difference, too, that any usage of a *growth and development* term has to make, no matter how casual and unreflective the usage: it renews the existence of the *growth and development* network. Like typing a keyword into a computerized library retrieval system and bringing onto the display screen all the titles connected with that word, just naming a word from the *growth and development* set brings the set into existence once again — though there's no display screen for us to see it on. And in that instant of naming, we not only renew the existence of the set but we also place ourselves in it, connect ourselves to it; so that while no single casual usage of one of its terms is likely to thrust us into action or to redefine our sense of the world, each usage renews our attachment to this network of meaning, putting us in the position of being led by it wherever it goes.

This way of imagining our relation to our culture's language and thought — as an often unconscious attachment to a network of meaning, an attachment renewed with each passing use of any of the language that the network passes through — is not entirely unlike the more common metaphor of the "absorption of ideas." The image that "absorption" gives us is of a sponge: when, for example, psychologist Richard Coan says in *Hero, Artist, Sage, or Saint* that "Western thought as a whole has absorbed the evolutionary view of mankind," we get a picture of Western thought as a sponge and the evolutionary view as a liquid soaking into this thought (our thought) and permeating it. The language of evolution, in this image, "influences" us by "flowing" through everything we think about and do. While the "network" metaphor gives more delineation to this flow — shows it to us more as a flowchart with lines of direction and interaction that we can trace — the metaphor of absorption gives a nicely vivid sense of pervasiveness: of our thought being so permeated by evolution that wherever we squeeze it (ex-press it), evolution comes out.

It comes out, as we've seen, not just when we deliberately express evolutionary ideas (as in the study of natural history) or when we express our thoughts about other subjects in terms of evolution (as in the study of "the evolution of" or "the development of" any aspect of human history) but also in our daily practices, the day-to-day products of our thought: the way we run our government and our businesses, the way we act in our communities and in our homes. After taking note of the extensive influence of *growth, development, evolution,* and *fulfillment* in our public and private lives, we have to qualify a remark made recently by biologist J. Z. Young in reference to Darwinian evolution. "It is interesting," Young wrote, "that the scientific discovery that has had the greatest influence on human thought has no practical use whatever." This is perhaps true; but it could hardly have had a greater practical effect.

THREE

It's All Relative — or Is It?

Introduction to *Relativity* and *Relationship*

Relativity and *relationship* are etymologically the same, so I should explain why I treat them separately, looking at *relativity* in Part Three and *relationship* in Part Four. The reason for the separation is that the two words have come to have separate associations, to move primarily in different sets — so that while their meanings are certainly connected and the ends they lead us to ultimately coincide, along the way they move on considerably different paths.

Throughout their histories, *relative* and *relation* have moved both together and apart. Starting together from their common root *relatus*, past participle of the Latin *referre* ("to refer"), they both started off in late Middle English carrying the basic meaning of "reference." Both almost immediately took this basic meaning in a variety of directions, in some of which they stayed closely together and in some of which they went their separate ways. In their meaning of "kinship," for example, which both *relative* (as a noun) and *relation* had taken on by the Renaissance, the two words were so close that they were — as they remain today — interchangeable (our *relatives* are our *relations*). But in certain other early meanings, they immediately leapt far apart: *relative,* for example, into the usage it still has as a grammatical term ("relative pronoun," "relative clause"), *relation* into its meaning of "recounting" (as in recounting or relating a story).

In the widest and yet also the most complex sense of both words, the sense of general "reference" or "connectedness," *relative* and *relation* have had from the beginning a complex relation of their own. Together in pointing to what is apparently one of our most basic human perceptions — the perception of interconnectedness between things — they very early moved apart by focusing on different aspects of this interconnectedness. *Relation* focused from the start, as it still does today, on the fact of connection itself: as early as 1393 *relation* had what is still its central meaning, of "any connexion, correspondence, or association, which can be conceived as naturally existing between things" (*OED*). As particular kinds of connection between things, and especially between people, have come to be conceived over the centuries, *relation* is the word that has served to indicate them; so we have had (more or less in this order) "the relation between master and servant," "the relation of ruler and subject," "the relation between the individual and society," "foreign relations," "socio-economic relations," "sexual relations," "interpersonal relations" — all different conceptions of our relations, but all the same concept of *relation*.

Relative, meanwhile, although sometimes going along with *relation*'s sense of general "connectedness" (as in the interchangeable phrases "in relation to," "relative to," "with reference to," "in connection with"), has tended since about 1700 to take a somewhat different perspective on our connections. Instead of looking, with *relation,* primarily at the fact or mode of connectedness between things, *relative* has focused on the individual thing as connected to other things. That is, while *relation* has focused on the connections *between* things, *relative* has focused on the connections between *things* — on things as defined by their connectedness. Something that is *relative* is, in this most common meaning of the word, "dependent upon or interconnected with something else for intelligibility or significance; not absolute" (*American Heritage Dictionary*). Focusing on the individual thing as dependent upon other things, *relative* has, in effect, a double focus: it looks at the single item only to look immediately away from it, toward what keeps it from being single; it points to the independent entity only to point out its lack of independence; it posits the separate thing only to negate the separateness and to insist that the thing is *not* complete by itself, *not* independent, "not absolute."

This negating gesture that is part of its very meaning has led *relative* to form its closest association with — of all terms — its opposite, *absolute*. The *relative / absolute* pair has then moved (for reasons we'll see in the rest of Part Three) into contact with another opposing pair, *subjective / objective,* and also with an assortment of words including *opinion, alternative,* and *consensus*. *Relation*'s different and at least initially simpler and more positive focus, on connectedness itself rather than on a separate thing's lack of separateness, has meanwhile led it into association with words that share (in ways which Part Four will examine) its own point of view: words like *whole, interaction, system, environment, community*. The two sets of terms, the *relative* set and the *relation* set, have both played dominant roles in twentieth-century thought, but they have tended to dominate in different areas: *relative* in physics, historiography, anthropology, and ethics; *relation* in epistemology, sociology, business, environmentalism, and psychology. From these different areas they have brought us different concepts and values, which in turn lead us in different (though not, as we'll see, finally incompatible) ways. Despite their starting from the same etymological root, then, *relative* and *relation* have branched in such different directions that we can best keep track of their movements by observing them — as far as possible — apart.

8

Relativity's Lines

"Length and time are relative concepts"

Unlike *self* and *development*, *relative* hasn't accumulated meanings and concepts over the centuries. As we've just seen, *relative* is defined today essentially as it was almost three hundred years ago; and though it underwent a change of form in the mid-nineteenth century — expanding into *relativity, relativism,* and *relativist* — the expansion took place quietly, in philosophical discussions about the "relativity of knowledge" or the "relativity of beauty," and attracted little public attention. The dramatic events that thrust *relative(ity)* into public notice have all taken place in our own century, beginning in 1905 with the most dramatic of all, when *relativity* — like an actress who, after quietly playing bit parts as the same character type for years, suddenly bursts into fame as the star of a shocking new film — exploded onto the screen of the popular imagination as the Theory of Relativity.

Einstein not only gave *relativity* the title role in both of his theories (the Special Theory and the General Theory of Relativity), but he also made it play a big part in his explanations of what the theories were about. "There is no such thing as an independently existing trajectory," he wrote, for example, in *Relativity: The Spe-*

cial and the General Theory (1916), "but only a trajectory relative to a particular body of reference." Or, in the same book, in his summary of the infamous thought experiment in which two flashes of lightning are observed from an embankment and also from a moving train:

> Events which are simultaneous with reference to the embankment are not simultaneous with respect to the train, and vice versa (*relativity of simultaneity*) [italics mine]. Every reference-body (co-ordinate system) has its own particular time; unless we are told the reference-body to which the statement of time refers, there is no meaning in a statement of the time of an event.

"There is no such thing as an independently existing trajectory"; "there is no meaning in a statement of the time of an event": this firm negation, denying the meaning and even the existence of what had been perfectly acceptable concepts, is the central rhetorical gesture of Einstein's *relativity*. The broad outline of the gesture is clearest in what has become its familiar popularized form, which Martin Gardner (one of the most reliable of relativity's popularizers) calls "the key to Einstein's special theory": "there is no meaning to the concepts of absolute length and time"; "length and time are relative concepts." Seen in this form, *relative*'s main act as the star of Einstein's theory seems to be to strike a quick karate chop at the solid Newtonian concepts of absolute length and absolute time, splitting the *absolute* right off from them. Hurling *absolute* into the abyss of "no meaning," *relative* then picks up the pieces of "length" and "time" that are left and attaches them to itself.

The same devastating blow is struck by Einstein's *relativity* at "absolute truth": *truth,* previously assuming absoluteness to be so much a part of itself that the phrase "absolute truth" was almost redundant, is slashed from *absolute* and made relative. We can watch this shattering epistemological feat in action in Gardner's own account of the lightning flashes (which is useful, too, in assembling most of the key terms that Einstein's *relativity* brings with it into the act):

> The question of whether the flashes are simultaneous cannot be
> answered in any absolute way. The answer depends on the choice
> of a frame of reference. . . . This is not just a question of being
> unable to learn the truth of the matter. *There is no actual truth
> of the matter.* . . . There is no question of one set of measure-
> ments being "true," another set "false." Each is true relative to
> the observer making the measurements; relative to his frame of
> reference.

That emphatic denial of "actual truth" is the climactic epistemological moment for *relativity*. Casting all claims of absolute or actual truth into meaninglessness, *relative* thrusts a dividing line as
sharp as a sword between itself and *absolute* and stands triumphant — claiming *truth* for its own. But it can't stand that way
for long. While "absolute truth" can stand by itself (stands, in its
very meaning, by itself), "relative truth" would tip over into
meaninglessness without an object to complete it, without a specification of what the truth is "relative to." In relativity theory, as
Gardner's lines show, the object to which truth is relative is specified as "the observer" or "his frame of reference."

Since "truth relative to an observer" has long been called "subjective truth," we shouldn't be surprised to find *subjective* often
joining the *observer* of relativity theory — as in the following ex-
plication of the almost inexplicable lightning flashes, by another
superb popularizer of relativity, Bertrand Russell:

> We cannot therefore say unambiguously that two events in dis-
> tant places are simultaneous. Such a statement only acquires a
> definite meaning in relation to a definite observer. It belongs to
> the subjective part of our observation of physical phenomena,
> not to the objective part which is to enter into physical laws.

"To the subjective . . . not to the objective" is, of course, an opposition that is as much a part of the very meanings of *subjective*
and *objective* as the opposition between *relative* and *absolute* is of
theirs. What Russell is implicitly doing here — and most other popularizers of relativity theory do likewise — is bringing one inherent opposition (*subjective / objective*) into association, almost into
complete identification, with another (*relative / absolute*). This as-

sociation is strengthened elsewhere in explanations of relativity theory when *objective* is made to play the role often given (for example, by Gardner) to *absolute* and to *actual truth*, the role of what relativity physics forces us to abandon. As the *Encyclopaedia Britannica* puts it: while classical physics claimed to measure quantities that had an objective existence, after Einstein "the idea of something existing objectively which physical measurement revealed had to be given up."

We can now see the lineup of terms that play the major parts in the rhetoric of relativity theory; and we can see that the terms line up on opposing sides, distinguished as clearly as the bad guys and good guys of an old cowboy movie. Wearing black clothes and riding black horses are the clear losers *absolute* and *objective*, demolished so thoroughly that — in the mode more of recent psycho-horror films than of cowboy movies — their very existence is ultimately denied. Beaming triumphantly on the good side, accompanied by *observer* and *frame of reference* in supporting roles, are the white-clad *relative* and *subjective*, secure in their victory because they've got *truth* on their side.

What is perhaps even more striking about these terms than the clearness of the division between them is their odd familiarity — odd because here, in the key explanatory roles of the century's most extraordinary scientific theory, are some of our most ordinary words. *Relative, absolute, subjective, objective, observer, truth* have all been around as long as the English language has, and acting pretty much as they do in relativity theory (*relative* opposing *absolute, subjective* lining up with *observer, truth* being fought over, and so on). They've traditionally acted this way, furthermore, in what we consider our broadest discussions, covering areas of universal philosophical concern; and this wide-ranging and longstanding philosophical association of its key terms is largely responsible for the universal significance that relativity theory was immediately seen to have. Gardner's italicized *"there is no actual truth of the matter,"* for instance, has the ring of universality about it; the *matter* he is referring to, as he makes clear, is the very specific one of the meaning of simultaneity in a particular experiment, but nothing in his statement holds it back from spreading over much more general matters. And such a categorical denial of *truth* slips easily into any area where truth might have been thought to be found.

Such slipperiness is common to all the key terms of relativity theory; and though the best popularizers, like Gardner and Russell and Einstein himself, hold on to their terms tightly and handle them with a preciseness that is a pleasure to watch, in less careful hands the terms tend to slip out of their proper scientific bounds. For example, Gardner's carefully specified "set of measurements," each of which is true only relative to a frame of reference, spills over into an unspecified "thing" when picked up by a nonscientist who writes:

> One can epitomize the concept of relativity by saying that a thing derives its nature not so much by its isolated essence as from its relationships to other things in its frame of reference.

No concept conceived with the exactness of Einstein's relativity could ever be epitomized by a term as inexact as "thing"; nor does relativity theory have anything to do with so vague a notion as a thing's "nature." Yet when the most rigorous versions of relativity theory use terms as broad as *absolute* and *truth,* we can understand how popularizations of the theory could move, without even noticing that they were moving, into fuzzy philosophical language like "a thing's nature" or — as in the following jacket blurb for a book called *Relativity Theory: Its Origins and Impact on Modern Thought* — like "the nature of reality":

> Einstein's Theory of Relativity . . . did away with the conception of a simple mechanistic universe, open to objective interpretation and functioning according to Newtonian laws within Euclidian space. The interpretation became subjective, the nature of reality dependent upon how you viewed it from where you stood.

Besides (along with much other popular relativity rhetoric) taking Einstein's theory into a misty "reality" where Einstein himself would not have dared to tread, this blurb makes another move typical of popularized relativity: into the *subjectivity* of psychology. The move is a misleading one, and is responsible for some of the major misunderstandings of what relativity theory implies; but we can see why it gets made. *Subjective* has such long-standing associations with personal psychology and individual perception, that when Russell, for example, says that the meaning of a statement "belongs to the subjective part of our observation," all the psychological associations of *subjectivity* rush in. The particular point from which a lightning flash is viewed thus becomes the "point of view" of individualized perception; and what for Russell is "dependent upon the observer" becomes (as in the blurb quoted above) "dependent upon how you viewed it from where you stood." That vague "*how* you viewed it," suggesting that psychological factors like your mood or personality or past experience might affect your view, gives the false impression that if *you* stood on the train exactly where *I* had been standing, you would measure the time between the flashes differently than I would. But in fact — and as physicists and philosophers like Philipp Frank, Hans Reichenbach, and Russell himself have been at pains to point out — you and I as individual beings play no part in relativity theory at all. "It is natural to suppose," Russell acknowledges, "that the observer [of relativity theory] is a human being, or at least a mind; but he is just as likely to be a photographic plate or a clock."

The popular (false) impression that modern physics was saying something about the subjectivity of individual observation was reinforced, however, when the discoveries of physicists at apparently the farthest end of the field — physicists measuring not the astronomically large distances of outer space but the infinitesimally small ones in atoms — were presented to the public in almost exactly the same terms as relativity. Heisenberg himself, when putting his Uncertainty Principle in popular terms, put it in terms of the *objective / subjective* opposition and the identification of *subjectivity* with an *observer*. "What one deduces from an observation" of an atomic event, he wrote in *Physics and Philosophy* (1958), "is a probability function" which "combines objective and subjective elements. It contains statements about possibilities" which "are completely objective"; and "it contains statements about our knowledge of the system, which of course are subjective in so far as they may be different for different observers." "So we cannot completely objectify the results of an observation"; "the observation plays a decisive role in the event and the reality varies, depending upon whether we observe it or not."

Heisenberg's *observer* is, of course, not a person gazing unaided at an atomic event but an instrument measuring the movements of electrons. And the *reality* he refers to is extremely limited: it is either the position or the velocity of the electron, each of which varies in the act of measurement ("observation") of the other. But *reality* is such a huge term in its possible range of reference, with *event* and *observation* not much smaller, that a statement like "the observation plays a decisive role in the event and the reality varies, depending upon whether we observe it or not" almost instantly swells to cover the full range of human psychological and epistemological experience. Like Gardner's *"there is no actual truth of the matter,"* Heisenberg's statement expands by itself into universal significance — and into what sounds like the same significance, the same meaning, as Gardner's. Proclaiming uncertainty a principle sounds very much like making relativity a theory; in both cases an opposition to the certain, the absolute — and a simply semantic opposition (one inherent, that is, in the ordinary meanings of *uncertain* and *relative*) — is raised to the level of a scientific Principle or Theory. From the farthest ends of its field, then, modern physics has seemed to proclaim a single message: that reality is subjective, that absolutes have no meaning, that everything is relative.

Against the force of terms so large in their range of reference and so sweeping in their grand gestures of affirmation and denial, voices of reasoned qualification can have little sway. So the message that relativity theory had destroyed all absolutes spread in the 1920s and 1930s with the inexorability of a Homeric army, undeflected by Gardner's objection (as wise and well reasoned as the voice of Odysseus) that "nothing could be further from the truth" because relativity theory in fact replaces Newtonian absolutes with absolutes of its own, like the speed of light. And the slogan "everything is relative" swept right over Russell's common-sense reminder that such a statement was "nonsense, because if *everything* were relative, there would be nothing for it to be rela-tive to."

Russell's own statement that "the theory of relativity has altered our view of the fundamental structure of the world" — concurred in by other famous philosophers like Ortega and Bachelard — probably helped spread the slogan though, by adding *world* to the terms of wide-ranging reference already in *relativity*'s ranks. *World* can obviously cover quite a lot of ground, and popular writers on relativity in the 1930s made sure that it did so, eagerly pulling it from its physical context and blowing it up into an ab-stract all-encompassing "outside world" which, they claimed, rel-ativity gave them an expansive new view of. "To see the outside world primarily in terms of relations rather than in terms of ab-solute substances," Stuart Chase exclaimed typically, in a popular 1938 book on language, "seems to develop an intellectual keen-ness hitherto unknown."

Actually, a similar intellectual keenness had been known less than half a century earlier, when another new scientific theory had set off excited speculation about a "new world view." (The an-nouncement of a new world view always seems to make us jump for joy and scramble to take a look: we'd rather shake up all our ideas and turn our minds upside down to get a new perspective, than stand still and look carefully at a view we already have.) To see the "outside world" in terms of relativity or, earlier, in terms of evolution was intellectually exciting because these terms — hav-ing taken over their particular fields so triumphantly, as the vehi-cles of a specific new scientific truth — seemed to carry the prom-ise of a more general truth as well. Like the jousting knights of King Arthur's court, for whom a victory was a sure sign that their cause had been right, these terms of *evolution* and of *relativity* seemed to have general validity — to be right — just because they had conquered a single scientific field. Triumphant in their respec-tive arenas, the terms of evolutionary theory and of relativity theory thus went forth to conquer other intellectual fields and the whole world of popular thought: *evolution* and its companion terms carrying, as we've seen, the new concepts of evolutionary theory; *relativity* and its comrades carrying not the new concepts of physics (maybe because almost no one except some physicists could understand them) but their own old concepts and attitudes, given new validity and prestige from their connection with a universally acclaimed scientific theory. Proud and confident — and waving the banner of *truth* — *relative* and *subjective* thus marched forth from physics, dragging *absolutes* behind them in the dust.

"Historic truth is relative and subjective"

One of the first places that *relativity* and *subjectivity* marched was into the American Historical Association meetings of the 1920s and 1930s, where they threw the field into disarray. With the battle cry that "historic truth is relative and subjective, not absolute and objective," champions of "historical relativism" tried to explode the historian's belief in the existence of historical fact, which he had assumed it was his job to uncover, and vigorously attacked the whole idea of objective historical truth, thus undermining the very grounds on which the historian did his work. Though some fighters for historical relativism drew on Einstein's relativity in (mistaken, as we'll see) support of their cause, they needn't have relied on such mercenary measures, since native to historical practice were forces strong enough to ensure *relative* and its concepts their day in the field.

Any intense preoccupation with time and change is bound to lead to at least a restricted relativism; and modern historical consciousness since Hegel has been preoccupied, as we noted in Part Two, with history as *change* — especially the *change* of *development*. In Hegelian *development,* the relativity of each historical fact is restricted by the course of the Absolute, whose particular stage of development is what each historical fact is relative *to*. But for Wilhelm Dilthey, who took over the relativism of Hegel's concrete historical picture but would have nothing to do with the abstract Absolute — insisting that in fact (in history) there *was no* Absolute — relativism was freed from the restrictions of any absolute being or absolute body of standards. Everything in history, Dilthey declared with the excitement of a liberating vision, is free to develop uniquely, relative to the particular experience of its own time and place.

This applied, in Dilthey's view, to *our* own time and place as well: our own present values and *Weltanschauungen* are as subjective, as relative to our own experience, as those of the past were to theirs. Dilthey thus made the logical extension — which has to be made in any honest historical relativism — from a relativism of the historical object to a relativism of the knowing subject (of the historian himself, as knowing subject perceiving the object of the past). These two relativisms, though following from the same premises and logically inseparable from each other, have very different consequences for the practice of historians. A relativism of the object just says that we can understand each historical fact only relative to the historical circumstances that produced it — which seems close to common sense and is what good historical practice has probably always done. But a relativism of the subject says that our understanding itself is relative to our own historical circumstances because these circumstances alone have produced it — which comes close to making historical practice impossible because it says that the historian looking into the past will never see anything except the reflection of his present experience. This self-reflexive epistemological doctrine, declaring the subjectivity of all historical knowledge, is what is generally meant (and what I mean) by "historical relativism." It is obviously subversive of the historical profession and so is bound to stir up historiographical controversy whenever it surfaces; and it is bound to surface from time to time, just by the force of logic, as long as history is seen in terms of *change* and *development*.

The particular forces that combined with the logic of *relative* and *development* to push historical relativism to the surface of American historians' consciousness in the 1920s and 1930s were (as historical relativism itself would have it) forces particular to the American experience of the time: evolutionary theory, the immensely popular philosophy of pragmatism, and the spirit of political reform. Evolutionary ideas, on which the American Historical Association had been founded, led historians like Carl Becker to see truth, reality, and the "very facts themselves" as subject to change. Pragmatism led to the same view, adding that what changed the "facts themselves" (the facts of the past selected by the historian) was their present social usefulness: Dewey measured all knowledge by its instrumental social value and found historical knowledge an especially useful instrument, "a lever for moving the present into a certain kind of future." This reformist edge in pragmatism — the eagerness to "move the present" — was sharpened for historians like Becker and Charles Beard by their participation in the general reformist spirit of the time. When Becker said that historical synthesis (the way the historian puts together his understanding of the past) was "true relatively to the needs of the age which fashioned it," he meant primarily the socio-political needs. And when Beard made his famous statement about the "frame of reference" according to which the historian selects all his facts, the frame referred to was the historian's hopes for the future, shaped by his present "experience" and projected back on the past.

In denying that the historian could ever be a detached, objective observer or that absolute historic truth was ever possible, and insisting that historical understanding was subjective and relative to the historian's own frame of reference, Beard and Becker were thus only drawing for historians the inevitable conclusions toward which relativism was heading in their field. (Yet to draw inevitable conclusions can be harder than it sounds; to take the lead in, paradoxically, merely following the forces of reason requires courage and strength of mind when those forces threaten to undermine one's own assumptions and career.) They were also drawing into historiographical debate the same division of terms that we saw in relativity theory: *relative, subjective,* and *frame of reference* claiming validity on one side and denying the claims of *absolute truth* and *objectivity* on the other.

But though the lineup of language is the same for historical relativism as for relativity theory, the referents of these terms are so different in the two fields that the many analogies from physics that rushed along with the language of *relativity* into the American Historical Association papers of the 1920s and 1930s were almost all false ones. When Becker wrote, for example, that "the form and significance of remembered events, like the extension and velocity of physical objects, will vary with the time and place of the observer," he was slipping from his usual clear thinking into a confusion between the physicist's and the historian's meanings of *event, time, place,* and *observer.* For the physicist, these words point to objectively existing realities which relativity theory allows him to measure more truly than ever; for the historical relativist, these words point to a subjectivist questioning of the very existence of any knowable reality or objective truth. There is thus a very different epistemological slant to *relativity* in each of these areas — toward skepticism in history, toward intellectual certainty in physics — which can be seen further in what *frame of reference* means for each. The historian's *frame of reference* is defined as his own personal experience and hence tends toward a pluralism of irreconcilable private views, since no one person's frame of reference can be exactly equivalent to another's. But in physics, as philosopher of science Hans Reichenbach points out, the plurality implied by multiple *frames of reference* "is not a plurality of different views or of systems of contradictory content; it is merely a plurality of equivalent languages. . . . Relativity does not mean an abandonment of truth; it only means that truth can be formulated in various ways."

With *relativity* in physics and in history heading in opposite epistemological directions, one wonders why historical relativists didn't fight to keep analogies from physics out of their arguments instead of eagerly drawing them in. The reason is probably that most historians (like most physicists at the time) didn't yet understand the new physics very well, and the similarity of language made relativity theory look like a natural ally for the historical relativists' embattled cause. In their eagerness for this powerful "scientific" support, they forgot their own lesson that historical products (including words) develop differently in different places and made the mistaken assumption that *relativity* would be the same wherever it was found.

"Evaluations are relative to the cultural background out of which they arise"

The doctrine of "cultural relativism" that emerged in anthropology in the 1940s didn't make history's mistake of looking to the alien field of physics for support; it recognized that it had ample roots deep in anthropology's own soil. Three-quarters of a century before cultural relativism came to be declared as a doctrine, the seeds of a relativism had been planted with the field's first concepts of culture: for instance, in Edward Tylor's seminal definition of culture as "that complex whole which includes knowledge, belief, art, morals, laws, customs, and any other capabilities and habits acquired by man as a member of society." Cultivating this concept of the "complex whole," Malinowski went on to specify the nature of the "complexity": in his famous functionalism, a culture was conceived as an independently integrated "functioning whole," each part of which was determined by — and hence relative to — all the others. This relativist functionalist conception then reached its full flowering in Ruth Benedict's brilliant and colorful *Patterns of Culture* (1934). Though, like her predecessors, making little use of the word *relative,* Benedict drew (for what proved to be a large public, well beyond the boundaries of her field) an implicitly relativist picture: of each culture as a unique configuration of traits which shapes its members along the lines of its particular pattern — and thus of each individual's personality, behavior, and attitudes as relative to his own culture.

When Melville Herskovits and his followers made their move in the 1940s to what they explicitly proclaimed a "cultural relativist" position, they were therefore just taking, initially, a small and natural step from the accepted relativist position: they themselves were stepping into the relativist picture of culture. In fine modern self-reflexive fashion, they recognized that if values are indeed (in Herskovits's words) "relative to the cultural background out of which they arise," this must apply to their own values as well as to those of the cultures they were studying. And since, they went on to reason, their own values are not absolute but relative to their own culture, these values have no more validity than those of any other culture. The anthropologist must therefore, they concluded, detach himself from his own necessarily subjective "cultural frame of reference" in order to understand the values of another culture objectively; and he must not pass judgment on any other cultures' values or practices but must recognize "the dignity inherent in every body of custom" and "the need for tolerance of conventions though they may differ from one's own."

In proclaiming *detachment* and *tolerance* as imperatives, cultural relativism had come a long way from that initial self-reflexive step of simply recognizing the anthropologist's cultural bias. It had moved to what it proudly presented as an "ethical position," summarized in one textbook as the insistence that "since cultures are diverse and unique, and embody different conceptions of the desirable, they can be understood and evaluated only in terms of their own standards and values." What had mainly motivated cultural relativism to take this firm ethical position was its disgust at the (un)ethical anthropological position of "ethnocentrism": the "fallacy" — derived from an outmoded concept of cultural evolution — of measuring "primitive" values by Western standards, which were assumed (falsely) to represent a higher and hence superior evolutionary stage. Ethnocentrism was indeed a fallacy, anthropologists were quick to agree; but they also soon found that cultural relativism was full of fallacies of its own. Far from being a clear ethical position, it was actually (as we'll see when we look in Chapter 9 at some problems of relativism in general) a muddle of sensible methodology, confused logic, and questionable morality — all hazed over by a certain ethical aura.

What made cultural relativism appear to its proponents as a single, solid ethical position, however, was that it put almost everything it said in the same terms, or term — and that term was *values*. Anthropology does have a lot to do with *values,* in several senses of the word. Anthropology studies cultural *values* — in the sense of *morals* (a culture's moral ideals), in the looser sense of *standards* or *norms* (the importance a culture places on certain conventions of behavior), and in the even looser sense of general *worth* (the worth or value implied in every activity or artifact just by the fact of its existence). And anthropology also *evaluates* the cultures it studies according to some standard or *value* system. When a word has so many relevant meanings, one probably does best to avoid it altogether in one's reasoning; unless the various meanings are deliberately and explicitly distinguished, they'll inevitably run together and blur one's thinking. This is unfortunately what happened with cultural relativism's attachment to *values*. Eager to make a moral contribution to anthropology, cultural relativism was apparently fooled by *value*'s importance in the language of ethics into thinking that the more it mentioned *values*, the more ethical its argument would be. So every available term in cultural relativism's discourse — *morality, standards, norms, worth, judgment* — tended to be joined or even replaced by *values*. The premise of cultural relativism, for instance, was formulated as "values are relative"; its main imperative as "respect for the equal value of all values." The result of this indiscriminate use of *values* was that the fine distinctions developed in anthropology's concept of culture were lost. The "complex whole" of culture — which for Tylor (who wisely avoided *values* in his definition) included the carefully distinguished "knowledge, belief, art, morals, laws, [and] customs" — was reduced by cultural relativism to an undifferentiated, *value*-laden clump.

With all this talk of *values* and of *tolerance*, cultural relativism brought to the language of *relativity* a considerably different vocabulary than history had. It's fascinating that despite their initially identical self-reflexive steps, from a relativism of the object to a relativism of the perceiving subject, historical and cultural relativism moved to such different sorts of positions. Historical relativism became, as we saw, primarily an epistemological position denying the existence of absolute truth and insisting that all historical understanding is necessarily subjective. Cultural relativism became primarily an ethical position denying the existence of moral absolutes and insisting that anthropological understanding and evaluation *must not* be subjective. In both fields, then, *relative* remained true to its meaning by firmly opposing an *absolute*. But — probably because of the fields' traditionally different concerns (history's with discovering the truth of the past, anthropology's with understanding the variety of current cultural values) — the *absolute* was *truth* in one case, *values* in the other.

Cultural relativism's strong command against *subjectivity* (thou shalt not be subjective) is the other major way that its language stands out from the *relative*s we've seen so far. Though initially acknowledging *relative*'s connection with *subjective*, cultural *relativism* goes on — even rushes on — to shake off its subjectivist associations and to embrace *objectivity* (*relative*'s traditional opposite!) instead. Similarly, the anthropological *observer* is directed by cultural relativism to *detach* himself from his own frame of reference — a command that not only contradicts the assumption of Einstein's and history's *relativity* that *detachment* from the relevant frame of reference is impossible, but also conflicts with the inherent meaning of *relative* as "*not* independent, *not* ultimately detached." What moved cultural *relativism* to make these inherently uncongenial associations was anthropology's desire for scientific status. Like a teenager taking on uncongenial companions in order to identify himself with a coveted social group, cultural *relativism* took on the terms *objectivity* and *detachment* in order to sound properly scientific in its method — and snubbed its own sister *subjectivity* because of her embarrassingly unscientific appearance.*

For cultural relativism to insist that anthropologists try to understand another culture apart from their own preconceptions did,

---

* The *relativity* of physics had no qualms about being called *subjective* because physics' status as a science is secure. And history, though occasionally going through periods of scientific longing (as in the Rankean fetishism of fact, or in the current craze — in one corner of the field — for quantification), has enough confidence in the value of its speculative activity that it could be comfortable, at least to some extent, with the *subjectivity* of its *relativism*.

as all workers in the field soon acknowledged, make good meth-odological sense; it just made little semantic sense for a *relativism* to be insisting on *detachment* and *objectivity*. This inconsistency in cultural relativism's language suggests that maybe if *relative* hadn't been so much the going term of the times, anthropology might have gone with some other terms in formulating its objec-tion to ethnocentrism. After all, for years relativist conceptions had been developing fine in anthropology with no *frame of refer-ence* and almost no *relative*. So if, in the 1920s and 1930s, the language of relativity theory hadn't inundated the popular press and the papers debating historical relativism hadn't flooded the journals of a profession conceptually close to home, anthropology in the 1940s might very likely have proclaimed a principle not of "cultural relativism" but of "cultural determinism" or "cultural pluralism" or "value-free functionalism." And in that case, the language and concepts of anthropology might not (though, of course, we can only guess) have slipped as easily as they did into the *relativism* of ethics.

" 'Right' and 'good' are relative terms"

Ethical relativism is, most simply and generally, the belief that moral values are relative to something variable rather than being absolute or fixed. The *absolutes* that ethical *relativism* opposes itself to are therefore "moral absolutes"; and the general rhetori-cal form of ethical relativism is "values are relative to X," where the *values* are moral values (ethical norms, definitions of what is good or right) and where "X" can be any variable of human ex-istence.

When the variable is "cultural background" or "cultural pat-tern," ethical relativism is identical to cultural relativism. In the past half-century the variability of cultural patterns has been so much talked about by anthropologists and (following them) poli-ticians and the public — and *values,* as we've seen, so much the center of this talk — that *cultural relativism* and *ethical relativism* are often treated as interchangeable terms, as if each fully implied the other. *Cultural relativism* does imply *ethical relativism;* but ethics can be seen, and indeed have been, as relative to many other variables besides culture. "To the evolutionist," Julian Huxley tells us, "ethics are relative to . . . evolutionary progress." For Marx the variable to which values are relative was "class interest" (our morality being that of the ruling class); for Nietzsche the variable was "power" (our morality being that of the ruled). And the many variables of the human psyche — emotions, temperament, tastes, desires — have been seen off and on at least since the Sophists as the basis of moral judgment and hence as what our values are "relative to."

This tradition of moral philosophy that sees values as relative to psychological variables has usually been labeled *subjectivist* or *skeptical* (because it questions whether our moral beliefs have any objective basis). But with Edward Westermarck's philosophical treatise *Ethical Relativity* (1932) — a "defense of ethical subjectivism and relativity" fortified by the same massive anthropological researches that later led to *cultural relativism — relative* became the title term for the subjectivist philosophical argument. And with *relative* ("with" it because *relative* can't do without a term to oppose, to beat down, like the puppet Judy, whose character consists in clobbering poor Punch) came *objective,* knocked down by the usual *no:* "Ethical relativity implies that there is no objective standard of morality"; "there are no moral truths in the ordinary sense of the word, which attributes objective validity to moral judgments."

Westermarck's argument — which is formulated, as the *Encyclopedia of Philosophy* says in its approving article on him, with "considerable care" and with much more sophistication than these summary lines suggest — also has its positive side, to balance and justify the negatives. Moral judgments have no objective validity because they "are ultimately based on emotions, the moral concepts being generalizations of emotional tendencies." " 'Good,' " for example, "is a concept rooted in the tendency to feel the emotion of moral approval." But Westermarck doesn't mean the emotion of the moment or even the emotions of a mere individual.

Drawing on an evolutionist line of reasoning similar to that still followed by ethical relativisms like that of Willard Gaylin in *Feelings* and E. O. Wilson in *Sociobiology,* Westermarck finds the origin of moral judgments in the emotions "felt by the society at large" and directed by the society's sense of its "needs."

The *Encyclopedia of Philosophy*'s receptiveness to Westermarck isn't surprising, since the twentieth-century philosophical mode of which the *Encyclopedia* is the perfect and probably culminating expression, the analytical-linguistic-logical mode, is strongly relativist in its assumptions — more strongly even than explicit relativisms themselves. While explicit *relativism*s are always shouting "there are no absolutes," the denial of *absolutes* is so strongly assumed by this modern philosophical tradition that no mention is even made of it. Following logical positivism's dictate that any assertion about *absolutes* (including the assertion that "there are no absolutes") is meaningless because unverifiable, analytic-linguistic philosophy maintains a strict silence about all *absolutes,* whether of metaphysics or ethics, and about anything touching on the transcendent. Even *values* are too close to transcendence for comfort, so this tradition of moral philosophy — if such a name can be given to a philosophy that refuses to talk about morals, and will talk only about talk about morals — implicitly alters the ethical relativist formula from "values are relative" to "statements about values are relative."

What statements about values are relative to, in this philosophical tradition, are either the speaker's attitudes (as in Westermarck) or the speaker's intention to effect certain attitudes or actions in others. Either way, values (that is, statements about values) are given a subjectivist basis, which is carried also into a modern doctrine called "metaethical relativism." Concerned primarily with the process of moral reasoning, metaethical relativism claims in typical relativist style that "there are no objectively sound procedures for justifying one moral code or one set of moral judgments as against another."

In the few schools of twentieth-century philosophy where morals themselves (rather than moral language or moral reasoning) are talked about, notably in pragmatism and existentialism, the ethical talk is explicitly — and similarly — relativist. Both pragmatism and existentialism teach openly that "there are no absolutes," and both frequently denounce what Dewey calls the "fiction . . . of a fixed transcendental world wherein moral ideals are eternally and immutably real." The very unfixed world of "concrete acts" and "experience" is the place, for both, where values are made — and remade with each new "situation." While for existentialism it is the individual and for pragmatism the society that creates values, for both the big words in ethical (and nearly all other) discussion are *concrete, actions, experience,* and *situation.* Both would subscribe to the general ethical relativist formula filled in as "values are relative to the situation"; and from both came "Situation Ethics" and other attempts by Christian thinkers in the 1960s at formulating a Christian ethical relativism.

The idea of a Christian ethical relativism is actually self-contradictory. While the basic secularism of twentieth-century philosophy — shaped by such aggressive atheists as Nietzsche, Russell, Dewey, and Sartre — logically leads to relativism's denial of absolutes, such a denial should make no sense to believers in God, since God is nothing if not absolute. There's no contradiction, of course, between Christianity and a limited relativism: one can accept Jesus' claim that "I am the Way and the Truth and the Life" while acknowledging that we poor mortals (as George Eliot endearingly calls us) have a far from perfect perception of what that Way is and have devised a multitude of ways of trying to follow it. One can recognize these many ways that people have tried to act morally as relative — relative to time and place and temperament and all the other variables of human life — while recognizing too that they need not (and should not) be only relative, but should be in touch also with God, the Absolute. The so-called Christian ethical relativism of the 1960s, however, insisted that human values are only relative because only human; such a belief is indeed relativist, but it isn't really Christian.

Nor did these Christian proponents of ethical relativism, the most influential of whom were Joseph Fletcher in *Situation Ethics* (1966)

and Harvey Cox in his best-selling *The Secular City* (1965), seem
to want to sound particularly Christian. They seemed much more
eager to sound like good academics, up on the latest relativist reasoning in all areas. "No twentieth-century man of even average
training," says Fletcher, showing that he's keeping up with the
Professor Joneses, "will turn his back on the anthropological and
psychological evidence for relativity morals." Cox not only won't
turn his back on this "evidence"; he turns to face it eagerly, to
welcome it with open arms:

> The awareness that his own point of view is relative and condi-
> tioned has become for secular man* an inescapable component
> of that point of view. His consciousness has been relativized. He
> knows that not only his language, his customs, and his clothing
> style, but also his science, his values, and his very way of per-
> ceiving reality are conditioned by his personal biography and the
> history of his group. In our time the Copernican revolution has
> reached out to incorporate everything into its sweep. All things
> are relative. Everything "depends on how you look at it."

This is a vision as sweeping as that which Cox attributes to the
Copernican revolution: the various conclusions of cultural, historical, and epistemological relativism are swept up into a single grand
everything and *all*. When people say *everything,* though, they rarely
have everything in mind (it's hard, in any case, to have everything
in mind at once, or even over a lifetime); and Cox makes it clear
in his next paragraph that what he really means by *everything* is
values, the relativity of which he announces enthusiastically:

> Secular man's values have been deconsecrated, shorn of any claim
> to ultimate or final significance. . . . They have become what
> certain people at a particular time and place hold to be good.
> They have ceased to be values and have become valuations. . . .
> Simple ethical certainty . . . will never be possible again.

---

* "Secular man" is Cox's plus term for modern man, who has discovered "that he
has been left with the world on his hands" and that "the world has become man's
task and man's responsibility" (pp. 1–2). In making *secular* positive, Cox is deliberately wrenching it from its traditionally negative place in Christian thought and
attaching it to the humanist value system which sees man's *control* of his life as
certain — and as certainly good.

While it's doubtful whether ethical certainty was ever simple, there's no doubt about Cox's approval of its loss. He recognizes, though, that the loss of ethical certainty presents a certain social problem, which he puts in Durkheimian terms:

> The relativization of values does cut the ground out from under many people. It melts the paste of traditional social cohesion and things begin to fall apart.

For Durkheim this problem of social collapse was tragic. But Cox solves the problem with a technique typical of dramatic comedy: like *dei ex machina,* two terms (*maturity* and *consensus*) suddenly appear on the page to salvage the collapsing social structure. If man has "real maturity," says Cox, he

> can accept the fact that value systems, like states and civilizations, come and go. . . . But insofar as they represent a consensus and provide a fabric of corporate life, they should not be tampered with frivolously or capriciously. Secularization places the responsibility for the forging of human values . . . in man's own hands. And this demands a maturity. . . .

I've quoted so much of Cox because his words were, for years, much quoted, and also because so many of them are quotations from other lines we've heard. *Maturity* we're familiar with from *growth and development* language, so we can recognize that it's playing in (and on) Cox its typical trick: appearing to be full of meaning about achievement, when really it's an empty plus — full only of the pretense of achievement and empty of any indication of what exactly is to be achieved. *Consensus* we heard a hint of in Westermarck, where values were seen as derived from a society's common feeling; and we'll hear more of *consensus* later, in connection both with the general structure of relativist language and with the relativist nature of current activities like the taking of surveys and the teaching of values. The rest of the lines quoted above from *The Secular City* are familiar because they're almost exactly the ones we've been hearing since the beginning of this chapter on the language of *relativity.* The purpose of quoting them yet again is to note how these relativist lines from different areas —

from history, anthropology, philosophy, psychology, and ethics — could be drawn together into the single vision that man's "consciousness has been relativized." What's also noteworthy about *relativity*'s lines as they appeared in *The Secular City* is that they reached in this book a sort of peak of their power: they showed themselves strong enough to penetrate a place, Christianity, which stands for their very opposite and persuasive enough to be bought by the hundreds of thousands of Americans who made the book a best-seller.

We should note, too, that while the line that "all things are relative" reached as wide an audience in the 1960s as it had in the 1920s, the "things" included in "all" were almost entirely different at the two times. The relativity of the things listed by Cox — language, customs, clothing style, values, perception — had become major subjects of attention mainly *since* the 1920s; whereas the relativity mainly referred to by the line in the 1920s, the relativity of space and time, is the only major one that Cox omits. (The "science" that he includes in his list of items "conditioned" by "personal biography" and "history" is obviously scientific activity in general, not the particular theory of physics.) Cox omits any reference to relativity theory because, to his credit, he recognizes — as not all ethical relativists have — that Einstein's relativity has nothing to do with "the relativization of values."

Yet Einstein's relativity does have something to do with the continuing popularity of the line "it's all relative," and even with *relativity*'s appearance over the years in one field after another. It's as if the line, thundered out by physicists from the peak of the Mount Sinai of science, has stayed (as we say) in the air of our century, hovering over the various relativisms as they've grown up indigenously in different areas and pulling them into line — into, that is, this particular line that "it's all relative" and accompanying lines like "there are no absolutes" or "everything depends on how you look at it." As these lines have then been uttered by authorities in more and more areas, they have come to sound more and more authoritative, to carry increasing weight — so that they carry by now the weight of a general truth. People now say "it's all relative" without giving a thought to what they're saying, yet with the confidence that they're saying something true. Meanwhile though, with an irony typical of the life of leading language, as the line has become increasingly accepted as a popular truth, it has become increasingly rejected as probably an error in many of the fields where it was first formulated; and many people in these fields who *have* thought about what they mean by saying "it's all relative" have — for reasons we'll see in the following chapter — come to the conclusion that they'd better stop saying it.

9

Relativity's Tangles and Other Troubles

The Structure of *Relativity*

Having followed *relativity*'s lines as they've made their way through some areas of twentieth-century thought that they've helped to shape, we should now step away for a broader view of what shape, in fact, these lines give to our thought. We should move, that is, from a close-up focus on particular lines of *relativity* to an overall view of their general structure, which is also the structure of relativism. For *relativity*'s standard lines have come to represent the concept of relativism — even though *relativity* need not by definition be an ism (since it can refer simply to the state of being relative) and even though the *relativity* of the field responsible for the word's fame is not strictly relativist itself. Einstein's relativity, despite the impression given by some of its popularized versions and by much of its own language, does recognize certain absolutes; whereas relativism is the uncompromising insistence that "there are *no* absolutes," that "it's *all* relative." Relativism is therefore essentially an extreme position, and a belligerent one: it is the word *relative*, which primarily means "dependent on something else, not absolute," taken to the extreme where it sees nothing in the world *but* dependence and denies absolutes any existence at all, the extreme from which — asserting itself as an unequivocally positive term — it shoots murderous minuses at the *absolute*. This attack of the self-asserting *relative* against the negative *absolute* is relativism's central rhetorical gesture. Relativism is most concisely represented, we could say — even more concisely than by the converse pair of lines "it's all relative" and "there are no absolutes" — by just this pair of words in their *relative / absolute* opposition, where all the positive value is on the *relative* side.

The rest of *relativity*'s main terms group themselves on either side of this *relative / absolute* division; so that what we see when we move to an overall, sort of aerial view of relativism's structure is two columns of terms standing opposed to each other, as if on opposite banks of a river that divides them like a slash. The two columns are not, however, of equal length or strength. *Relative*'s side is clearly dominant, waving a proud plus sign and including in its ranks a long list of terms like *subjective, observer, frame of reference, experience, situation, opinion, consensus, agreement, tolerance, pluralistic, alternative,* and *options* — some of which we can recognize as recruits from relativism's march through various fields earlier in the century, others (as we'll see) picked up by *relative* more recently. By contrast, *absolute* has behind it just a few terms like *objective, ultimate,* and *certainty;* and though the *absolute* side couldn't be said to be waving, showing off, a minus sign (how could a term as inherently positive as *absolute* be celebrating its own negation?), we can see the signs of defeat written all over it. But this is because what we're seeing, we must remember, is the *absolute* of our century's relativisms, in which naturally — relativism being what it is — *absolute* fights a losing battle. (To see *absolute* in its glory we would need only to look at the language of absolutisms and idealisms from Plato through Christianity to Hegel.)

If we look more closely at the losing side of relativism, we see that the *absolute* is actually of two sorts. Either *absolute truth* or *absolute values* can turn up, or be turned down, in relativism's cry that "there are no absolutes." *Absolute truth* is what appears (but appears, of course, in order to have its existence denied) in all forms of epistemological relativism: we've come across examples in historical relativism and in popularized relativity theory, and we'd find others in the recent isms of a variety of academic fields — in the "deconstructionism" of philosophy and literary criticism, in the post-Kuhnian "historicism" of the philosophy of science and the sociology of knowledge, in the "experientialism" of George Lakoff's linguistics. *Absolute values* (or *moral absolutes*) are what is attacked in all versions of moral or ethical relativism, such as we've seen in cultural relativism and would find nearly everywhere in twentieth-century ethics.

On the positive side of relativism's *relative / absolute* split, the distinction between epistemological and ethical relativism doesn't seem to make much difference to the organization of terms. Instead, the terms in *relative*'s column tend — while shifting around quite a bit — to cluster according to certain concepts associated with relativisms of all kinds. *Relative*'s association with the concept of subjectivity (in the idea that truth and values are relative to the individual person and are hence subjective) brings in as positive terms not only the *subjective, observer,* and *frame of reference* that we found along with the *relative* of every area we looked at in Chapter 8, but also the currently ubiquitous *experience.* Though *experience* was once associated (in the seventeenth century) with the scientific method and meant the same thing as *experiment,* it has moved today into close association with the subjectivity of the *self* set; and while no longer containing anything firm enough in most of its users' minds to be called a meaning, it does carry strong connotations of subjectivity, individuality, and uniqueness. *Experience,* that is, tends now to imply *personal* experience — with the further implication that every person's experience is different and unique. This subjectively based and infinitely varied *experience* is what relativism tries, in turn, to base our understanding and values on, often by means of construction talk: *experience* is the basis on which we "build" a value system, "construct" a world view, and so on (which perhaps is why we have so many *workshops*).

The concept of subjectivity brings *opinion,* too, into the ranks of *relative*'s positive terms. Since relativism denies *absolute truth* any existence and gives personal *experience* prime value, personal *opinion* takes the place of *truth* as the positively valued product of the human mind. The opposition between *opinion* and *truth* is a long-standing one in Western philosophy, but philosophers (lovers of knowledge as they literally are) have traditionally seen *truth* as the positive term of the pair and have looked down on *opinion*, lashing it with a minus as "mere opinion." Relativism's switching of the value carried by *opinion* has had, as we'll see in a later section on opinion polls, substantial effects not only on our public decision-making process but also on our society's general sense of what a human mind is supposed to do.

Since both opinion and experience are notoriously changeable, these terms join in connection with another concept celebrated by relativism: the concept of impermanence. *Situation* comes in here too in the same (positive) way: our values, perceptions, opinions, understanding, and so on are relative to the *situation* or to our *experience*, and both situations and experience are assumed by relativism to change — since otherwise they would be fixed and absolute. Relativism praises all this variability, as it does the closely connected concept of diversity (which is variability at one time instead of over a period of time). And in its praise of diversity, relativism picks up a string of positive terms associated also with the theory and practice of democracy: *consensus, agreement, pluralism, tolerance, alternative,* and *options*.

Consensus is really just *opinion* taken collectively, which is how relativism has to take it when a whole society's decisions are being made. Since, that is, relativism denies any absolute standard of truth or value that might be appealed to, public decisions must be based somehow on *opinion:* either by adding up individual opinions to find the majority opinion (called a *consensus*) or by finding an area of common agreement, the place where most opinions overlap (also called a *consensus*). We reach for a *consensus* so often these days that it's startling to learn from Raymond Williams's *Keywords* that we've been doing so with our current obsession only since the mid-twentieth century, and that *consensus* has been available to reach for in English only since the mid-nineteenth — though the concept it stands for has been around, and celebrated, much longer. If de Tocqueville is right (and his remarks certainly have the ring of truth), the celebration of public opinion has been part of all "ages of equality," because when people sense their resemblance to each other this "gives them almost unbounded confidence in the judgment of the public" ("for it would seem probable that, as they are all endowed with equal means of judging, the greater truth should go with the greater number"). In our current age of both equality and relativism, we have confidence in nothing *but* this collective judgment that we call *consensus*. So we panic if a *consensus* can't be "found" or "arrived at" and wouldn't consider making a public policy decision or a moral judgment without one. And once we've got a *consensus*, we treat it as something sacred, issuing stern warnings like Harvey Cox's that "insofar as [value systems] represent a consensus, . . . they should not be tampered with."

Another unquestioned good that relativism won't let us tamper with is *tolerance*. Relativism has to insist on *tolerance* as a prime good because it insists that there are no absolutes by which one opinion (attitude, practice, whatever) might be judged better than another, so all must be treated as equally valid. *Equality, respect,* and *tolerance* thus become imperatives for relativism, which exhorts us — as we heard cultural relativist Melville Herskovits doing — to recognize "the need for tolerance of conventions though they may differ from one's own."

The more they differ, even, the better. Praising *pluralism* and delighting in *diversity,* relativism has come — especially recently — to love *alternatives* and *options. Alternative's* recent rise to prominence as a positive term is intriguing, since *alternative* just means "other" and so is inherently neutral. But ever since the success of the counterculture of the 1960s in promoting its lifestyle as an *alternative,* the word has flourished as a promotional term — usually still for projects counter to the existing culture, like "alternative cinema" and "alternative birthing centers," but also for some well-established enterprises like "alternative newspapers" and "alternative energy," which evidently find *alternative* valuable enough to want to keep it as a name. In fact, *alternative*'s positive value is now so firmly established that people find the word worth stealing: a recent *National Review* article arguing for private inner-city schools brazenly calls them "alternative schools," ripping the word off from the public inner-city schools that it is arguing against and that have been advanced as *alternatives* for years.

This example illustrates, too, another quirk of *alternative*'s fate. When people now offer something as an *alternative,* they usually mean it to be taken not as just one possible choice but as the only one. The book called *The Humanist Alternative,* for instance, doesn't suggest humanism as just another alternative; it firmly believes that humanism is the only answer. And the "positive, constructive alternatives" repeatedly put forward in *The Humanist* magazine are obviously intended as the ones we should (as humanism itself, sharing relativism's fondness for construction talk, would put it) "build on." I take my examples from humanism because it's so full of *alternatives;* but the same sense of certainty is carried by most *alternatives* (and *options*) these days. *Alternative* comes on sounding open and tentative, but often it's as fixed as an absolute.

The same is true for many of relativism's plus terms. *Opinion, experience, consensus, tolerance,* and even *relative* itself take on such firmly positive value these days that they tend to be treated as absolutes. All positive terms have this tendency, but for relativism it poses a special problem because *relative*'s very meaning lies in its opposition to *absolutes.* When the terms on *relative*'s side of the opposition turn into absolutes, the slash dividing the columns of *relative* and *absolute* therefore blurs — like a river flooding its banks and washing together everything from the separate sides, in a rush of confusion.

Self-contradictions of *Relativity*

It's certainly one of the central confusions of relativism that while casting aside all *absolutes* with one hand, with the other it grabs onto certain terms with an absolute grip. It even pounds the podium with these favored terms in its fist, as when Harvey Cox declares a *consensus* something that "should not be tampered with" or when Melville Herskovits insists on *tolerance* as the anthropologist's prime "need" and on *mutual respect* as "the very core of cultural relativism." All relativisms have at their core particular terms and concepts like this, which they assume to be prime goods and absolutely refuse to tamper with, as well as all having as their common core an absolute trust in relativism itself. This central trust in their own truth makes all relativisms therefore rotten at the core, or at least mushy in their central meaning — because they state that there is no absolute truth, yet accept that statement as true.

Besides suffering from this self-contradiction of holding absolutely to a denial of absolutes, relativism is plagued as well by another (almost reverse) problem: seeing everything as relative, it must see itself as merely relative too. Philosopher Max Black, in his criticism of Whorf's linguistic relativity, refers to this problem as "the familiar paradox that all general theories of the relativity of truth must brand themselves as biased and erroneous." The paradox is indeed familiar. Critics of the relativist nature of Marxism have long wondered, for example, "how Marxism alone among social opinions could escape being vitiated by its relations to a given class and age." And the more recent relativisms of every field have been reduced in the same way to their own terms: "anthropologists now understand," the *Encyclopedia of Anthropology* comments typically, "that the dogma [of cultural relativism] itself is the product of a particular ideological and historical tradition."

This paradox of relativism's own relativism has an added twist, which acts like the turn of another screw in relativism's self-made coffin. As a critique of a kind of epistemological relativism called "historicism" puts it:

> The main claim of [cultural] relativism, and historicism, is just that the intellectual products of *all* cultures, and of *all* historical periods, must . . . be accorded equal intellectual status. Therefore, the antirelativist and antihistoricist positions are the intel-

lectual equals of relativism and historicism. So no relativist, and no historicist, can coherently argue the intellectual superiority (or preferability) of relativism or historicism without (implicitly) denying the very doctrine which he seeks to defend.

Nor can a relativist coherently argue that relativism, or any other theory, has any intellectual value at all. Relativists claim that all beliefs and values have equal worth; but (in the words of a critic of cultural relativism) "it is equally logical, as many a philosopher has seen, to reach the conclusion that all cultural values [and, we might add, all other social-cultural-historical products] are equally worthless."

As if these various logical tangles and self-made traps that all relativisms get into weren't trouble enough, particular relativisms also have particular logical problems of their own. The ethical relativism derived from cultural relativism suffers from the common fallacy of turning an "is" into an "ought." Diversity of moral values around the world might be a fact; but — as the supremely logical *Encyclopedia of Philosophy* points out — "nothing in particular about what ought to be, or about what someone ought to do, follows" from this fact. In reasoning that because different cultures prescribe different behavior, people therefore ought to behave differently, relativism is reasoning falsely — as it is when it makes the related mistake, sometimes called the "naturalistic fallacy," of assuming that because something (in this case, diversity) is apparently natural, it is therefore unquestionably good.

Another logical problem from which cultural relativism suffers is one which is inherent in all epistemological relativisms and which leads for all to a practical problem as well. The problem has been put — with reference to historical relativism, which has been especially plagued by it — as follows. While the historian's aim is to understand the past, the relativist's assumption is that he can see only the present, only what his subjective frame of reference shows him. Therefore, to the extent to which the historical relativist succeeds in carrying out his aim, he refutes his own assumption. Conversely — and here's where the practical difficulty comes in — to the extent to which he accepts his relativist assumption (that historic truth is relative and subjective), he can't carry out his aim as historian (the discovery of historic truth). Acceptance of relativism therefore makes the work of the historian impossible, as it does the work of the anthropologist investigating other cultures, or anyone else professionally engaged in the pursuit of truth. To engage in the pursuit of truth while holding relativist assumptions is to ask for trouble: the relativist pursuing his object of investigation will inevitably run up against his own mind instead.

Retreats from the *Relative:* "Relativism is not a position one can ultimately live with"

Forced to choose between being historians and being relativists, most historians have decided that there's more of worth in the practice of their profession than in the theory of relativism. They've sensed, contrary to relativist claims, that an object of investigation does exist outside their own minds and that this object is worthy of pursuit. But they don't claim to be able to grasp the absolute truth of their object. They don't try to make rigid claims on either side, for either the *relative* or the *absolute;* in fact, they don't say much about, or with, these words at all anymore. The debate over historical relativism has subsided without being really settled. Or it has settled into a casual compromise. The aggressive line that "historic truth is relative and subjective," which once pierced the historical profession like an attacking spear, has softened, slackened. Historians now hold loosely to part of the line — they assume that their understanding is relative and subjective to some extent — but, without fussing over exactly what that extent is, they stop well short of following the relativist line all the way to its skeptical and solipsistic end.

In anthropology, too, there has been a retreat from relativist extremes. Anthropologists have noted all the logical difficulties to which cultural relativism leads: the self-contradiction of treating its favored terms (like *equality* and *tolerance*) as absolutes, the blindness of not seeing its own dogma as culturally determined, the fallacy of turning the "is" of cultural diversity into an "ought," the incoherence of arguing for the superiority of a doctrine that declares all doctrines of equal worth, the nonsense of insisting that cultures be evaluated only in terms of their own values (since this is just to accept them on their own terms and not to evaluate them at all). And having noted all these problems that cultural relativism gets into when its reasoning is followed, anthropologists have — reasonably enough — pulled back and tried to find a more logically defensible position.

And more politically defensible as well: because it turns out that cultural relativism's strong stand for *tolerance* and *respect* can put one in a dangerously weak political position. The American Anthropological Association, in its initial excitement about cultural relativism, had enthusiastically advised the United Nations Commission on Human Rights in 1947 that:

1. The individual realizes his personality through his culture: hence respect for individual differences entails a respect for cultural differences.

2. Respect for differences between cultures is validated by the scientific fact that no technique of qualitatively evaluating cultures has been discovered.

3. Standards and values are relative to the culture from which they derive, so that any attempt to formulate postulates that grow out of the beliefs or moral codes of one culture must to that extent detract from the applicability of any Declaration of Human Rights to mankind as a whole.

Yet — such is the lag of institutional pronouncements behind individual awareness — while this confident relativist position was being officially proclaimed, many relativists were already finding it awkward and uncomfortable and were trying to squirm out of it. World War II had shocked them into discovering that an ultimate value of "respect for differences" provided no defense against a nation that treated individual and cultural differences with an aggressive *dis*respect. And many anthropologists, as well as politicians and ordinary people, discovered during the war that indiscriminate *respect* for all cultures was not their ultimate value after all. They found — despite the inability of science to find a "technique of qualitatively evaluating cultures" — that they nevertheless did evaluate their democratic culture as superior to Fascism, and that they did so not just because it was their own but because they believed it to be inherently better. Yet this belief in the superiority of democratic values could not be defended without abandoning the relativist position that proclaimed all values equal.

Since the war, cultural relativism has continued to be abandoned by politicians and anthropologists alike as it has come into conflict with other positions considered politically and morally more desirable. The advancement of the American and international human rights campaign, for example, has forced a retreat from relativism because the two doctrines — contrary to the American Anthropological Association's 1947 statement of their harmony — fundamentally conflict: a declaration of the absolute value of human rights is a denial of the claim that there are no absolutes; and a policy of (even subtle) intervention in cultures that violate the human rights of their members is a rejection of relativism's hands-off policy of complete *tolerance* of all cultural practices. This policy of nonintervention and even indifference implied by cultural relativism's imperative of *tolerance* is what is now generally found to be intolerable. "Cultural relativism leads us into moral impotence in a world where few are prepared to forsake the right to judge," is how one textbook puts the current indictment, concluding "many anthropologists would urge that cultural relativism is not a position one can ultimately live with."

Anthropologists no longer try, therefore, to live with cultural relativism ultimately. They're happy to live with it moderately, as a limited methodological tool. "Cultural relativism remains a necessary condition for gathering data," says the *International Encyclopedia of the Social Sciences,* and all textbooks written since the 1960s concur; "one cannot observe objectively if one's own ethical judgments . . . intrude and color the observation. But," they all go on, drawing a firm line between methodology and morality, "the suspension of value judgment is not indefinite"; "the moral corollary of cultural relativism — moral relativism — has been quietly discarded." So the cultural relativism that started off as a proud ethical position has been stripped of its moral validity and reduced to the methodological rule that one mustn't pass judgment on one's data while gathering it — a rule which, while certainly sensible, is not much more than common sense. In both history and anthropology, then, the extremist views to which relativism led have been generally abandoned for more moderate positions along the relativist line: the position that historic truth is indeed to some extent relative, but we can still know quite a bit about it; the position that cultural values are indeed to some extent relative, but we can still evaluate them.

Some people in both fields, and in all others where relativism has penetrated, have resisted going along with the relativist line even this far. They haven't so much retreated from the *relative* as stood firm against it from the start. Among these resisters, some have known immediately just what *absolutes* to stand their ground on, and — catching relativism's cry that "there are no absolutes" — have hurled right back "there are *so*, and here they are." (Though most of these immediate objectivist counterattacks have come, as we would expect, from people firmly grounded in religious principles, not all of them have: one of the earliest was from a historian who in 1938 heaved at historical relativism a massive secularized argument for "the ideal of objective historical knowledge.") Other resisters of relativism's advance, though not able to put their hands on any *absolutes* right away, have felt certain that there must be some somewhere, while fearing disaster for society if there aren't. In response to the claim that "there are no absolutes," they've cringed ("oh dear, there'd better be, or woe to us all") and have searched at once through life's diversity to find some.

Succeeding, they've reported their findings with a forcefulness unusual in academic articles. Anthropologist Ralph Linton, who began searching after World War II for some "universal ethical principles" on which an urgently needed worldwide value system could be based, sounded obviously relieved to be able to report in 1952 that "behind the seemingly endless diversity of culture patterns there is a fundamental uniformity." Linton's relief was evidently shared by the many people — not just anthropologists but philosophers and moralists as well — who grabbed up his findings from the brief article in which they appeared and who quickly spread the word, through encyclopedias and textbooks, that "there is an actual common core of cultural values" which "may be called absolutes as well as universals." The more vividly people have imagined the chaos — the social, political, intellectual, psychological, or moral confusion — that would come to a world with no source of stability, the more enthusiastically they have hailed the rediscovery of *absolutes*. The rhetorical emphasis given by one psychologist who had looked anxiously through the varieties of human behavior for a "basis of a stable and ordered society" is typical: "some individual patterns of behavior, such as those summarized by such words as 'courage,' 'temperance,' 'justice,' 'wisdom,' 'charity,' and 'friendliness' . . . can be seen," he announced emphatically, "to be preferred *absolutely* to their opposites."

Such forceful reaffirmations of the *absolute*, along with the eventual retreats from the *relative* wherever it comes on as an ism, suggest that there's something basically uncongenial about relativism, which pushes us sooner or later away from it. Unlike the concepts carried by the words *self* and *growth*, which seem to reinforce some element of human nature (our natural self-interest, our natural identification with organic growth), the relativism carried by *relative, opinion, consensus,* and their comrades when they assert themselves as uncompromising positives seems to violate something natural in us: what Plato called our natural desire for the truth and for the good. People have always, as far as we know, striven for certainty and perfection of "head" and of "heart" (as the places where we seek truth and goodness are traditionally symbolized); and so in denying the possibility of certainty in both "places," in attacking the existence of intellectual and moral absolutes, relativism is threatening vital human functions. This is why, in my sketch of *relative*'s career through our century, I've pictured it often in aggressive, militaristic terms: because the minus sign that relativism thrusts like a spear at the *absolutes* of head and heart is aimed, as we'd now put it, at the jugular.

That minus sign hurled by relativism at all *absolutes* is, however, starting to boomerang, to come back and stick to *relativism* itself. The word *relativism,* more and more these days, carries negative connotations. The word is getting a bad reputation because people have found, from living with relativism in one area after another and trying conscientiously to follow its implications, that doing so always leads to difficulties. Following the implications of moral relativism — that is, of the line that "all values are relative" — leads to moral chaos (because one has no grounds for judgment), to social instability (because society has no basis for its values), and to political impotence (because a nation has no moral justifications for action). Following the implications of epistemological relativism — of the line that "all knowledge is relative" — leads to skepticism, to intellectual immobility (because one can't get outside one's own mind), and to a practical impasse for all professions engaged in the search for objective knowledge. Both moral and epistemological relativism lead, when their logic is followed to its finish, to self-contradictions and logical fallacies. The people who reject relativism immediately when it enters a new area are, therefore, just sensing sooner what eventually becomes apparent to anyone who tries to go along with it to its (a)moral, (un)intellectual, and (il)logical ends: that — morally, intellectually, logically, as well as socially, politically, and practically — relativism is not a position one can ultimately live with.

10

It's All Relative Still, in Some Cases

Even though relativism is not a position one can ultimately live with, we are still — strangely enough — living with it in many ways. This section and the next will look at two areas of contemporary American life where we live on intimate terms with relativism: the institution of opinion polling, which practically runs our public life as a nation, and which persistently invades our private lives in the form of the surveys we're always being asked to respond to and the percentages we're quoted in the daily news; and the field of values education, which spreads its methods through our classrooms and hence touches the lives of nearly everyone in our schools.

Opinion Polls: "Our survey says . . ."

The language of the opinion polls, surveys, and questionnaires that continually impose themselves on our lives isn't explicitly relativist. Surveys don't come out and say "it's all relative" in their instructions; nor do they directly denounce *absolutes*. Yet "surveys show," along with their reported findings and throughout their operations, a firmly held relativism — implicit in the words they most depend on and in their basic assumption about what our minds are meant to do.

The word *opinion* itself, as we noted in the section "The Structure of *Relativity*," carries relativist concepts when it's put on a pedestal and worshipped — which it certainly is by the polling industry. Though the notorious changeability of opinion is acknowledged by pollsters (and is their excuse for surveying opinion so often), they treat *opinion* as if it were indeed as solid as a cement statue: "measuring" it with "instruments" that give them "hard data"; calling what they do "opinion research," as if *opinion* had the concreteness of an object of scientific investigation. They then raise this solid object, *opinion,* before us as an object worthy of our respect, as something worth not only our society's constant attention but also large amounts of its tax money. And something presumably worth more to us as individuals than knowledge or information: surveys encourage and even force us — at the drop of a letter through our mail slot or at the ring of our phone — to "have an opinion" on every subject whether or not we know anything about it.

This persistent request for our *opinion* rather than our knowledge is relativist because it asks us to engage, as our primary intellectual activity, not in the pursuit of truth but in the (instantaneous) production of opinion — and thus implies that the truth, if there is such a thing, isn't worth pursuing. But surveys go even farther than this in their epistemological relativism: they convey the clear if unarticulated message that "there is no absolute truth," that there actually is no such thing as *truth* apart from *opinion.* They convey this message by, for example, treating the two words and what they stand for interchangeably, as in the *Esquire* issue (October 1979) where "The *Truth* about Today's Young Men," proclaimed with red underlining on the cover, is revealed inside as the tabulated results of one of Gail Sheehy's surveys (a survey of *Esquire* readers — hardly a random sample of today's young men — about how much happiness they felt in their lives). Or the same relativist message can be conveyed by eliminating the word and concept of *truth* altogether and putting *opinion* in its place, as in the television game show *Family Feud,* where contestants are rewarded not for knowing the right answer to a question but for guessing what most people polled had considered the right answer, for guessing (as the emcee exuberantly announces) what "our survey says."

Children watching *Family Feud* (and the show is especially popular with children) and young men reading *Esquire* are thus being taught the opposite of what Rousseau recommended in *Emile:*

> First teach a child things as they really are; afterward you will teach him how they appear to us. He will then be able to compare popular ideas and truth [*comparer l'opinion à la verité*] and be able to rise above the vulgar crowd. . . . But if you begin to teach the opinions of other people [*l'opinion publique*] before you teach how to judge of their worth, . . . your pupil will adopt these opinions whatever you may do.

Surveys, however, not only teach opinions before teaching how to judge of their worth; they teach that there *is* no judge of worth apart from opinion, no right or wrong apart from what "our survey says." And we in modern American society have learned this lesson so well that we've forgotten other lessons that history has taught us. Forgetting that slavery, for example, would have received high approval ratings on an attitude survey done less than two centuries ago, we let polls guide us on all questions of public policy and can't imagine that a consensus might be mistaken, that the majority polled might approve of something wrong. What "our survey says" is gospel; * we have no ears to hear any other voice; and the vulgar crowd (which includes not only the audience polled in *Family Feud* but also that part of each of us which is our mere opinion) is raised above us all.

This contemporary faith in *opinion* merges, in the characteristic wording of survey instructions, with another dominant faith of our time: in *feelings.* Questionnaires make no distinction between

---

* In a revealing moment, pollster Louis Harris actually bore witness to this faith. Testifying before a House subcommittee, he complained that often in the press "some polling outfit nobody has ever heard of . . . is quoted as the gospel, as though it were the Gallup or Harris polls."

the two words, asking "what is your opinion of?" interchangeably with "how do you feel about?," and typically slipping *opinion* and *feelings* — as well as *belief* and *thought* — in place of each other randomly:

> Some people *feel* that the government in Washington should see to it that every person has a job and a good standard of living. Others *think* the government should just let each person get ahead on his own. And, of course, other people *have opinions* somewhere in between. Suppose people who *believe* that the government in Washington should see to it that every person has a job and a good standard of living are at one end of this scale. . . . [italics mine]

Questionnaires' blurring of *thought, belief,* and *opinion* is another expression of the relativism we've been noting in surveys: their sense that the various products of our mind are indistinguishable, and are as good as truth itself. The further blurring of all these terms with *feelings* then shows this relativism run into — dissolved into — the subjectivity that we've seen (in Part One) carried by *feelings* and other words associated with *self.*

Opinion, of course, already carries some subjectivity on its own, as we noted in Chapter 9. And other terms associated with *relative,* like *experience* and *subjective* itself, have long carried the concepts of relativism and subjectivity together. So surveys aren't making a new connection by equating *opinion* and *feelings.* But they're reinforcing this connection at certain points: at the points where current *opinion* and *feelings,* both conceived as valuable, carry the same particular — and particularly celebrated — values. The immense positive value that we grant today to *personal,* for example, presides over both *opinion* and *feelings* and links them by a common plus: even when this value isn't explicitly evoked in the (almost redundant) form of "personal opinion" and "personal feelings," one's opinion and feelings are assumed to be valuable, special, just because they are "one's own." The positive value of *change,* too — celebrated today (as we saw in the case of *growth and development*) even to the extent of *instability* — is carried by both *opinion* and *feelings* when they themselves carry plus signs.

Opinion and feelings are both notoriously unstable; we might even say — since opinion is a phenomenon of mind, and since feelings, though not simply physical, are intimately involved with our bodies — that opinion and feelings are respectively the most transient products of head and heart. When these equally slippery phenomena, *opinion* and *feelings,* are equally celebrated (as they are today) and are also equated (as they are, for instance, on surveys), the highly valued flux of our minds runs together with the highly valued flux of our bodies into a single highly celebrated ooze.*

People have always had feelings and opinions. What's new in recent times is that we celebrate them so exuberantly and throw ourselves so eagerly into their flux, instead of trying to stand back from their inevitable ups and downs to let them pass as undisruptively as possible. Our present inability to keep apart from their confused and muddied current — our desire, even, not to keep apart at all but to dive right in with heart and soul — comes largely from our combined Romantic and relativist heritage. Romanticism (we saw in Part One) swelled the positive value of *feelings* in all their flux, and hence increased their attraction immensely; relativism has done the same for *opinion,* and in the process has joined Romanticism in conveying those subjectivist values that, we've noted, *personal feelings* and *personal opinion* both carry.

These values, conveyed as they are by such strong cultural forces as Romanticism and relativism, are bound to show up in many other contemporary phenomena besides surveys. They appear every evening, for example, in the "personal response" interviews that have become an integral part of television news: as the camera focuses respectfully on randomly chosen people "reacting" — expressing their ordinary personal feelings and voicing their always predictable opinions — our own just as ordinary and predictable

---

* Other typical survey language goes even further in turning *opinion* into a simple physiological phenomenon: pollsters like to talk about "taking the pulse of the public"; and they often ask, especially in phone or face-to-face interviews, for "your immediate reaction," as if coming up with an opinion were as instinctive as reacting with a jump to a sudden crash of thunder or vomiting when someone sticks a finger down your throat.

"personal" feelings and opinions are swelled to the status of national news, and the immense value that we as a culture confer on *feelings* and *opinion* is projected back at us. While one reason that news programs find "personal response" interviewing attractive is that it's inexpensive and easy to do, another (probably unconscious) reason is that it dramatizes vividly a complex set of values that our society is much attracted to: those relativist–Romantic–subjectivist values that surveys show as well.

I've restricted this brief discussion of surveys to the way they say "it's all relative" — and by extension, "it's all subjective" — because the leading language of relativism, and not surveys themselves or even all of their language, is my main subject. There are certainly other things that surveys say, and other ways that they lead us, that are just as significant as their relativism: their way, for instance, of bossing us around at election time, or of ordering our thinking at all times into pigeonholes (and so really treating us as pigeons, as beings made not to reflect freely but to be programmed into a limited number of fixed responses). Fortunately, these and other manipulative practices of polling, outside my subject here, are examined in Michael Wheeler's *Lies, Damn Lies, and Statistics* and in an increasing number of newspaper and magazine articles. One other feature of surveys, however, does fall within my general focus on how certain leading words affect our lives.

Whatever the leading words of the day happen to be, surveys act as one of their leading vehicles, and even give these words an extra push into prominence. That is, since surveys try to measure already existing public opinion, they tend to formulate their questions in already popular terms; and just by questioning us in these terms, they imply that these are terms of special value, the ones in which we *should* be questioning our lives. So, for example, when a poll from the prestigious National Opinion Research Center asks, "In general, do you find life exciting, pretty routine, or dull?," respondents are encouraged to think that entertainment is what they ought to be looking for in "life." Or when Gallup does a "global survey" of "human needs and satisfactions" and establishes an international data bank to measure "levels of personal happiness" around the world, the position of *personal happiness* and *satisfaction* as leading words in (and goals of) our lives is reinforced — as it is by the previously mentioned *Esquire* survey of the amount of happiness felt by today's young men. Even apart from their findings, then, polls affect us by conferring value on what they're looking for. What surveys ask, we have to conclude, can be as influential as what surveys say.

Values Education: From "personal values clarification" to "consensus" to "_____"

When I was first planning this book in the late 1970s, I thought of using as my main example of current moral relativism the widely favored method of teaching values called "Values Clarification." But now that I come to writing this section in the early 1980s, Values Clarification has fallen out of favor. Raved about by teachers less than five years ago, Values Clarification is now — if mentioned by teachers at all — raged against, and mainly for its relativism. There's no need, then, for me to follow my original plan of examining at length the relativist nature of the language of Values Clarification, since educators themselves have already whipped Values Clarification soundly with the minus of *relativism* and expelled it from the schools. Yet, oddly, what they seem to be inviting in its place, in their thinking about values education, is another version of relativism disguised in only slightly different terms. So it seems worthwhile just to take note of the language of Values Clarification and the concepts it carried, in order to see how some of these concepts are carried on in more recent moral-education programs. After all, despite the eagerness in modern American society to write off the follies of each closing decade with an easy label (the "Turbulent Sixties," the "Me Decade" of the seventies) so as to begin the new decade with eternally recurring innocence, the fundamental concepts of the 1970s — in the field of education or anywhere else — are not likely to have simply disappeared so soon. And the very fact that a method of moral instruction that was all the craze in one decade could be considered crazy in the next is a sign if not of madness then at least of the sort of instability that a continuing relativism can cause.

Values Clarification was presented to teachers — mainly in the two books *Values and Teaching* and *Values Clarification,* but also in numerous articles and, of course, workshops throughout the 1970s — as a solution to the problem of "value confusion" caused by the "bewildering array of alternatives" with which "the children and youth of today are surrounded." Insisting for a start that "values are a product of personal experience" which "evolve and mature as experiences evolve and mature" and that "for any one person, [values] are not so much hard and fast verities as they are the results of hammering out a style of life," Values Clarification offered "tools" with which the student could "build" or "forge" "his own personal values." The toolbox or Values Clarification "kit" consisted of a set of "strategies" in which the teacher "tries to give students options," on the assumption that "the more alternatives open to us in a choice situation, the more likely we are to find something we fully value." While directing these "games" and other deliberately "contrived" activities, the teacher was to make sure not "to impose his or her own views (although they may be shared)," since the purpose of Values Clarification was "to help individuals learn a particular *valuing process*" and "not . . . to instill any particular set of values."

The particular sets of values that the whole approach of Values Clarification was itself instilling are, however, readily apparent, especially since they're the same ones that we've seen, in our study of our century's leading language, being carried by the three sets of leading terms we've looked at so far. The set of values associated with *self* was promoted by Values Clarification not only (and most obviously) in the *personal values* which the method was designed primarily to clarify, but also in many comments in specific strategies along the lines of: "An important question to ask in the search for values is, 'Am I really getting what I want out of life?'" The values of *growth and development* were carried by the *evolving* and *maturing* that Values Clarification saw both our experience and our values as constantly doing, as well as by the repeated emphasis on the valuing *process* — rather than, say, the discovery of ultimate values or the practice of certain virtues — as where the action is in our moral life. And, of course, the relativist set of values was there in full force, represented by most of its familiar terms. *Experience* was brought in as usual, as the source of all values. *Absolutes* were kept out as usual, in the form of the "hard and fast verities" that values definitely "are not" — and also in the form of the rejected authority of the teacher, whose values were granted no more validity than the students' (despite his greater experience). There was the typical toolbox talk of "hammering out a life-style" and "building a value system," which seems to come these days with the relativist view that since values can't be passed from one generation to the next, they must be built over and over again from scratch by each person. And there was the typical proliferation of *options* and *alternatives* almost as ends in themselves ("the more the better"), common in recent relativisms but a bit confusing in one that cited "the bewildering array of alternatives" as the problem it set out to solve.

Finding all these leading terms together in a single fad of a single field shouldn't surprise us. Nothing is more likely to make a theory or a proposal in any area instantly attractive, instantly fashionable, than putting it (consciously or not) in the leading terms of the day — whatever they are. These are the terms that people are already drawn to, led by, so any proposal put "in" them will automatically have a large following. (Conversely, a list of the key promotional terms of any fad will read like a catalog of the leading terms of the time.) In the case of Values Clarification, though, the attraction felt initially by teachers to its familiar language and concepts — an attraction probably increased by teachers' natural fondness for methods, programs, strategies, and so on which promise to simplify their overwhelmingly complex job — was bound to weaken and even to turn into a repulsion.

Teachers were bound to recoil from Values Clarification after they had tried out this method of systematized relativism for a while in their classrooms because — as we've seen, as we keep seeing again and again — when people try to go along with any relativism in any area of their lives, they eventually run into trouble and, naturally, try to pull back. The troubles that teachers found Values Clarification causing — moral confusion (instead of the clarification it promised), unrestrained subjectivism, social chaos — were the same ones that people had found in or feared from relativisms before. And the energetic retreats from Values Clarification, once the evils of its relativism had been recognized, followed the same lines as previous retreats from previous relativisms — as we can hear in one particularly eloquent example, from an editorial in the March 1981 issue of the professional education fraternity's journal, *Phi Delta Kappan*. I quote from the editorial at some length because it expresses with special candor the general dismay among teachers by the early 1980s at the disastrous social consequences of the relativism that had run rampant through education and morals during the previous two decades and had manifested itself (they now saw) in such embarrassments as Values Clarification.

> . . . For reasons I haven't yet fully grasped, U.S. society seems to have been sundered from moral certainties. . . . Not only is there doubt about what credo to pass along to our youngsters; there is confusion, too, about *who* is to hand down whatever set of values we are willing to say we stand for. The result is a moral vacuum. . . . The schools, caught amid conflicting views as to their proper role . . . , seek neutral ground so that they can educate without bias. Thus values clarification and related phenomena.
> But such exercises provide no moral leadership. In a society that has few certainties, they are simply an affirmation that each person's creed is as valid as any other's — and that is not true. . . . There *are* legal — and moral — certainties. We must consent to be governed by them; we are entrusted with transmitting them to our children. Without those certainties as a foundation, our system of education is hollow at the core, a castle built on sand. Without those certainties, our motions are random and essentially meaningless.

The impassioned plea for "certainties" recalls other protests we've heard against relativism's denial of absolutes, as does the almost desperate insistence elsewhere in the editorial that we'd better find some solid "core values" on which to build a moral education program *or else:* "No such core values exist, you say? They must, else we cannot hope to continue as a society." There's nothing like living with the consequences of relativism to shock us into noticing the need for standards and certainties in our lives. Yet when the editorial gets specific about where to find these vital "core values" and "certainties," it turns — as a large part of the field of moral education seems to be turning — to (of all terms) *consensus.*

The title of the editorial is "Toward a Moral Consensus"; the title of the special section in this issue of *Phi Delta Kappan* is "Moral Education: An Emerging Consensus"; the lead article, called "Community Consensus Is Available on a Moral Valuing Standard," begins "Community consensus is imperative in a democratic society" and ends "we still have time to discover and affirm a consensus on a desirable and acceptable moral norm," a consensus which will halt "the disintegration of the West." Yet if *consensus* is indeed what is emerging as the savior of moral education and of the West, then the sooner it recedes, the better, since — as we've seen — when *consensus* comes on as the key to our salvation, it's really the devil of relativism in disguise.

Consensus isn't always relativist, of course. When absolute truth and values are assumed to exist, then a *consensus* about them isn't relativist at all, but is just common recognition of what is true or good. And even without a basis in absolutes, a *consensus* needn't be relativist: *consensus* means simply "common agreement," and people can (and do) agree on all sorts of things without either believing first in certain absolutes or trusting in the agreement itself as absolutely good. When, however, common agreement itself, *consensus* itself, is treated with absolute trust and sought as an unquestioned good, no matter what is agreed on, then *consensus* is carrying all the assumptions (and problems) of relativism because it's making mere collective opinion the measure of truth and value, and recognizing no standards outside itself. And this relativist *consensus* is, alas, what educators seem to be asking for. In their desperate desire to stop the social disintegration that they see caused by the loss of shared values, they seem willing to seize on any values at all as long as they're shared. Schools must "rally around a set of values," exhorts the president of Johns Hopkins University in a *U.S. News and World Report* interview, implying that one set is as good as another. "Anger, confusion and cynicism . . . will spread unless we restore some common framework of values," he continues, as if all that matters is that the framework be "common" and then any values hung on it will be fine.

The relativist nature of the *consensus* sought by educators becomes even more apparent when they start to describe in detail what they're seeking, because the favored method of finding a "values consensus" on which to build a moral-education program sounds very much like the notoriously relativist methods of Values Clarification and of surveys combined. When, for example, the Phi Delta Kappa Commission on the Teaching of Morals, Values and Ethics — commissioned to "identify a means by which schools could determine the core values" they should teach — began to develop "instruments and processes" for finding out what the core values of a given community already are, they drew on a mixture of standard "values survey" and Values Clarification processes. One "game-like process" chosen, a "values meeting" in which "a representative group of community members" is invited to participate, sounds like a typical Values Clarification Strategy. Other "instruments and processes" chosen to "identify community value consensus" are adaptations of the "values assessment" surveys popular now in the field of values measurement: methods, like the Rokeach Value Survey and the Echo method ("a simple, straightforward process for the generation and analysis of data regarding the idiosyncratic values present in a given community"), which already conceive of values in the same subjectivist way, and in much the same language, as Values Clarification. The Echo method, for example, "asks respondents to complete the following value-relevant questions: For a person like you, what is a good thing to do? If you did such a thing, who would praise you?" The purpose of collecting all this "values data" and subjecting it to sophisticated statistical analyses, says the Commission, is to provide "a clear, up-to-date understanding" of "what is 'good' and 'bad' *in that particular community*," so that schools can then base their moral-education programs on exactly what their particular community values. "If self-respect is a major core value of the community, for instance, educators can make sure the curriculum relates to and enhances self-respect."

Presumably if self-respect is not a core value of the community, then educators are not to enhance it, but are to make sure the curriculum does *not* relate to self-respect or even systematically destroys it. Such is the silliness to which morality by *consensus* inevitably leads. The mad scientism of presuming to measure values just adds to the folly because what all the pseudo-scientific instruments for generating values data and all the elaborate statistical procedures and semantic differential processes and the like add up to is the simple relativist statement that "good" and "bad" are relative to the community; and such a statement, like all statements of ethical relativism if their inferences are really followed, leads — as we find yet again — to obviously unacceptable ethics. Obviously unacceptable, no doubt, even to educators — when they leave their values inventories and valuing analysis workshops and return to common sense.

The fundamental relativism of consensus morality is, furthermore, reinforced by the sort of *community* that educators keep insisting on in their repeated calls for "community consensus" and "community values." This *community* (like many *community*s these days, as we'll see in Part Four) is conceived of as a collection of *individual opinions,* as a plural form of *personal values;* and so it carries all the relativism of the *personal values* it was called on to transcend. And it carries, too, all the relativism of surveys, since they are the chosen instruments by which community consensus is found: the "core values" of *community consensus* are whatever our survey (our values assessment process) says. So although educators' original longing for solid "core values" and "moral certainties" was a move away from relativism, the search for those values and certainties in *community consensus* is, sadly, a plunge back in. The *Phi Delta Kappan* editorial called urgently for the moral certainties without which "our system of education is hollow at the core, a castle built on sand"; yet core values derived from *community consensus* can't fill the hollow with anything more solid or certain than the shifting sands of public sentiment.

When the inevitable reaction against *moral consensus* has set in (as probably it will have by the time these pages are in print, given the speed with which terms move in and out of fashion in the field of education); when educators have retreated in dismay or horror or despair from the relativism of *consensus*, as people eventually do from each relativism they've rushed to embrace; when, having gone unsuccessfully from *personal values clarification* to *consensus*, educators are looking for a new basis for their moral education programs, where will they go next? I wouldn't presume to guess what term will be the next one favored; but in an educational system derived from John Dewey, and in a society apparently determined to recognize no source of meaning outside itself, the next term — and the next, and the next — is likely to be relativist still.

Continuing Confusions: Adhering to Absolutes; Hanging on to Relativism

One school day recently, a ten-year-old black boy from a poor neighborhood in my city received a lesson utterly at odds with any relativist one that his teacher might have presented in her Values Clarification exercise for the day, or that his school's administrators might have been preparing in their search for community consensus. On his way to school, as the local newspaper reported it, Derrick found a bag of money. After hesitating briefly about what to do with the money (wishing he could buy a bike), he asked the crossing guard, who told him to turn it in to the school principal. Derrick did so; the principal immediately phoned Derrick's mother at work; his mother, when she finished work at the end of the day, took the money to the police. A photo of a smiling Derrick accompanied the newspaper story, which also quoted Derrick's father as saying that the money would have been handy for groceries but that if Derrick had brought it home he (the father) would probably have told him to turn it in to the police. Two days later the newspaper published a photo of a beaming Derrick sitting on a new bike, with the story that the owner of the moneybag, a vending-machine operator who had lost it on his rounds, had claimed it from the police but had used the reclaimed money, about $125, to buy Derrick a bike. Along with the bike, delivered to Derrick through the police because the man wished to remain anonymous (since he often carried cash, he said), Derrick's benefactor sent a message saying that Derrick deserved the bike for having done the right thing but that he shouldn't always expect to be rewarded in this way for doing right.

Besides being given the bike and this message that "virtue is its own reward," Derrick had received from this episode a clear lesson in absolute values. He had been taught in no uncertain terms that "there are moral absolutes" — because one such absolute, "thou shalt not steal," was obviously firmly believed in by every adult he had encountered. No one had said to Derrick "what's right to do here is relative" or "it all depends on how you look at it" or "you have to figure out what's right for a person like you, in your own personal value system" or "we'll have to do a survey to determine whether there's a community consensus on this matter." Everyone looked at the matter the same way, knew for certain exactly what was right, and acted on that certainty. Even Derrick's father, though forced by poverty to see the matter for an instant from another perspective, concurred in the common message that "Derrick did the right thing in turning in the money." Passing this message on to the rest of the children of the community was probably the newspaper's main reason for printing the initial report: the story was most likely considered newsworthy not because (as cynics might say) it's news when someone does the right thing, but because here was a perfect model of what we all recognize as right conduct. A corollary message, especially in the sequel about Derrick's reward for his virtue, was that while we all know what's right to do, we also know that doing it is hard.

The story of Derrick shows that at least sometimes we as a society act as if we firmly believe in certain absolutes. We sometimes speak as if we do, too: not just when we actually say "there are absolutes" (which we don't have occasion to do very often) but whenever we assume the positive value of nonrelativist terms like *justice, kindness, love, peace.* These terms are nonrelativist because they refer to ideals outside of any particular situation or application. When we call for *justice,* for example, we don't primarily have in mind (as our concept of the word itself) what is fair for a particular society or what is the best alternative in a particular situation; we have in mind an abstract concept of an absolute good, to which we urge each particular society in each situation to strive to conform. So when columnist Sidney J. Harris says that what we need to make a better world is "more compassion, a keener sense of justice" and "people who are kinder to one another," he's expressing a firmly nonrelativist belief — as is Orwell in his nightmare vision of the undoubtedly worse world of *1984,* where belief in such concepts as *justice* and *love* and *truth* has been systematically obliterated.

But while we sometimes speak and act in a decidedly nonrelativist way, we still keep on speaking and acting in an apparently endless variety of relativist ways as well. And we keep doing so even though, as the preceding sections have indicated, following relativist lines and adhering to relativist terms always gets us into trouble in the end. Yet — oblivious or reckless or just stuck in a rut — we keep jumping on one relativist bandwagon after another. We bounce along enthusiastically on a *relative* or a *subjective* or a *tolerance,* playing titillating relativist mind-games and tooting relativist horns under the bright "it's all relative" banner, until suddenly we notice that we're headed for disaster, that the *relative* is riding us to ruin. So we leap off, resentfully slashing with a now negative *relativism* the tires we've just been rolling on with positive pleasure; then we leap right on an *alternative* or an *opinion* headed in the same relativist direction. For all the value we place on *experience,* we don't seem as a society to learn from experience — maybe because the values we've placed on *experience* are subjectivist and relativist ones which prevent us from accepting as certain anything we've learned.

Evidently, we as a society can't figure out whether it's all relative or not. Certain individuals among us are clear about the need for *absolutes,* but their clarity is not reflected in our popular language or our powerful institutions. In fact, the institutions we count on to think clearly for us about complex intellectual matters — our academic institutions — have not only not led us out of the confusions of relativism but have been instrumental in leading us into them. And the institutions we count on to keep faith in the eternal verities — our religious institutions — have been unable to keep from flirting with a denial of *absolutes.* No wonder then that most of the rest of us are muddled about these matters: shouting for a return to "standards" while shrugging "it's all relative," looking for "solid core values" in a constantly shifting *consensus,* calling for *justice* and *compassion* while insisting "everything depends on how you look at it," longing for truth and goodness while listening obsessively to what "our survey says."

This is an extraordinary time in human history. Having rejected the source of absolutes that Western civilization up to the previous century assumed, having determined to prove that we can live entirely on our own (human) terms, we keep finding that we can't live without absolutes after all and race around looking for a reliable source for them. We're like adolescents who have determined to throw off parental authority and rules (no mere obedience for *me!*) and then dash all over the place, desperately trying to find standards and values to regulate their behavior.

The word *relative* itself isn't responsible for our contemporary confusion. There's nothing confusing about the word, which points — as we noted in the introduction to this part — to a basic perception about the world, the common-sense perception that something can be "dependent upon or interconnected with something else for intelligibility or significance." And there's nothing confusing about applying this perception generally: saying that everything is to some extent dependent upon something else for intelligibility. Common sense tells us that everything in this spatial-temporal existence of ours is bound to be dependent upon, relative to, its place and time to some extent. The confusion comes when no limit can be seen to the extent, when everything is seen as only relative, when all intelligibility seems to depend completely on relativities, when the basic but partial truth that *relative* points to is blown up into a presumed whole truth, so that the *relative* — stretched into a dogmatic *ism* — becomes rigidly (and absurdly) *absolute*.

Such confusion about the *relative* can come at any time, since it's a sort of mistake the human mind is always prone to: mistaking the part for the whole, stretching a single fact over everything we see. But in our own time this particular *relativist* confusion has come upon us with special force. Attracted increasingly since the Renaissance by the idea of our *self*, delighted after Darwin with the theory of our own *development*, we were determined to prove that we could live fine on our own, that we could develop ourselves fully without ultimate certainties or fixed absolutes, when physics suddenly seemed to announce that there weren't any absolutes anyway. This apparently scientific proof of what we were already trying to prove in less scientifically secure areas was too appealing to resist. We grabbed onto the line "it's all relative" and let it swing us along, even though it was soon swinging us in circles and whipping our heads against the wall. By now we've had enough sense knocked into us that we're starting to let go of the line itself (people don't say "it's all relative" in so many words as much as they did up through the 1960s) and to keep our hands off the actual word *relativism* except as a term of abuse. But we still hang onto relativism in other terms: partly out of habit (we're used to relying on *personal experience* or on a *consensus* or on what "our survey says"); partly because it's tied to other concepts we're currently stuck on (concepts of *subjectivity*, of *development*, of — as we'll see in Part Four — *relationship*); partly because, despite relativism's difficulties, we still want to believe in it.

FOUR
Relationships

Introduction

The story of our current fondness for *relation(ship)s* * doesn't have quite the drama that the stories of *self* and *development* and *relative* do. *Relation* wasn't dramatically thrust on the scene by a single scientific discovery, as were *development* and *relative;* and it didn't steadily increase in psychological significance like a good novelistic character, as did *self.* There's not even a clear chronology of *relationship*'s claim on our attention or a clear single source for the value we find in the word: our current sense of the importance of *relationships* seems to come almost at once from several places which value *relations* in sometimes different and even conflicting ways.

The method of presentation in this part therefore has to be a bit different from that of the rest of the book. We'll look in turn at the *relationships* that seem to mean most to us today: wholistic *relations,* sociological *relations,* the *relations* of the modern systems method, interpersonal *relationships* (including those of *community*), and environmental *relations.* For each of these *relations,*

* There's no significant difference between the forms *relation* and *relationship,* so I treat them (as they're generally treated) interchangeably.

we'll look into the main words that help give it whatever meaning it now has; and though we'll find some overlap among the sets of words, each chapter will be almost a separate study.

The order of the chapters is necessarily almost arbitrary, though there's a loose logic behind it. Wholistic and sociological *relationships* go back, for their current significance, to the nineteenth century, so they're examined first. The words that are the focus of the remaining chapters — *system, community,* and *environment* — go back even farther as common words in our language; but they were each suddenly loaded with new significance in the 1960s, so they're examined last — with *environment* last of all because the way that *environmental relations* are now talked about does both draw from and add to the meanings of the other terms in which *relations* now tend to be seen. What these terms and their meanings have in common, despite their many differences, is then considered in a concluding chapter which also attempts a summary sketch of what the world looks like when seen in such terms.

11

Wholistic *Relationships:* *Relations* Perceived as Meaningful *Wholes*

(W)*holistic* Values

We're starting to hear a lot about *holistic* or *wholistic* values. The spelling makes no difference, since both versions have etymological validity. The Indo-European root from which our English *whole* comes is one of those fundamental phonetic forms that shaped words with similar meaning in nearly all the derivative languages. From it came, via Old Teutonic, English words like *heal* and *health* as well as *whole;* and from it came the ancient Greek word for "whole," ὅλος. When *holism* was coined in English in 1926, its inventor — J. C. Smuts, South African philosopher-statesman and author of *Holism and Evolution* — chose this spelling because he derived the word from ὅλος, which is transliterated "holos." While Smuts's spelling is the more common one today, the *wholistic* spelling shows more clearly what the word is basically about (wholes, not holes); so in the following pages I use *wholism* unless referring to actual usages of *holism*.

The *holism* that Smuts had in mind when he coined the word was a creative evolutionary force that he saw as "the ultimate principle of the universe," a force drawing life into the form of new wholes whose parts are "not merely put together" mechanistically but are combined "in a specific internal relatedness, in a creative synthesis" making the whole "more than the sum of its parts." The *holism* that we hear about today, however, has nothing to do with this grand (and forgotten) philosophical theory — nothing, that is, to do with its evolutionary content. What has been carried on in the word, curiously enough — and what has evidently made the word seem worth keeping — is not its original content but its inherent value structure: its opposition of a negatively seen mechanical association of parts to a positively valued *whole* whose value lies in its parts' special *interrelatedness*.

This is the value structure that the various current enterprises called *holistic* have in common, despite their different activities. Practitioners of *holistic* medicine criticize the established medical profession for viewing the body "as a machine with parts that can be treated separately" and claim instead to treat "the total person" as "an integrated whole" of body, mind, and spirit. Teachers who practice *holistic* grading refuse to break down a student's essay into separate problems like punctuation and paragraphing, but base their grade on their immediate "sense of the whole" derived from a deliberately "nonanalytical" reading. Proponents of what's coming to be called *holistic* science criticize the "overly analytical, atomistic, mechanical" world view that has dominated scientific thinking since Descartes and — seeing all entities as "holistic systems greater than the sum of their parts" — urge instead a view of the world as "one indivisible, dynamic whole whose parts are essentially interrelated and can be understood only as patterns of a cosmic process."

While passages like this last one sound right out of *Holism and Evolution*, current proponents of *holistic* science don't at all see themselves as disciples of J. C. Smuts. In fact, none of the ideas and activities now calling themselves *holistic* derives either from Smuts or even from the word *holism*. They've all taken the word as a handy label for their characteristic value structure — their vision of a *whole* that's more (and better) than the mere sum or mechanical association of its separate parts — but the view of a *whole* valued in just this way has been around much longer and is much more widespread than the use of the word *holistic,* which so far has been limited to a few anti-establishment enterprises. It's hard, though, to pinpoint the source of this widespread *wholistic* view (to switch now to the spelling I've chosen to distinguish this general — and generally unnamed — view from specifically self-proclaimed *holisms*). Two concepts especially seem to have filled *whole* with the meaning and value it has for us today, the concepts of Gestalt theory and of organicism; yet the *wholes* they conceive of — though described along similar lines — aren't really the same.

Gestalt, Organic, and Other *Wholes*

The concept of the Gestalt *whole* comes from what was originally a theory about visual perception. Developed in Germany in the 1920s, the theory of Gestalt psychology insisted that when we look at something, we perceive not (as the current associationist theory claimed) "isolated" elements which our brain then connects, but an *organized whole* whose parts are "experienced" in relation to the whole. Such an *integrated whole,* in which "what happens to a part of the whole is determined by intrinsic laws inherent in the whole," was what the Gestalt theorists — giving their own technical meaning to the ordinary German word for "form" or "structure" — termed a "Gestalt."

They were soon using the term for other "relational configurations" besides those of visual perception. Eager to apply what they had discovered about the visual field to as many fields as possible, they set out to extend their deliberately general terms to other areas, particularly (at first) the area of psychology concerned with "productive thinking" and "intellectual perception." This extension from visual to intellectual perception could be made especially smoothly because "perception" and other words about "seeing" already have (in all Western languages, not just in German) the common metaphorical meaning of "understanding." So without altering any of the main terms of their theory of visual perception, the Gestalt psychologists were able to talk about intellectual perception: to define "understanding" as "an awareness of a required relation between immediately given facts," to define "intelligence" as "the perception of relations," and to treat "productive thinking" as "the development of new structures or organizations" in which "parts and relations previously unnoted or in the background emerge . . . and parts previously separated become united." They were also able to propose a general Gestalt theory of meaning in much the same terms: "a whole is meaningful when concrete mutual dependency obtains among its parts."

This meaningful *whole* is essentially what Gestalt theory, wherever it's applied, is all about. "The chief tenet of the Gestalt approach," explains the *Encyclopaedia Britannica*, "is that the analysis of parts, however thorough, cannot provide an understanding of the whole. . . . A whole that is a Gestalt is not simply the sum of its parts." The "mere sum," the "isolated" element, the "separate" part — these are always put down as analytically worthless by the Gestalt *whole*, which insists on its own positive value as an *integrated total* of *interrelations*.

Yet the Gestalt *whole* wasn't the first to promote itself like this. For a century before the Gestalt *whole* was conceived of, the organic *whole* had been coming on in what sounds like exactly the same way: putting down any mere mechanical assemblage as (in Coleridge's words) "nothing more than a collection of the individual parts," while exalting its own *integrated unity* in which "dependence of the parts on the whole" is combined with "dependence of the whole on its parts." Despite this congruence of their main defining lines, and despite the fact that the organic *whole* was famous well before the Gestalt *whole* was thought of, the organic *whole* can't be said to have molded or shaped the Gestalt *whole* conceptually — because behind their shared terms and shared wholistic values, the two concepts have little in common. The referents of the two *whole*s are fundamentally different, so the two have different conceptions of where their *wholeness* comes from. The terms of the organic metaphor refer primarily to plants, and an organic *whole* is the result of the growth of a living organism; the terms of Gestalt theory refer primarily to human visual perception, and a Gestalt *whole* is the result of the activity of the human mind. Put most simply, organic *whole*s grow (in nature); Gestalt *whole*s click (in our minds).

Two *whole*s so different in concept and yet so similar in the terms in which they're described are bound to be hard to tell apart at times. Not all of the terms describing the two *whole*s are the same, of course. When we come across a *whole* described as *growing, developing,* or *living,* we know it's an organic *whole.* And when we come across a *whole* that's an *emergent pattern* or a unique *configuration,* it's clearly a Gestalt. But if a *whole* is promoted, in opposition to a "mere sum of isolated parts," as an *organized integrated system* whose *interdependent* parts *interact* with each other and with their *environment,* then it could be either a Gestalt or an organic *whole.*

Or it could be getting some of its positive value from each. Anyone using language has to choose his words, but he doesn't have to choose his concepts or even be aware of what they are, since concepts are invisible. Fundamentally different and even conflicting concepts can therefore hang on to a word at the same time, vaguely adding to its sense of meaningfulness without forcing it to take a particular meaning; and — as we've found for other leading language — all the highly prized concepts attached to a word are likely to hang on to it in just this way unless they're deliberately cut off. When, as in the case of organic and Gestalt *whole*s, the concepts attached to a word not only carry the general positive value of being considered important concepts but also carry the same specific positive (in this case, wholistic) values, they're even more likely to add their combined weight to the word, making it sound unquestionably valuable.

Many of today's most valued *whole*s do seem — as far as we can tell from the surrounding terms — to be deriving their positive value in this way from both organic and Gestalt concepts, as well as from other more or less specified sources. The *whole person* celebrated by popular psychology, for example, certainly derives much of its value from the organic metaphor: organicism is the deliberate model for the "personal growth" psychologists like

Rogers and Maslow, who have done so much to promote the *self* as an *integrated whole*. Yet *wholeness* is also the goal of Gestalt therapy, which superimposes explicitly Gestalt terms and concepts on those of organicism ("making gestalts is making wholes . . . as we grow, we become capable of organizing more and more of the field into wholes"), and of the therapeutic process conceived by Jung, whose archetype of *wholeness* as a union of opposites is radically different from both organicism and Gestalt. All of these ideals of personality *wholeness*, as well as the vaguely Buddhist ideal of "oneness" behind California's brand of *holism*, seem to add, then, to the positive value of today's *whole person* — and probably to the hip ideal of "togetherness" with reference to oneself alone, as when someone claims to be "feeling together" or to be "hanging together" or to be just "together." "Hanging together" as an aesthetic ideal, we might note, seems to derive from some of the same sources as the personality ideal. The *unity* valued in a work of art has been assumed since Coleridge to be (at least metaphorically) organic, and since Arnheim to be (at least for visual art) literally derived from the laws of Gestalt; so today organic and Gestalt concepts probably both lie vaguely behind the aesthetic *wholes* that art critics talk so much about.

The cultural *whole*s that anthropologists talk about also have something of both organicism and Gestalt theory behind them. Ruth Benedict specifically mentions Gestalt psychology as a precedent for her view of each culture as a unique *pattern* or *configuration*, an *integrated whole* which "is not merely the sum of all its parts, but the result of a unique arrangement and interrelation of the parts that has brought about a new entity." But anthropologists before her had drawn on organicism for much the same view. Malinowski, who had insisted that cultural traits be viewed not (as the diffusionists saw them) as isolated entities moving from one culture to another but as parts of an "integral whole," had derived his "functionalist" view from biology's study of organisms. And Radcliffe-Brown deliberately drew on organic concepts for his influential hypothesis that a culture, as a network or system of social relations, is a functional unity all parts of which — be-

cause they contribute harmoniously to the working of the whole —
must be studied "not in abstraction or isolation, but in their direct
and indirect relations to social structure."

Relations Perceived as the Whole of What's Meaningful

The intellectual values expressed in Radcliffe-Brown's insistence
on studying *relations* within a whole system, as opposed to "isolated" phenomena, are obviously a variant (a highbrow version)
of what I've called the wholistic value structure. This intellectual
version of wholistic values — or epistemological version, really,
since it's an evaluation of what constitutes "understanding" and
"knowledge" — still forms an operating premise for the field of
anthropology, which, according to the *International Encyclopedia
of the Social Sciences,* "considers an 'explanation' achieved when
it has shown how each part" of the "culture pattern" contributes
to the functioning of another part or of the "overall configuration." This wholistic epistemological value structure can be found
today, further, in all areas influenced by Gestalt theory (which, we
recall, became essentially a theory about intellectual perception
defining "understanding" as the perception of relations) and indeed almost everywhere that understanding is defined or explanation is considered worth achieving or knowledge is valued.

Throughout our century, in fact, definitions of knowledge and
meaning in various fields of thought and various theories of how
to think have dismissed "separate parts" as not worth looking at
while valuing the "perception of relations" as equivalent to
knowledge itself. Many of the relativisms that we heard so much
of in Part Three, for example, put their epistemology in just these
terms, stressing the value of *interrelations* over *isolated elements*
(when they aren't stressing the value of *relative* over *absolute*). A
summary of Carl Becker's historical relativism says, typically: "It
is not the isolated particularity of events that makes them meaningful for the historian; on the contrary, they are meaningful only
because they play a role in a web of relationships." Relativity

physics, too, with its conception of time and space as "systems of relations among physical events and things," can sound as if it's defining knowledge in these same relational terms — especially in popularized versions claiming the "epitome" of relativity theory to be that "a thing derives its nature not so much by its isolated essence as from its relationships to other things in its frame of reference." Even recent structuralist theory, though scorning the idea of "frames" and "wholes" as too confining for its vision of infinite regress, still gives a privileged epistemological place (as structuralism itself would say) to *relations,* declaring that "the meaning of individual elements" in all human structures — of literature, of unconscious thought, of social custom and social institutions — "arises out of *and only out of* the relations of the elements to one another and their mutual interdependency."

These *relations* given positive intellectual and epistemological value in so many areas have more in common — as we can see from the quotations above — than their opposition to "separate parts." They tend to be *relations* of *mutual interdependency* and of *reciprocal interaction;* and they tend to be pictured as a *pattern* or a *network* or a *web.* This way of picturing epistemologically meaningful *relations* * seems to be special to our century, or at least to the last century and a half. While *relations* have always played a part in Western concepts of knowledge, they haven't been *relations* of this kind. The *relations* that Aristotle conceived of as the object of knowledge, for example, were those of classification, *relations* of greater and lesser inclusiveness; to know something for Aristotle was to know its genus and species. The *relations* that gave meaning and purpose to the world in the Middle Ages were those of the great hierarchical Chain of Being; to know something in the Middle Ages was to know its place in this fixed, finite system of vertically ordered *relations.* The *relations* that Francis Bacon defined scientific knowledge in terms of were primarily those

---

* "Epistemologically meaningful" as distinguished from another sort of currently meaningful *relation,* the *meaningful interpersonal relationship,* which we'll look at in Chapter 14.

of causation; to know something for Bacon was to know its antecedents or causes. The *relations* that we currently see as meaningful, however, are neither classificatory nor fixed nor hierarchical nor (in Bacon's sense) causal. In our picture of meaningful *relations* as those of *mutual interdependency,* the *interrelated* elements seem to slide around along a *network* imagined if not as exactly flat, then certainly not as vertical; and causation within the network is a matter not so much of antecedents as of simultaneous and reciprocal cause and effect.

The fact that widely different areas of contemporary thought see the "understanding" of their area in terms of a *network* of simultaneous and reciprocal *interrelations* doesn't mean, however, that all these areas have the same concept of knowledge. They "see" or "picture" their knowledge in the same terms; but behind the picture, beneath the surface similarity of the terms, lie considerably different concepts of what is being known and of what knowing it involves. Just as talk about an *integrated whole* might have either Gestalt or organic concepts behind it, talk about "the perception of relations" might have behind it the epistemological extensions of either of these concepts — or other epistemological concepts altogether.

The main difference among modern concepts of "relations perceived as knowledge" lies in where they assume the *relations* to be formed: whether outside our minds, or inside, or somehow in both places. Organic *relations* are, of course, formed outside our minds, in nature; so knowledge of organic *relations* — of the *interrelations* among parts of a tree, for example — is knowledge (epistemologically old-fashioned as this may sound) of a reality that exists entirely apart from our minds and would go on existing even if we knew nothing about it. Gestalt *relations,* however, depend on our minds for their very existence, since they're made in the mind at the moment of perception. Different Gestalts, different patterns of interrelation, can even be made at different moments of the same reality: one can see trees as part of a forest, or not see the forest for the trees, or switch back and forth between seeing a forest and seeing separate trees. (So Gestalt *relations* can't even be said to be "known," since knowledge implies an object with at least conceptually separate existence; Gestalt *relations* can only "emerge" or "develop" or be "formed" — or be "perceived," if perception is understood as the act of forming them.) When the trees have been cut down to make houses and anthropological knowledge about them is sought, the *relations* to be known — relations of trees, when turned into cultural artifacts, to the whole network or pattern of culture — are independent of the human mind in one sense but not in another. They're independent of the mind seeking to know them, because they exist in the culture whether or not any anthropologist finds them; but they're dependent on human minds collectively for their very existence, since culture itself is a human product. Structuralism, however, would say that cultural *relations* (and all other human *relations*) aren't even independent of the mind seeking to know them, since the same unconscious network of *relations* structures the individual human mind and all collective human products and activities. Knowledge for structuralism is knowledge of the *relations* both within this unconscious network and between it and the observable patterns of human life — *relations* conceived by Lévi-Strauss, for example, as those of mathematical logic. A tree mentioned in a primitive myth is for Lévi-Strauss neither a living organism nor a cultural artifact but a term in a set of binary oppositions, an element in the system of logical relations by which the culture makes meaning for itself. The *relations* of modern mathematical logic, we should note, are even further removed from what we usually think of as reality. The "reality of relations" that Bertrand Russell insisted on vehemently was a purely abstract reality; the *relations* that he conceived as constituting knowledge in math and logic have nothing to do with trees and are proud *of* it.

There's something odd about finding so many different concepts (of knowledge or of anything else) expressed in the same terms. People who talk about knowledge as the perception of a *network* of *relations* often aren't talking about the same thing, but they're talking in the same way; and this seems contrary to our usual assumption about how thought and language work together. We tend to assume that we "have an idea" and then "express" it, but here the expression seems to come somehow before the idea. Or at least to come independently of any of the ideas or concepts it has expressed, and to exert an influence apart from them. If these terms for talking about knowledge, these lines about knowledge being "not of separate parts but of the reciprocal interaction and mutual interdependence of parts within the whole," came originally from organicism, they "came from" there only in the sense of being first formulated there; and they were soon cut off from that source in the formulations of Gestalt theory, which attached the lines to its own basically different concept. The lines have gone on expressing both organic and Gestalt concepts in the many areas of professional and popular thought into which these two leading concepts of our century have spread. But the lines have also gone on through the century exerting an influence of their own; they've seemed to float above our various currents of thought, forming a picture of *relationships* to which many of these currents and their concepts are drawn.

Why this picture of *relations* perceived as meaningful *wholes* has proven so attractive for modern epistemologies is hard to say. Human thought has always been drawn, of course, to the general idea of the *whole;* it's one of those ideas that seem inherently good. And Western thought has always, or at least since Plato made the One the highest good, perceived the *whole* as especially meaningful and reached for it as the object of knowledge. The desired *whole* can be imagined in various ways, however; and the way it has been pictured in the past century and a half, while owing much to the wholistic relational concepts of organicism and Gestalt theory, seems to have an attraction beyond either of them — and an attraction not only for esoteric epistemological thought but also for thought about *wholes* as apparently different as the "aesthetic unity" desired by art critics or the "total person" treated by holistic healers. To find out where else our image of the desired *whole* — our *whole* prized for its internal *interrelations* among mutually *interdependent* parts — might have gotten its attraction, we should look at other places where *relations* have recently been prized.

12

Sociological *Relationships:* Reified *Relations*

When American sociologists talk about their work, they often talk in terms of *relations, systems, interaction, interdependence, function, structure, wholes:*

> What is specifically "sociological" in the study of any particular feature of a total society is the continual effort to relate that feature to others, in order to gain a conception of the whole.
>
> C. WRIGHT MILLS

> Of all contributions that sociology has made to contemporary thought none is greater than, if indeed as great as, its envisagement of human behavior in terms of social structure . . . [or] in terms of wholes — systems, organizations, ecological relationships, institutions, structures. . . .
>
> ROBERT A. NISBET

> The most inclusive sociological unit is the *social system,* which is constituted by the interaction of a plurality of actors whose relations to each other are mutually oriented by institutions.
>
> *International Encyclopedia of the Social Sciences*

> Sociologists with a structural-functional approach [the "most prevalent" American approach] study the way each part of a society contributes to the functioning of the society as a whole. . . . [They] view society as a system of interrelated parts. . . .
>
> *Sociology* [college textbook]

But what does it mean to "see" one's object of study in such terms: to "envisage" human behavior in terms of *social structure,* to "view" society as a *system* of *interrelated parts?*

For the founders of sociology, seeing society as a system of interrelated parts meant seeing it as a living organism. Comte, Spencer, and Durkheim all had biological concepts clearly in mind when they projected their grand visions of something new called the "social organism": something definitely "out there" that hadn't been seen before, something immense and powerful with a life of its own, obeying (for Comte and Spencer) natural laws, exerting (for Durkheim) a measurable force on human behavior. All of these great visionaries deliberately drew on the biological concepts of *function, structure, interrelation,* and *system* not only to describe the "social organism" but also to argue for the legitimacy and autonomy of sociology as a science. Social life, the argument went, is every bit as real and natural as biological life; and its reality, its very existence and life, consists — like the life of biological organisms — in the *interrelatedness* of its elements. Just as "there are in the living cell only molecules of crude matter," Durkheim argued, "but these molecules are in contact with one another and this association is the cause of the new phenomena which characterize life," so the "association" of people in contact with one another causes the new and distinct phenomena of social life. "Society is not a mere sum of individuals," Durkheim insisted in 1895 (obviously drawing on organicism for this formulation, which Gestalt theory would make famous a quarter-century later); "rather, the system formed by their association represents a specific reality which has its own characteristics."

Sociologists since Durkheim have continued to insist on the specific reality of the social system, but they've lost the firm nineteenth-century sense of this reality as specifically organic. When they refer to "the social organism" or to society's "organic unity" (as they still do, but mainly in passing, as if out of habit), the image of an actual organism seems to have faded from behind their words.

Also faded from the minds of most twentieth-century sociologists when they talk about the social *system* and its *interrelations* is the vividly detailed picture — of a plethora of particular social phenomena *in* their interrelatedness — that filled the capacious minds of the first great sociological thinkers. Filled, at least, the minds of Marx and Durkheim and Weber. Comte and Spencer were less successful at focusing on the minute and messy particularities whose precise interconnectedness Comte himself had challenged sociology to take as its subject: the most complex of all subjects, he declared, because "not only are political institutions and social manners on the one hand, and on the other manners and ideas, necessarily interdependent, but in addition the whole system is attached to the corresponding state of development of humanity, with all its modes of activity — intellectual, moral, and physical." Minds like those of Marx, Durkheim, and Weber could meet the challenge of picturing such interdependencies. They could manage to plunge into what Weber called "the tremendous confusion of interdependent influences" and come out not only unconfused but possessed of a clear conception of at least some segment of the web of social relations. But, as Comte warned, only "the best scientific minds" would be able to sustain such "continued speculative effort" as sociology demanded; and for most sociologists, quite understandably, "the whole system" has been too much to try to imagine.

What then is left in the minds of sociologists who continue to talk (as nearly all do) about social *structures* and *systems* and *relations*, when these words have lost both their concretely imagined content and the organic images with which they were originally conceived? Unfortunately, what threatens to be left is a heap of hollow abstractions, since these words are inherently abstract. Of course, all words are to some extent abstractions. But so-called concrete nouns (*girl, tree, house*) are less abstract than so-called abstract ones (*development, relativity, relationship*) because the former refer directly to concretely existing entities while the latter don't.

How far *relation* is from referring to anything concrete is clear from its basic *OED* definition: "that feature or attribute of things which is involved in considering them in comparison or contrast with each other; the particular way in which one thing is thought of in connexion with another; any connexion, correspondence, or association, which can be conceived as naturally existing between things." A *relation,* then, is a way of conceiving things; it's an interpretation, a mental construct, a "particular way" in which things are "thought of" together. A *relation* is definitely not a "thing," but an abstraction from things, an interpretation of the imagined space "between" things. As all the *inter-* words that go along with *relations* indicate (*interaction, interdependence, interrelation*), *between*-ness is where the action is in *relations.* But, again, it's the action of our understanding. When we examine *relations* — as in books written during this century with titles like *The Relation of Wealth to Welfare* or *The Relation of Parental Authority to Children's Behavior* or *The Relation of Latin to Practical Life* — we're looking literally at nothing. We're looking strictly in the metaphorical sense of intellectually perceiving, focusing our minds on the materially empty space between things (or even between abstractions) and filling it with the lines of our understanding.

When we talk about *relations* of *interdependence,* for example, we're understanding the *relations* as being those of mutual need and support. When we talk about *interaction,* we're keeping the sense of mutuality in the *relations* but adding a sense of effective movement, of back and forth influence. *Pattern* gives an aesthetic sense to *relations; network* (an exceptionally concrete *relation* term, with its image of a net) a picture of intersecting lines. *Function* gives a sense of purpose and assumes a whole *relational system* for the sake of which each part operates. *System,* in turn, gives a sense of arrangement and complexity and also boundedness, a sense of order within a complex whole.* So does *structure;* but while *system* (from the Greek "to stand together") gives a sense of self-

---

* More has been added to the sense of *system* since modern systems analysis has gotten hold of it, as we'll see in the next chapter; I refer here to the general sense had by *system* until about twenty years ago.

sufficiency to the *relations, structure* (from the Latin "to construct") suggests a firmness and fixity in their arrangement.

All these abstract *relation* words refer to particular ways in which (to go back to the *OED* definition) things can be thought of in connection with each other; but these words need not — in order to work perfectly well together — make any reference to particular things. We can go on, that is, for days (or pages) talking about *systems* of *interrelated parts* and *networks* of *functional relations* — or, as sociology especially does, about "the *social system*, which is constituted by the interaction of a plurality of actors whose relations to each other are mutually oriented by institutions," or about "the structure of the relations between the actors as involved in the interactive process," or about an individual's "status" as "his place in the relationship system considered as a structure," or about "general patterns of norms that define behavior in social relationships" — we can go on like this with perfect logical consistency but without anything in mind except these mutually referential abstractions, without any thought of a single concrete "thing" being related. In fact, these *relation* words, when they pile up in lines like those just quoted, work to keep us from thinking about concrete things. The words themselves, referring back and forth to each other and building up in our minds a set of subtly distinguished senses, tend to form together a wall of abstraction that blocks anything more concrete from entering our minds. Convincing us of their solidity and substantiality, the abstractions come to seem like concrete things themselves; they become reified.

All disciplines tend to reify their abstractions, to mistake their main conceptual terms for concrete things. From long residence in our minds, our most familiar terms — no matter how abstract they are — are likely to seem closer to home and hence more concrete than whatever we're supposed to be investigating "through" them. The likelihood is especially great for a field such as sociology, whose object of investigation — the "association" of individuals (in Durkheim's phrase), the social "bond" (in the title of a recent introductory book) — has no concrete reality or material existence itself. This isn't to say that social relations aren't real or don't exist. After Marx's analysis of the capitalist system, or Durkheim's of the inverse relation between suicide and social cohesion, or Weber's of bureaucratic structure, no one would deny that social systems and relations and structures exert a definite force on human behavior and represent, as Durkheim said, "a specific reality." But their specific reality is nonmaterial and invisible. And since the sociologist's chosen subject is essentially invisible, since he can't in any literal sense "see" it, the conceptual terms he sees it "in" acquire an undisputed presence and unchallenged authority in his mind. Seeing society "in terms of a system of interrelated parts," he's sure before peeking at a single part (or puzzling over what a "part" of society might be) that he'll see *interrelations* and a *system*. Viewing "society as a whole," he's sure that society *is* a whole without even looking (maybe deliberately not looking, because who could really see the whole of anything as sprawling and complex and essentially unbounded as "society"?). Starting off to observe human behavior, he assumes from the start that what he'll see is *interaction;* setting out to examine some social phenomenon, he assumes he'll see *patterns* and *relations*.

The parochialism of such assumptions is apparent in a standard formulation like the following by a current eminent sociologist:

> . . . The fundamental and inescapable subject matter of sociology — and of all the social sciences — is human beings and how and why they behave as they do.
>
> But it is equally true that we see human beings only in the roles, statuses, and modes of interaction which are the stuff of human society.

Now while it's true that sociologists see human beings only in "roles, statuses, and modes of interaction," and while it's true that "we" today see human beings this way when we adopt sociology's perspective, it's not true that "we" — in the generalized human sense evidently meant here — either now see or in the past have seen human beings only in these modern sociological terms. Nor is it true that these sociological abstractions are unquestionably, as the statement assumes, the reified "stuff of human society."

The ancient Greeks, for example, neither saw human beings in

roles, statuses, and modes of interaction nor saw these terms as
the stuff of human society; in fact they didn't see "human society"
at all. Thinking so little of what we call "society" that they had
no word for it (the words *society* and *social* are Roman inven-
tions, as Hannah Arendt points out), the Greeks saw human beings
as bound together in a "political community" for the purpose of
promoting virtue in both the individual and the community. An
inherently nonpurposive term like *interaction* would have made
no sense to them in reference to human behavior. As for *roles* and
statuses, while Plato imagined his ideal state divided into classes
with separate functions and hence (we might say, though he didn't)
with separate roles and statuses, such divisions were merely means
to the end of designing a community in which virtue would thrive.
Far from being the "only" way of seeing human beings, any such
categories were just an intermediate way. And in Aristotle's view
of the political community, nothing like *roles* and *statuses* played
any part, since the members of the political community as he saw
it were equals, all participating in the same way in the process of
promoting and living the good life.

Even today, influenced by sociology as we are, we hardly see
human beings "only" in sociological terms. In fact, each discipline
that examines human behavior does so in its own set of terms,
which it then tends to take as the "only" ones in which human
beings can be seen. Focusing its attention exclusively on the aspect
of human behavior that it wants to understand — focusing on man
as a social being or man as an economic being or man as a sexual
being, on man as a power seeker or a status seeker or (most recently) an information processor, on man as maker of myths or
maker of meaning, as a creature of instincts (or today of needs)
or a creature of passions (or today of feelings) — each discipline
tends to forget about the rest of man that remains outside its particular focus. The rest slips from view, dissolves; and what man is
seen *as* in each discipline becomes for that discipline what man *is*.
Man's essence gets put in terms of a partial view; and being put
in certain terms that refer to just part of his nature, man is necessarily shrunk in the process, reduced (as we say) to those terms.

This is why disciplines express such maddeningly partial truths, why each seems to tell us things about ourselves that are in a sense right but are, when they're treated as all there is to say, essentially wrong.

What sociology tells us is that our *relations* have a specific reality, that our association forms definite structures in which we live (or *function*), move (or *interact*), and have our (essentially social) being. Yet in talking so much about *relations,* in viewing human behavior in terms of *interaction* and *structure* and those other abstractions that point to varieties of between-ness, sociology risks being beside the point. It risks losing touch with all the specific realities of human behavior that exist entirely apart from these terms, all the particular stuff that goes on in our lives together and was going on long before society was seen as a system of interrelated parts, and even before our collective life was seen as society. These particularities of social life are no doubt partly patterned and functional but are probably also more free of systems and less structured than sociological language suggests. The sociological imagination, as C. Wright Mills inadvertently implies in the first quotation of this chapter, takes on the *total society* and reaches (valiantly but maybe too ambitiously) for the *whole* at the risk of losing touch with life's odd particularities and slippery parts. "What is specifically 'sociological' in the study of any particular feature of a total society" is indeed, as Mills says, "the continual effort to relate that feature to others, in order to gain a conception of the whole": the effort, that is, to get at once to the *relating* and the *whole* (brushing with un-Comtian effortlessness past the *effort*); the confidence that a conception of the whole can fairly easily be gained (as if even such partial conceptions as were grasped by the great sociological thinkers aren't easier lost than gained); the rush — above and before all else — to *relate.*

13

Systems Analysis:
Quantified and Controlled *Relations*

Systems' Spread

Social *systems* are far from the only *systems* around these days. We have information *systems,* control *systems,* communications *systems,* support *systems.* We have more computer *systems* than we know what to do with: word-processing *systems,* data-processing *systems,* digital *systems,* disc *systems.* We have career-development *systems* at work and stereo *systems* in place of our old hi-fi sets at home — where we also hook up to the cable-television *system.* Ma Bell's familiar homey telephone *system* has turned, in its ads, into an information *system;* another firm familiar at home, Singer, has spread out into stellar inertial-guidance *systems.* A company without *systems* evidently isn't worth its salt; so Rockwell International has its Switching *Systems* Division, Cast Shipping Company its Blue Box *System,* Burroughs Corporation its Respond *System.* IBM, hiding its old-fashioned business machines under its acronym, now proudly promotes its business *systems* instead — in line with the trend toward management *systems* and office *systems* everywhere. So many *systems* are moving into offices that the very walls are being replaced by Privacy Panel *Systems* and the old light bulbs by General Electric's new Optimizer

System; while in other markets fire-suppression *systems* are now sold instead of fire extinguishers, heating *systems* instead of furnaces, skin-care *systems* instead of lotions. Diet centers now offer nutri-*systems;* and Kodak, which once sold cameras, now sells its new disc-photography *system.*

Why are *systems* suddenly so salable? Nearly all of those just mentioned have come on the scene, or maybe we should say on the market, since World War II; and, in fact, the war is where *systems'* current success story begins. *Systems* of many kinds — political *systems,* circulatory *systems,* value *systems,* and so on — have been around for centuries; but when the British High Command during World War II hired teams of scientists (physicists, biologists, mathematicians, and engineers) to devise strategies for incorporating technologically advanced equipment like radar into the air defense system, *systems* made what turned out to be crucial new connections. Radar worked and the Allies won and *systems* shared in the success because the new high-tech strategy-devising and decision-making methodology came to be known as "systems analysis."

The name "systems analysis" wasn't actually settled on until the 1960s: during the early postwar years the methodology — which spread quickly through the American military into strategic war games like MAGIC, logistic simulations like SAMSON, and computerized information systems like SAGE* — was more often called "operations analysis" or "operations research." "Systems analysis" seems to have become the preferred name partly because weapons systems were what was being analyzed; partly because the nice orderly sense of *systematic* tended to sneak into *systems* and make them sound especially good; partly because the methodology was merging with that of "systems engineering."

Though systems engineering had originally developed indepen-

---

* The acronyms — obviously chosen for their connotations of extraordinary (even superhuman) power, strength, and wisdom — stand for Manual Assisted Gaming of Integrated Combat, Support-Availability Multi-System Operations Model, and Semi-Automatic Ground Environment System (designed to keep constant track of all flying objects, friendly or otherwise, in — and above — the world).

dently to deal with the design of complex man-made systems (like electric power systems), it was used to design weapons systems during the war and aerospace systems afterward, so that by the 1960s the work done by systems engineers and systems analysts was often indistinguishable and was described by both in a nearly identical series of steps called the "systems approach":

1. formulate the problem
2. identify the parts (or components) of the system and their interrelationships
3. develop a mathematical model of the system and determine the system equation
4. analyze system performance and study alternative means for accomplishing objectives in terms of such criteria as cost, effectiveness, and risk
5. choose the optimum system and implement or (especially for engineers) design and build it.

Emphatically wholistic (focusing always on *"total* system performance") and fundamentally quantitative (putting all system parts and purposes in measurable terms), the systems approach of both analysts and engineers continued to adopt — and to help engender — postwar developments in cybernetics and mathematical optimization techniques and computer technology, as well as to share the glory of NASA's dazzling space-exploration systems' achievements.

Together, systems analysis and systems engineering made *systems* a subject as it had never been before. Suddenly in the 1960s *system* burst into card catalogues as a subject heading, under which the glossy new cards nearly all named "systems analysis" or "systems engineering" or "the systems approach" in their titles. And this new subject of *systems* was one with definitely high-tech associations: associations with computerized simulations and information *systems,* with the successful design of almost inconceivably complex defense and aerospace *systems,* with sophisticated mathematical models and "scientific" decision-making techniques.

The association of the new *system* with "scientific" and hence "objective" decision-making, together with its reputation for rationally choosing among alternative means to the same goal and maximizing effectiveness in relation to costs, made the *systems* approach look like the ideal way to make difficult decisions of a great many kinds, especially the complex budgeting decisions of large organizations. This was how Secretary of Defense Robert McNamara saw it when, as head of the largest organization in the government, he brought in RAND Corporation weapons-systems specialists to turn the systems method into the Planning-Programming-Budgeting System now well known to fiscal managers all over the country as PPBS. And this was how President Johnson saw it in 1965 when he seized on PPBS almost before the ink on its flow-charts was dry and made it mandatory for all major federal agencies. But Johnson saw even more in the new *system* than a scientific method for increasing governmental efficiency. He saw it as a modern, technologically advanced means for improving the *quality* of governmental decision-making: as a technique to provide "the alternatives and the information on the basis of which we can together make better decisions," even as a light to "illuminate our choices" among Great Society programs. Here at last, it seemed — not only to Johnson but also to the social planners who in the 1960s poured out books like *Cure for Chaos: Fresh Solutions to Social Problems Through the Systems Approach* — was a scientific means for deciding how best to promote public welfare, a systematic procedure for bringing order to perennially chaotic and competing social concerns.

Also propelling *systems* thinking into social policy concerns in the 1960s was its connection with outer-space achievements. The connection was made repeatedly in political speeches that traced the rhetorical path followed, for example, by Senator Gaylord Nelson's "Space Age Trajectory to the Great Society" speech introducing a bill "to mobilize and utilize the scientific and engineering manpower of the Nation to employ systems analysis and systems engineering to help . . . solve national problems":

> Mr. President, why can not the same specialist who can figure out a way to put a man in space figure out a way to keep him out of jail?

Why can not the engineer who can move a rocket to Mars figure out a way to move people through our cities and across the country without the horrors of modern traffic and the concrete desert of our highway system?

Why can not the scientist who can cleanse instruments to spend germ-free years in space devise a method to end the present pollution of air and water here on earth?

Why can not highly trained manpower, which can calculate a way to transmit pictures for millions of miles in space, also show us a way to transmit enough simple information to keep track of our criminals?

Why can not we use computers to deal with the down-to-earth problems of modern America?

The answer is we can — if we have the wit to apply our scientific know-how to the analysis and solution of social problems with the same creativity we have applied it to space problems.

The senator is wrong, of course. The answer is "we can't" — because the two sorts of problems he's connecting rhetorically are in reality worlds apart. Figuring how to put a man in space has no more in common with figuring how to keep a man out of jail than figuring how much material to buy for a dress you're making does with figuring how to help a close friend who's dying of cancer; and in any case, the "man" who goes to jail is hardly — despite rhetorical appearances — the same "man" who goes into space. The scientist who can cleanse instruments for space can't solve our earthly pollution problems because these aren't, unfortunately, simply scientific problems but are at least as much political and economic problems. And so on.

These limitations in applying *systems* terms and techniques to social matters were quite evident to many systems analysts of the time. But words aren't private or professional property, and professionals' awareness of a word's limited applicability can't keep the word from being grabbed up and stuck on to all sorts of inappropriate places if it has strong popular appeal. Like the earlier new scientific-sounding words *evolution* and *relativity*, *systems* sounded too good to the public ear to be left to the scientists. So although many of the most creative systems thinkers were as cautious as Darwin and Einstein had been about making large claims for their central terms, panacean powers were claimed for *systems* nonetheless — especially by the politicans who seemed really to believe that "the techniques that are going to put a man on the Moon are going to be exactly the techniques that we are going to need to clean up our cities," as Vice-President Humphrey proclaimed in a typical 1960s promotion of "the *system analysis approach*."

But to be fair to the politicians and social planners who fell under the spell of what a less enchanted observer called "the man-on-the-moon magic," certain tricks of language do make the *systems* method sound exactly suited for social matters. The word *system* itself is the main culprit. Systems analysis is analysis of *systems*, and all our social enterprises and operations (our education systems, our sanitation systems, our welfare and health-care and criminal-justice systems) are indeed *systems* — or so we call them. In calling them this, we're already letting ourselves in for trouble though, since social systems can appropriately be labeled *systems* only in the loosest sense of the word and not, we now know, in the tight sense of organic structure that nineteenth-century sociologists had in mind when they took the term over from biology. The *system* of systems analysis has an even tighter sense of structure than does a biological *system*, so in applying systems analysis to social systems, we're applying a specifically technical sense of *systems* to what are *systems* only in a very general sense. But the difference doesn't show up in the word itself: the application looks right, as in the "System Analysis Study of the California Welfare System" proposed in 1966 by Lockheed Aircraft, because every appearance of the word *system* looks the same on the surface.

So does every appearance of *complexity;* and this is another word that makes systems techniques look more applicable to social matters than they are. The hardware systems designed by engineers and the social problems faced by politicians are both routinely, and aptly, called *complex*. But *complex* means one (fairly technical) thing to engineers and another (extremely vague) thing when applied to socio-political problems, which are indeed com-

plex but just in the general sense of being overwhelmingly complicated. And while complex hardware systems are "designed" from
scratch by engineers, who therefore have nearly complete control
of them, complex social systems aren't, alas, designed by anyone;
they're given to us in all their sprawling complexity and frustrat-
ing near-uncontrollability to do the best we can with. Turning to
technology for help is certainly understandable, especially in this
time of general trust in what has been termed the "technological
fix": our trust, built up steadily over the century, that everything
troublesome can be defined as a "problem" and that technology
is the universal solution. Many social matters really are problems,
and the converging reasoning of the technological fix and the all-
purpose systems approach makes complex social problems look
like "systems problems" solvable by "systems technology." It's
faulty reasoning, based on false analogies and facilitated by the
slippery meanings of *complex* and *system;* but we can see why
politicians under pressure from a populace demanding quick solutions, as well as from the less cautious members of the systems
profession who were offering them, might have been persuaded by
it.

Meanwhile, what had originally attracted the Defense Department to the systems method as a fiscal decision-making method
had drawn *systems* thinking, and all that went with it, into the
private sector as well. Business management *is* basically the art of
decision-making; and the chance to turn this art into a science —
in an era when the longing to be scientific possesses every human
endeavor — wasn't likely to be passed up. The "management science" that became the nationwide trend in business schools by
1960 was fundamentally the science of systems analysis. Set up to
deal with numbers, systems analysis was a natural for an enterprise that already conceived of its objective in quantitative terms,
that is in terms of profit. Promising increased efficiency, precise
measures of performance, and exact calculation of cost-benefit ratios, the systems concept appeared to its proponents as the business manager's dream come true.

The skepticism of many managers didn't stop the spread of *sys-*

tems. Twenty years later, businesses have so absorbed *systems* thinking that they've actually been transformed — in much of the talk about them — into "business *systems.*" Organization charts show *subsystems* in place of the old *departments,* and the ideal organizational structure is pictured as a connected series of *systems:* the accounting *system,* purchasing *system,* marketing *system,* production *system,* inventory *system,* and so on — linked by clear lines into an overall information *system.* Even interpersonal relations among employees are increasingly *system*atized, with businesses buying up the "Skill-Building Systems" of operations like Interaction Management and with promotions being programmed by career-development *systems.* Business dependency on *systems* is so great that if the word were suddenly pulled, *1984*-style, out of management vocabulary, the conceptual structure of the business world would collapse.

But what exactly are managers — in business and also in government — depending on when they depend on *systems*? It's not just the computer capability to handle complex data-processing tasks that makes managers rush into *systems* dependency, nor is it just the efficiency and (for the private sector) profits promised by the *systems* approach. These are real advantages and are certainly strong selling points, but they don't tell the whole story of *systems'* attraction. If we read not even between the lines but right on the surface of articles and ads in *Business Week* and *Fortune* and of government brochures and reports, we can see what else decision-makers are hoping for when they take the *systems* approach, what they're counting on when they buy the *systems* concept.

Systems Control

Basically what decision-makers are counting on is complete control. "We don't intend to waste your time by explaining the need for control," says a Qantel Corporation ad in the July 1981 issue of *Infosystems* magazine; "you know full well that lack of controls marks the difference between success and survival." Qantel's "business computer systems" give you "total control," the ad promises, linking *total, control,* and *systems* in the way that has become standard in today's *systems* concept. It's a way that was unknown until forty years ago; before then the concept of *system,* though suggesting *totality,* had almost nothing to do with *control.*

The two main meanings of *system,* ever since the word came into English in the seventeenth century (via the Latin *systema,* from the Greek word for "organized whole"), have been "a set of associated things forming a complex whole" (like the solar system or the circulatory system) and "a set of correlated ideas or an organized method of procedure" (like a system of philosophy, a system of government, or — at least in 1663 — "a systeme of Iniquity"). Both meanings, the physical set of things and the conceptual set of ideas, suggest (as does the original Greek) orderliness and completeness, suggestions which systems analysis has made much of. The orderliness implied especially by conceptual *system* as conscious method (and made a positive attribute in *systematic*) is what the systems approach capitalizes on when it offers itself as a "cure for chaos," as the answer to the "problems of today's complex organizations." The wholeness implied by definition in *system* is what the systems approach turns into the positive value of *total,* as in the (probably redundant) "total system" whose "total system objectives" and "total system performance" it's always claiming to consider. This *total system* is, however, taken into consideration at some cost, as the diagrams and flowcharts that regularly represent the "total system picture" show: while complete, the *system* represented by simple geometric shapes and arrows is completely abstract; the systems view, while claiming in these diagrams to encompass *subsystems* and *intrasystems* and *feedback loops* and even the *total environment,* still appears essentially flat.

The total systems picture projected by flowcharts and models gives an impression of control in a sense maybe hinted at in *system*'s traditional meaning of "method": the sense of intellectual mastery achieved by seeing or imposing patterns. But the main sources of *control* in today's *system* concept are engineering and computer technology and cybernetics. An engineering system is designed to control itself and therefore naturally (or maybe we should say artificially, designedly) does so. Cybernetics (which *is* "control theory") and computer systems have so much to do with *control* that the word *control* has over two hundred entries in the *Data Communications Dictionary:* technical compounds like *control card* and *control action, numerical controls* and *open-loop controls,* and, of course, *control systems* as well as *systems control.* In the engineering and computer worlds, *controls* are both the purpose of *systems* and their principal operating devices; *controls* are linked to *systems* as both means and end.

When *control systems* move into management, the links are multiplied and the compounds compounded. *Control* and *management* are already loosely connected in their general meanings: managers have always controlled, or tried to; control is a traditional function of management. But computers mechanize the *control function,* and systems analysis makes *control* a matter of measurement: "controlling implies measurement," say management textbooks, defining *control* as "the managerial function of measuring and correcting performance." As a result, the once loosely redundant *management control* takes on the tighter high-tech sense of computer hardware systems and cybernetic feedback loops and complete quantification; and the success of multiply compounded *management control systems* sounds assured by the multiple guarantees of sophisticated mathematics and modern technology.

Compounding the sense of *control* in *management systems* even further is the *information* of *management information systems,* which seem somehow doubly powerful because they sound as if they'll both manage your information and give you information to aid in your managing. This *information* that today's managers take as "the basis of control" was first brought into *systems* thinking by Norbert Wiener, for whom the *information* central to cybernetic control theory was a highly technical, mathematical term whose "amount" was measurable by precise formulas. But such a common word wasn't likely to keep its other connections out of its technical usages for long; and the meaning of the *information* assumed to be basic to the *control* of current *systems* has become considerably confused. On the one hand, *information* is often confused in *systems* thinking with knowledge, especially the knowledge required for making sound decisions. On the other hand, *information* tends to be treated in computer talk (despite resistance to this confusion by the more precise management thinkers) as indistinguishable from *data,* that is, from numbers suitable for processing. The two hands then come together — in *systems* slogans like "data for a decision" — to press the two sorts of *information* into the idea that numbers are all that's needed for sound judgment, and to reach jointly for the *control* that the *systems* approach is ultimately after. ("The gist of the control process," says a formula-filled book called *The Modeling of Complex Systems,* "is to learn enough about a system so as to gain control of it.")

Behind the *systems* grasp for *information* as *control* probably lies also, as a shaping force, the classic idea that "knowledge is power," along with the Faustian twist that power is the very purpose of knowledge. For there is indeed something Faustian about the *systems* greed for more and more information, especially when its express purpose is the power over the future sought not only in the "feedforward control systems" designed specifically for "future-directed control," but also in much general *systems* talk. People have always wished for the superhuman power to predict the consequences of their actions, so that they could know in advance how best to act; and the systems approach seems finally to fulfill this age-old wish. Promoted as a tool for getting "a better grip on the future" and as "a whole new way of . . . testing in advance the consequences of alternative actions," the *systems* method promises to "measure" precisely "factors such as chance and risk" and to "predict and compare the outcomes of alternative decisions." How many decision-makers actually buy this line when they contract for their new *systems* is impossible to know. But in the professional journals and the textbooks and the sales materials alike, this is how *systems* are sold.

Systems' Costs

If we believe the *systems* line and do buy *systems* as a decision-making technique, we're giving up more than money in exchange. In turning our decision-making over to *systems*, we're relinquishing our responsibility as decision-making beings, so we're in danger of selling our souls. What Kodak Chairman Walter Fallon stressed about the new disc camera when he announced it in 1982 — that it's a "decision-free photography system" — is a big selling point for many of today's *systems;* they're decision-free, they promise to free us of the burdens of decision-making. In the case of taking pictures, it's probably better for most of us to make as few decisions as possible; but there are other cases in which freeing ourselves of decision-making is giving up more than we've bargained for. Or more than we ought to be bargaining for: because we can't be freed of the burdens of decision-making without being freed in the process of our freedom of choice, our free will.

While many *systems* proponents are aware of this danger and make a point of insisting that systems should never supplant human judgment but should only serve to aid it, many others seem oblivious to this crucial distinction. A textbook called *Business Systems* practically crows that thanks to the new information system technology, now "judgment may be removed from the process" of decision-making — as if it's a blessing that managers won't need to rely on their own judgment in making decisions. A glossy self-promoting brochure put out in 1976 by the Justice Department's Institute of Law Enforcement and Criminal Justice sounds just as proud of the way its Advanced (and obviously *systems*-inspired) Technology Division

> helps criminal justice agencies harness the most promising technology by:
>> analyzing their needs
>> developing sophisticated new equipment
>> evaluating and setting performance standards

— as if there were no difference between harnessing technology to do what technology is made to do (develop sophisticated equipment like the "truck-mounted protective systems" and the "home burglar alarm systems" pictured on the page) and harnessing it to do what people are made to do (analyze their own needs and evaluate and set standards for their own performance).

We're all faced at work and at home with conflicting needs and confused standards, with difficult decisions and painfully imperfect evaluating processes; and we've all wished at times that we "had a system" to sort things out. The temptation to give in to ready-made gimmicks can be great, as the authors of *Finding Your Best Place To Live in America* (a how-to book that temptingly offers "a system for choosing a place to live") know well. But in our rush to become *systems*-dependent we're in danger of losing what independence we really have as human beings: the freedom to judge, to choose, to decide. In counting on *systems* to give us "total control," we're in danger of giving up the (admittedly partial but still special) control we already have.

In counting on *systems* to take over our social policy concerns, we're in another sort of danger as well: the danger of distorting the very nature of our social problems and twisting the main purpose of our social programs. The *systems* approach (to anything) is an essentially quantitative approach; its standard techniques, like mathematical control theory, assume that "the analyst can specify completely and quantitatively the characteristics of a system and the required system performance." But the characteristics of a social system can never be completely specified because no social system is ever complete (who can say where the education system stops and the criminal-justice system begins?), and our requirement for system performance will depend entirely — and subjectively — on where we stand in relation to the system (whether we stand before our well-fed subordinates, pointing proudly to improved cost-benefit ratios on a chart, or whether we stand in line, waiting anxiously for a welfare check). Nor can the characteristics or the goals of a social system usually be quantified, as systems analysis demands. "In important areas of social concern," admits an early *systems* developer, Congressional Budget Office Director

Alice Rivlin, "objectives are vague and measures non-existent"; yet systems analysis goes right on measuring and right on dealing with social problems in quantitative terms because that's the only way, by its very (mathematical) nature, it can deal with them.

The most common quantitative terms applied to social action programs, since all cost money, are, of course, dollars. So in order to be properly analyzed the welfare system becomes an "income maintenance system" and the health care system a "health financing system"; and the primary purpose of such social action programs — as well as the controversial questions about them, like what we mean by welfare or whose health should be most cared for — get lost in the cost-benefit analysis process. And nondollar benefits of social programs get so twisted by being forced into measurable terms that even Rivlin, who finds the popular cost-benefit technique of estimating future income fine for measuring the success of programs where increased income is actually the aim, expresses impatience with naive *systems* practices like measuring the success of Headstart by guessing the future income of four-year-olds.

Rivlin also expresses impatience with the tendency of *systems* thinking to tell us, after long study and expensive analysis, what we already knew, or to come to conclusions that are no more and sometimes less than common sense. Citing several cost-benefit analyses of education — studies elaborately designed to measure which inputs into the education system yield the best output (the best-educated student) — which conclude that the quality of teachers is the main factor, Rivlin wryly comments: "most people suspected that teachers were important in education." Most people, we might add, already suspect much of what they hear from *systems* studies of most human-related matters; and it's sad that we rush to apply expert-sounding *systems* approaches to matters that we can manage fine by ourselves. A *Training and Development Journal* article, "Applying a Systems Approach to Personnel Activities," seriously advises implementation of a "dimensionally organized personnel system," complete with "selection / promotion subsystem" and behaviorist "performance measures" jargon, because "specialists have discovered they obtain better results through a system of interrelated and coordinated elements rather than single elements taken independently." But do we really need specialists and costly systems analyses to tell us that an organization should train its prospective supervisors for the tasks it wants them to perform? And do we really need, as the article also recommends, a mechanized *system* for making employees aware that their jobs are interrelated?

Such *system*s seem more likely to inhibit this awareness, as is painfully evident from an article in a how-to magazine for middle managers called *Supervisory Management*. In eager recommendation of the "systems approach to resistance among workers," the author tells the story of his friend, a supervisor unfamiliar with systems thinking, who one day without warning installed wall-like separators between his female assembly operators to reduce their talking. The uproar and near strike that followed could have been avoided, says the author, if his friend had known how to

> . . . think systems when he made the decision to change the work environment. If my friend had analyzed the probable impact on the behavioral subsystems of his employees, he could have foreseen that the stress anxiety from the sudden change (psychological subsystem) and the threat to group unity from the barrier to communication (sociological subsystem) added up to trouble.

But from this specimen it seems as if using some common sense would have helped the friend more than "thinking systems," which sounds more likely to cause trouble than to prevent it.

What's likely to be especially troublesome for employees who are surrounded by this sort of *systems* talk is the way it threatens to close in on them, to invade their very beings and transform even them into *systems*. The standard "systems approach to resistance," as this article says matter-of-factly, is to break people down into "system components"; "people in work situations are not simply employees but rather systems of behavior." *Systems* thinking at all levels, whether taking this practical how-to approach or staying on the esoteric abstract plane of works like *The Logic of*

Social Systems, turns people (with the help of behaviorism, whose mechanistic terms click perfectly with those of *systems*) into "behavioral systems," "personality systems," and so on — because it has to. For a *system* to be *total* it must transform everything it touches into its own terms. People therefore present a problem for *systems* because people have minds and wills of their own, and *systems* can't handle that. The textbook *Business Systems* puts the problem quite frankly:

> Perhaps the greatest detriment to the proper functioning of a management information system is inconsistent human behavior. Few systems can operate without people, and people are unpredictable.

People might say, in return, that perhaps the greatest detriment to the proper functioning of (inherently unpredictable because ultimately free) human behavior is management information *systems* and most other *systems* as well. People and *systems* are evidently not made for each other, not when *systems* insist on *total control.*

Such *systems* and people are bound to become mutually and increasingly irritating to each other — especially in places where, as in modern offices, *systems* must seem to be approaching rapidly and inexorably from all directions. Office workers find their personal selves transformed into behavioral *systems,* their jobs redefined as functions of accounting *systems* or marketing *systems* or other organizational *subsystems,* and more and more of their office equipment replaced by the new office *systems* that are moving in to take over office communications (*totally,* of course): the stand-alone *systems* and the more sociable-sounding clustered *systems,* the hybrid *systems* that sound ready to reproduce on their own, the Honeywell *systems* that not only "talk to each other" but will (if put on the spot) talk to rival *systems* like IBMs, the proudly promoted user-proof *systems* designed to withstand mere human meddling. In this *total system environment,* workers can hardly avoid feeling uneasy and out of place. Even the chairs they're used to sitting on are turning into furniture *system* components right under them.

Evidently, converting to *systems* isn't the unmixed blessing that all the *systems* promotion suggests. The *total system* package has some unpleasant surprises inside; and if we tally up (in a defiantly unscientific and unmathematical manner) the main benefits and costs of the *system* approach, we might wonder if we want to take it quite so often. On the plus side, the new technological *systems* do provide definite benefits of a purely technological nature: engineering *systems* and computer *systems* do make good on their promise of *total* (or almost total — the human element still keeps intruding, as *Dr. Strangelove* dramatizes) *control* over purely technological *systems*. And the quantification techniques of systems analysis are certainly useful tools for finding the most efficient way to reach goals that are clearly quantifiable. But, as we've seen, there are many fewer quantifiable goals in our lives, and many fewer purely technological problems, than *systems* proponents assume. And when *systems* thinking is applied to nontechnological and nonquantifiable problems, its pluses switch to minuses, its benefits become (not in its own but in what are generally called "human" terms) costly, and the dark underside of our shiny new *systems* shows up.

Today's *Systems* Concept

Maybe we should think twice before thinking *systems*, or at least be clearer about what thinking *systems* involves — because *systems* aren't quite what they used to be. Systems analysis, with the aid of computers, has made subtle changes in the very meaning of the word.

One change is the blending of the two separate meanings of *system* noted earlier: the physical (*system* as a set of interrelated things) and the conceptual (*system* as a set of interrelated ideas or as an organized method or procedure). Dissolving the physical / conceptual distinction makes sense in the case of computer *systems*, since computers are hardware systems providing organized procedures. But in the case of systems analysis, the merging of the two previously separate meanings of *system* is more problematical. Systems analysis deliberately drops the distinction among *systems* in order to make its method sound broadly applicable. Such at least is the hope of the abstract theorists whose premise is that "the notion of system is widely applicable to many kinds of things." In actual application to particular things, however, such a widely ranging *system* can run wild and lose all sense of its boundaries:

> Almost all life is a system. Our bodies certainly are. Our homes and universities are, as are our government agencies and our businesses. These, in turn, are interconnected with various other systems, and each has within it a number of subsystems.

So says a management textbook, applying *system* so broadly that it becomes meaningless.

Another change in the meaning of *system*, this one made mainly by computers, is a new hardware sound to the word. General definitions of *system* are increasingly taking on computer characteristics, with the old *parts* of the definition being replaced by mechanical-sounding *components;* and in discussions even of social and other nontechnical systems, *system* has started to be defined as "any set of interrelated components." This new technological ring to *systems* joins with the mathematical techniques implied by systems analysis to make the "method" that has always been part of *system*'s meaning sound now like a scientific method, and the concept of systems sound as never before like a scientific concept.

As a high-tech term, loaded with all the good we perceive today in science and technology, *system* has lost the innocence it once had as a fairly value-free (or value-flexible) word. Previous *systems* could be positive or negative or (usually) neutral, depending on their context. Hegel certainly made his all-embracing philosophical *system* sound positive, just as Marx made the capitalist *system* sound negative. But the capitalist *system* would sound positive in the mouth of a Carnegie; and most *systems* we've had in the world — most political *systems* and value *systems* and *systems* of thought and so on — have been neutral, merely descriptive. They haven't implied that the "value system," for example, had any special value *because* it was a *system*. When *system* did carry a value sign in the decades before World War II, it was likely to be the exasperated or despairing or resigned minus of "What a crazy system!" or "You can't beat the system." We still use such expressions when the occasion demands, but their negative *system* is practically an anachronism in a world where *system* is so loaded with positive value and good promise that it's a must in every marketing expert's vocabulary.

The enormous promotional value of today's *system* — its strongly, overwhelmingly, positive sense — hasn't come entirely from its postwar technological connections. I've emphasized these because they've been decisive in making *system* what it is today, but other influences have helped to swell *system*'s value for us.

The esoteric philosophy of "general system theory" has played some part, though not nearly as big a part as it presumes, in making *system* seem a valuable scientific term. Modernizing the age-old dream of "a synthesis of scientific knowledge," general system theory combines the old biological organic *system* with new mathematical cybernetic *systems* to form an updated, all-purpose general *system* into which all the problems of the world can, it claims, be translated. In the process it declares not only *system* but also its other superpositive terms like *interaction* and *relations* and *organized whole* to be "new scientific categories."

These are, of course, the same terms granted wholistic relational value earlier in the century by Gestalt theory. Despite general system theory's claim of coming straight from the brain of Ludwig von Bertalanffy in the 1940s, the general system "world view" can look exactly like the view of Gestalt perception. And both can look, in their abstract (which is their usual) form, like the dominant view of twentieth-century sociology. Viewing society regularly, almost obsessively, "as a whole" and "as a system of inter-related parts," sociology grants the *wholistic–relational–systems* view the privileged intellectual status of being especially comprehensive, complete, even congruent with knowledge itself.

What general system theory and Gestalt theory and sociology have contributed to our current sense of *system* is mainly this intellectual value: the sense that seeing something as a *system,* which means understanding something in terms of the *interrelations* that make it a *whole,* is attaining the highest sort of knowledge. The *systems* of engineering and computers and the systems method involve knowledge too, of course, but it's a more practical knowledge. Computer *systems* and *systems* analysis do concrete work: they solve problems and increase profits; they manage information flow and measure the impact of alternative actions. Finally, they not only project a wholistic view of the world but also promise *control* — even, in their extreme statements, *total control* — of the whole world within their grasp.

The promise of *control* is passed on implicitly to all the *systems* sold today, including those that have nothing to do with technology, and all are capitalizing on it just by calling themselves *systems.* Nutri-*systems,* in their very name, promise the control over our diet that we've never been quite able to manage; skin-care *systems* ensure in a single word complete victory over our pimples; personnel *systems* promise smooth management of the awkward business of hiring and working with people; learning *systems* guarantee schools the complete success that no teachers, mere mortals that they are, could ever ensure. It's this sound of guaranteed success, backed in some unspecified way by the marvels of modern technology, that (to return to the initial question of this chapter) makes *systems* currently so salable — this implicit promise of total control over whatever in our complex chaotic lives seems out of hand. This is the sales pitch of all the *systems* being pushed at us like patent medicine from the soapbox; and in grabbing for them and swallowing them whole, we're showing how much we long, and how much we'll pay, for some sense of control.

14

Human *Relationships:* Longed-for, Heartfelt *Relations*

The *relationships* we've looked at so far — the wholistic *relations* of modern epistemology, the reified abstract *relations* of sociology, the managing *relations* of *systems* thinking — all carry, as their positive values, the values of the intellect. They all carry, that is, the positive sense that has always been attached to acts of mind when these acts are appreciated: the sense that reason, abstraction, mind over matter, the intellectual grasp of reality are good. But the intellect has also often been seen as too grasping, the mind as too distant from what matters, reason as too rational: as cold, detached, unfeeling. When the values of the intellect turn sour in this way and the plus sign over *mind* becomes a minus, the positive values that emerge in opposition to the negative *intellect* are usually those of *emotion, feeling, the heart.* These positive values of the heart — the warmth and softness of close feeling and of the personal touch, as opposed to the cold distance of abstract theories or the hard calculating edge of mechanized systems — are, amazingly enough, precisely those carried by the *relationships* we'll look at in this chapter: *community relations* and *meaningful, sharing, interpersonal relationships.* These leading terms for our human *relations* convey, that is, a sense of good directly opposed to the good of other *relations* that are equally prominent.

Community

Community's particular sense of good is part of its very meaning and always has been, though this part has swelled in the past couple of centuries. Coming originally from the Latin word for "common," *community* entered English in the fourteenth century already carrying, from the medieval Latin *communitas,* the two related yet distinct general senses it still has: a qualitative sense, referring to the quality of common ownership or other common interest and hence the quality of fellowship; and a concrete sense, referring to a body of people having in common some external bond like social rank or socio-political organization or geographic area. The concrete sense of *community* is inherently neutral, but the qualitative sense tends to be positive because fellowship is a good feeling.

During the eighteenth and nineteenth centuries, the good feeling of fellowship that's associated with forms of social organization based on direct contact among people came increasingly to seem threatened by larger impersonal forms of social organization like those of the state or society in general. *Community* in its qualitative sense therefore gained in value, since it designated those positive qualities of close personal interaction perceived as absent from and endangered by the more abstract *society*. When the German sociologist Ferdinand Tönnies published his *Gemeinschaft und Gesellschaft (Community and Society)* in 1887, he gave official confirmation and influential theoretical elaboration to the contrast between these two terms and especially between the values associated with each. While *society*'s values weren't treated by Tönnies as entirely negative (he was contrasting the two terms but not simply opposing them), *community* came out of his treatment — and into our century — as overwhelmingly positive. "A young man," Tönnies wrote, "is warned against bad Gesellschaft (society), but the expression bad Gemeinschaft (community) violates the meaning of the word."

Community can't, that is, carry a minus sign. Nor, since Tönnies, can it remain neutral; even its once neutral concrete sense, of reference to a body of people related in some social way, tends to be overpowered by the positive sense of the word. As Raymond Williams puts it in his very useful entry on *community* in *Keywords*:

> Community can be the warmly persuasive word to describe an existing set of relationships, or the warmly persuasive word to describe an alternative set of relationships. What is most important, perhaps, is that unlike all other terms of social organization (*state, nation, society,* etc.) it seems never to be used unfavourably, and never to be given any positive opposing or distinguishing term.

Since the mid-1970s when Williams wrote this, *community*'s warm positive sense has become so strong that in many cases the word has ceased to be a term of social organization altogether and has been transformed into an entirely emotive term: a warmly persuasive word describing no particular set of relationships at all. There are still some *community*s that are careful to attach their positive value to the particular social structure designed to create it: *women's community health centers,* for example, are generally strict about insisting on participation by patients in the operation of their own clinics; and the popular new *community development* activities that involve people directly in the rehabilitation of their own neighborhoods are deliberately substituting a new sociopolitical arrangement for the old one of what was called "urban renewal," which imposed on neighborhoods the distant and often destructive decrees of city planners. But in many of today's new *community*s the word's concrete social content, its sense of responsibility to a social reality, has been completely lost. The only concrete change being made by the community relations offices that are replacing public relations offices in business and industry is in the plaque on the door. And the offices of community development rapidly appearing at all levels of government around the country rarely make the organizational and social changes that their title implies; they remain every bit as bureaucratic as the old offices of city planning. In fact, since *community* has traditionally designated structures *opposed* to formal government, these government community development offices are actually co-opting *community* for the very purposes — of official establishment — against which the word has traditionally stood.

Communitys like this — or like the *defense community* and the *intelligence community* with which (rather ludicrously, as William Safire observes) the military and the CIA try to give a sense of coziness to their operations — are taking advantage of the word's heart-warming good feelings. They're trying to give off *community*'s good vibes without bothering to build the concrete social structure from which those good vibes are meant to resonate. Or maybe, overcome by the warmth given off by the word, they're just forgetting that *community* ever meant anything more.

The good feeling that these self-proclaimed *communitys* hope especially to convey is the comfortable sense of belonging that has been central to *community*'s meaning for over a century. "The idea of community," writes Daniel Yankelovich, whose polling firm does an annual "Search for Community" survey, "evokes in the individual the feeling that: 'Here is where I belong, these are my people, I care for them, they care for me, I am part of them. . . .' This is a powerful emotion. . . ." And indeed it is — more powerful, deeper in its significance for our psychological well-being, than a survey can ever show us. But Yankelovich's mind reaches well beyond his method, and he nicely grasps the strength of *community* feeling by noting the sort of weakness people feel without it: "its absence is experienced as an aching loss, a void" symptomized by "feelings of isolation, falseness, instability and impoverishment of spirit."

Evidently its absence is experienced quite often, judging from the frequency with which *community* appears as the prepositional object of a *search* or a *quest* or a *longing,* as in the "Search for Community" survey. What's longed for in *community* is generally associated with an earlier and simpler age before relations between people had been mechanized by modern industrial society, so *community* contains a strong element of nostalgia. And of wish fulfillment too: in the call for *community* there's the wish, the deep desire, the almost desperate hope that we can call forth all that was once good — and is now felt to be gone — in human *relations*.

The good sought so desperately in *community* isn't just psychological though. While the sense of well-being that comes from feeling cared for does, as we've seen, make up much of *community*'s positive content, there's more to the good seen in *community* than good feeling. "Every privilege, every object, every 'good' comes to us as the result of a human harvest, the shared labor of others," claims Peter Marin in his now well-known 1975 *Harper's* piece, "The New Narcissism." Marin makes clear that included in "every good" coming to us from *community* is every moral good; his urgent appeal to *community* values is basically an appeal to *community* as the very source of our values, the source of our morality. Marin isn't trying here to make a new claim for *community*. Ever since Tönnies insisted that all the traditional virtues like loyalty and honor and friendship derive directly from *Gemeinschaft*, the appeal of *community* as the source of our moral values has been strong.

With *community* conveying such strongly positive meaning and promising so much good — the good warm feelings of belonging and of close human contact, as well as moral goods like loyalty and honor and the other virtues — no wonder the word is in demand as a name for any enterprise dealing with people and has become one of the leading grant-getting terms of our time. Add *community* to the name of your business (Community Insurance Agency, Community Savings and Loan) and you've automatically added that special touch guaranteed to draw customers. Call your project a *community* project in your grant proposal and your funding is practically ensured, because nothing with *community* ties — so it sounds — can go wrong. (To be safe, call it a *community development* project and draw on *development*'s considerable grant-getting powers too.)

But if, as we've seen, *community* has had this special appeal for over a hundred years, why has the word suddenly leapt to everyone's lips and letterhead in the last decade or so? I suspect there are two main reasons. In the *community politics* of the late 1960s, *community* was given what Raymond Williams calls "a polemical edge." With its distinction from established politics at both national and local levels thus sharpened, *community* shot high on the placards — and on the list of anti-establishment terms — waved by the aggressive activists of those years who poured onto the streets protesting conventions of all kinds. Then in the late 1970s *community* seems to have gotten a boost of another sort, this time from people tired of all the *self*-involved talk of that time. *Community* values began to sound, that is, like a good antidote to what had become a dangerously overvalued *self*.

This particular attraction to *community*, however, turns out to be entangled in ambivalences because the values seen in *self* and in *community* aren't simply opposites. The very meaning of *community* has become closely connected with that of *self*. But the meanings of both are tied up too with what's now considered a *meaningful interpersonal relationship*, so we should look first at the meaning of such *relationship*s before trying to follow the tangled lines connecting *community* and *self*.

Meaningful Interpersonal Relationships

The sort of *relationship* now popularly considered *meaningful*, the sort that pop psychology pushes us into, has quite a different meaning from the one that the word *relationship* has previously had. For centuries the main meaning of *relationship*, as we've noted, has been "any connexion, correspondence, or association, which can be conceived as naturally existing between things" (*OED*). But the *relationship* referred to in an encounter group or reported on by *Psychology Today* is far from "any" connection. It's a particular kind of connection, and it's conceived as existing just between people, and usually just between two people at a time. What Carl Rogers — who has done as much for the meaning of current *relationships* as anyone — means by "Being in Relationship" is a very specific kind of *relationship* which is "interpersonal" (even one-on-one), "intimate," "warm," "feeling-centered." What those who talk today about "having a relationship" mean is usually even more specific: a *relationship* with not only all the Rogersian attributes but one that's romantic and sexual as well.

No doubt people have always "had" such *relationship*s. But they've also always had many other kinds, and the way that the various kinds have traditionally been distinguished is by adjectives: warm interpersonal *relations* as distinguished from, say, equally prevalent cold impersonal *relations;* sexual *relations* as distinguished from Platonic or from filial *relations;* personal *relations* as distinguished from institutional or socio-economic *relations*. Similarly, since *relations* extend to much more than just people — since everything in the world is in some sense *related* (even if only in the largest sense, of being in the world) — the specific objects whose *relations* are receiving attention at the moment have traditionally been specified as prepositional objects: as in *relations* between husband and wife or between master and servant or between business and government or between life and death, or as in *relations* between friends or between enemies or between fairy tales or between species or between words. Nearly all these *relations* are simply ignored by today's pop psychology *relationship*, which sucks its own distinguishing adjectives ("warm," "intimate," "interpersonal," and so on) into the word *relationship* itself, making the meaning of *relationship* over into its own exclusive image and thus transforming one of the widest-ranging words in our language into one of the narrowest. What's now considered a *meaningful relationship* not only limits its meaning to human interpersonal *relations* but even leaves out of consideration all persons except one "significant other" (at a time). It thus relegates all our other *relations* with the things and people of the world — *relations* that are given to us with our humanity and are hardly the matter of choice that popular rhetoric about "establishing relationships" and "ending relationships" suggests — to implicit meaninglessness.

Yet at the same time that pop psychology's *relationship* takes over this general word for its own specific purposes, it also hangs on to whatever generality and vagueness in the word it finds convenient. The word's fundamentally general reference to "any" kind of association, its inherent lack of commitment to any particular kind, makes it sound like a convenient term for the fad — which began in the 1960s — of "not committing yourself." If you want love without the legal commitment of marriage, or sex without the emotional commitment of love, having a *relationship* instead of a wife or instead of a love affair sounds perfect: conveniently free, unrestrictive, noncommital.

It actually turns out, though, that if you think of yourself as "having a relationship," you're committing yourself to something much more coercive and restrictive than marriage. You're committing yourself, for a start, to expressing your feelings — openly, persistently, obsessively. The first instruction on the Practice Home Session sheet for a current form of therapy called Relationship Enhancement is to list "feelings expressed by my partner" and "feelings I expressed"; and this regimen of regularly expressing — and duly noting the expression of — your feelings is the prime requisite for a good modern *relationship*. "In a desirable relationship the participants openly express their feelings," asserts the textbook *Interpersonal Communication,* implying that if you manage most of the time to keep from burdening your partner with your feelings, your *relationship* is by definition undesirable. Also undesirable by such a definition is a *relationship* where participants silently and even secretly do small thoughtful things for each other: where a husband unobtrusively takes over a chore that he knows his wife dislikes, say, or where neighbors take the trouble to close their windows when turning on their stereos, so as not to disturb each other.

By current definitions, not only are you committed to expressing your feelings in order to have a good *relationship;* you're restricted to feeling a certain way in order to be considered "in" a *relationship* at all. "Relationship is a human being's feeling or sense of emotional bonding with another," says a recent book called *Relationship: The Heart of Helping People.* If this is true, then "having" a *relationship* is restricted to the times when you happen to have this warm, "mutually responsive" (the book also calls it) feeling; and the rest of the time — which is surely much of the time, since there's a limit to how long anyone can sustain a single emotion — you're presumably cut off from human *relations* altogether. The same restriction is implied by another slightly different definition in the book, where feeling is made not quite the equivalent but still the prime requisite of a *relationship:* "again one sees that essential condition of a meaningful ('moving') relationship, that like or empathic feelings shuttle between two persons, linking them." Under such a condition, a *relationship* where feelings are *un*like (where, say, you regularly and cheerily shop for a crochety elderly acquaintance) is meaningless; and the possibility of *relations* apart from shuttling feelings (like anonymous acts of charity) is completely cut out. Shuttling feelings are, in any case, a shaky basis for our *relationships:* while "like feelings" are certainly a lovely fringe benefit of many good relations, to link ourselves primarily by means of feelings is to subject our *relationships* to all the ups and downs of moods and emotions and to put our human *relations* at the mercy of what's most unreliable in human nature.

Relationships *and* Self *(with* Sharing*)*

The meaning of a *relationship* that's restricted like this to the realm of emotions, a *relationship* so full of *feelings,* is obviously close to the meaning of *self.* "To be tuned to the responses throughout one's body, as well as to be tuned to one's feelings in emotional relations with the world and people around him [*sic*] is to be on the way to . . . health," writes Rollo May in *Man's Search for Himself,* identifying the positive, health-giving values of *feelings, self,* and *relations* in the way typical of today's *self* promoters and *relationship* enhancers alike. Today's *self* promoters are, in fact, today's main *relationship* enhancers, and vice versa, because both see *self*-fulfillment and *relationship* enhancement as part of the same process. The authors of a book called *Relationship Enhancement* make their subject primarily a matter of *self*-understanding: "by our definition, . . . 'enhanced' relationships are those in which the participants have developed a greater capacity, within and by virtue of the relationship, to better understand themselves and each other." Carl Rogers, too, always connects his main subject of "being myself" with "being in relationship," although he isn't always clear about the nature of the connection. Sometimes he seems to value *self-growth* as a means to the end of good, i.e. "real" *relationships* (a "result which seems to grow out of being myself is that relationships become real"); sometimes he seems to value *real relationships* as a means to *personal growth* ("real interpersonal relationships are deeply growth-promoting").

The latter arrangement of means and ends is the most common one today. In the commonly expressed ideal of "personally fulfilling relationships," the implied purpose of the *relationship* is to reach the end of *personal fulfillment;* and the most often-stated purpose of Relationship Enhancement programs is "to increase the psychological and emotional well-being of the individual participants." So while we might have expected — from *relationship*'s original and basic meaning of "connection" — that the purpose of a *relationship* with others would be to connect us with something beyond the merely personal and thus to pull us out of the *self*, this isn't at all the case with today's *meaningful interpersonal relationship*, which is meant rather to be a pulling out, a stretching, an extension of *self* to cover the barely larger area of concern of two (mutually *self*-absorbed) people instead of one.

The *sharing* that's regularly involved in current *relationships* is also, oddly enough, an extension of *self*. I say oddly because *sharing* has in the past generally implied some sort of self-sacrifice. Etymologically, *share* is connected to *shear*, and suggests cutting up something and distributing it, with presumably less left for the person doing the *sharing*. This is still the implication of most transitive *sharing:* if I share my dinner or my income or my house with you, I'm making a definite sacrifice because less food or money or space is left for me. But when I share my feelings or my experiences or my opinions, I'm not giving up anything and am in effect making not less but more of (and for) myself: aggrandizing my*self*, spreading my*self* over you, laying it on you. The same *self*-indulgence is implicit, even imperative, in all the intransitive *sharing* that goes on these days, which is really reflexive in meaning: a *sharing* of oneself that seems to come from raising the flame under one's innermost feelings until they bubble up or ooze out, spreading their warm, *self*-expansive flow over all around.

Community (with *Relationships*) and *Self*

Sharing brings us back to *community* because commitment to *community* currently involves *sharing* as much as commitment to *relationships* does. While *community sharing* can be of fairly concrete objects like "tools" or "skills" or "resources," it doesn't really count as *sharing* unless the requisite feelings are there too: those warm mutually responsive feelings required also for a *meaningful relationship*. *Community*'s current meaning is in fact (in feeling) so close to that of *relationship* that the two words often come up in the same breath, the same longing sigh for "community and caring relationships" * — suggesting that much of our sense of *community* now is an extension, over a larger group of people, of the *interpersonal relationships* that are, in turn, an extension of *self*.

It's not surprising, then, to find that *community* is often conceived today as a direct extension of *self* and all it stands for. We've already found (in the section on values education in Chapter 10) that our much called-for *community consensus* is basically a collection of *individual opinions* added up in a survey, and that the *community values* reached in this way are no more than a plural form of *personal values*. The *community* currently seen by sociobiologists and other neo-Darwinians as a "biological necessity" designed for our survival is also a collective form of *self*-interest, a *self*-protective instinct linking the good of the individual with that of the group. And the "community self-reliance" so much talked about that it's now a *Reader's Guide* subject category shows

---

* *Care* has recently joined the jargon of *community* and *sharing*, probably as much because its spelling neatly links the other two words as because its meaning does.

from its rhetoric of *self-assertion* and *independence* that its concept of *community* is exactly that of an extended, multibodied Emersonian *self*.

In these various extensions of the concept of *self* into that of *community*, the two terms are treated (strange as this may sound) as roughly equivalent. They're pointing, of course, to slightly different referents (one singular, one plural), but they carry much the same meaning and an equally positive value. Sometimes though, while both terms are treated as positive, *community*'s value seems to lie mainly in the good of the *self*: *community* is valued — in the same way that we saw *relationship* now often is — as a means to the (presumably higher) end of *self-fulfillment*. This is the hierarchy of values, for example, in a recent how-to self-help book like *A Time for Caring: How To Enrich Your Life Through an Interest and Pleasure in Others,* in which the "Community Care Plan," "Caring Goals," and other apparently *community*-centered gimmicks are really aimed — as the subtitle suggests and the book often states — at helping people feel "more positive" about themselves.

The "ethic of commitment" pushed by Yankelovich in *New Rules: Searching for Self-Fulfillment in a World Turned Upside Down* is also a *community* commitment proposed as a "strategy for self-fulfillment." The *self-fulfillment* that Yankelovich has in mind, however, is far from — and is, in fact, a deliberate rejection of — the narrowly *self*-indulgent aim of merely "feeling good": he envisions *community* as a means to the fulfillment of a rich, world-embracing *self* deliberately opposed to the conceptually and morally poorer *self* promoted popularly in the early 1970s. This is the vision of *community* projected as well by Peter Marin, who argues with almost Hegelian logic in "The New Narcissism" that true "human fulfillment hinges on much more than our usual notions of private pleasure or self-actualization, for both of those in their richest forms are impossible without communion and community." In what has turned out to be the widely persuasive vision of "The New Narcissism" and *New Rules,* then, *community* stands between two images of *self:* a negative narrow narcissistic *self* which it rejects and a positive fuller *self* for which it reaches.

In the first part of this stance, the opposition to a narrow *self*-interest, *community* is just taking up what has been historically its traditional position. The concept of *community* first arose, according to Robert Nisbet, as a reaction against the "individualistic rationalism" of the eighteenth century, and conceptually "community . . . achieves its fulfillment in a submergence of individual will." Traditionally, then, *community* fulfillment and *self*-fulfillment are at odds; and this is the tradition behind Yankelovich's call for "an ethic of commitment" that "shifts the axis away from the self . . . toward connectedness with the world" and behind Marin's urgent warning that "in the worship of the self, life . . . gives way . . . to an exaggeration of the will" so that the "ground of community" disappears and "the web of reciprocity and relation is broken."

In moving on to urge a higher *self-fulfillment* that can be achieved through *community,* though, Marin and Yankelovich seem to be moving, at least in part, into another traditional value structure that happens to be the reverse of this opposition of negative *self* to positive *community:* they're moving into the Romantic value structure which opposes positive *self* to negative *society* (where *society* necessarily fills the negative slot in place of *community,* which we know can't be negative). They're not, of course, drawn at all to the negative side of this opposition; they aren't engaging in a Romantic rejection of *society.* But something of the Romantic celebration of *self* seems to be exerting its force on their minds. In their complex vision, that is, of *community* both as the positive salvation from a negative (narrow, selfish) *self* and also as the positive means to a positive (richer, higher) *self,* Romantic and community values seem to be superimposed. Positive *community* is placed firmly over negative *society,* while the *self* put down on one side reappears more richly fulfilled on the other, in the elevated position of a higher end to which the fulfillment of *community* leads.

In the popular sloganeering of the early 1980s about moving

from the "Me Decade" into the "We Decade," Romantic and community values also seem to be combined, but not so much neatly superimposed as just jumbled. In one way the movement from *me* to *we*, presented as a simple progression from narrow *self*-concern to broader *community* concern, is made to look like a simple positive step across the slash in the standard value structure of negative *self* / positive *community*. But at the same time the promotional *community relations* rhetoric announcing this move is so similar in tone to the old *self* promotion that it often sounds as if we haven't really crossed the slash at all but have bumped into it and been bounced back into *self* (with our *me* flipped over into *we*, so that we're under the illusion that we've made it into *community*). Or, at best, it sounds as if we've gotten into *community* but are marching there to the same old beat of *self*-interest, moving just in a slightly larger circle encompassing others with a similar interest — as if, that is, in going from *self*-concern to *community* concern we haven't gone very far.

And in a way, as the previous pages have shown, we haven't. When our call for *community* is a call for connection with other people for the sake of helping them, then what we value in *community* is indeed beyond (and, our moral tradition would say, better than) the *self*. But when what we really want in calling for *community* is a certain *feeling* of connectedness, when the purpose of *community* involvement is to make us feel better about ourselves, then we're still nearly as wrapped up in *self* as ever. The distinction of meanings and ends here is, I admit, one which is hard to perceive these days when the very meaning of *community* — primarily emotive as it is — is tied up with personal ends; and it's a distinction which has always been hard to hold on to in practice anyway, since our motives for doing what we hope is good are often confused. Yet the distinction exists nonetheless. It makes a real moral difference, or so the wisdom of mankind has always assumed, whether our help to our neighbors is given for their sake or for our own. To put the distinction in other (more modern) words: in our longing for the connectedness of *commu-*

nity and of human *relationships*, it makes a difference whether we long for this connectedness in order to leave the *self* or to enlarge it.

Meanings and Misplaced Ends

In another way though, it makes no difference whether what we ultimately long for is a sense of *community* or a fuller sense of *self*, whether we're searching for *community* as an end or as a means to *self-fulfillment*. It makes no difference because in either case, unfortunately, the search is futile: neither a sense of *self-fulfillment* nor a sense of *community* can be found by deliberately seeking them. Sociologist Dennis Wrong pointed out this paradox in his essay "The Idea of 'Community': A Critique" in 1966, when the longing for *community* was leading people en masse to the suburbs:

> The achievement of community, like the achievement of mental health (or, for that matter, of happiness, as John Stuart Mill argued a century ago), cannot come from pursuing it directly but only as a by-product of the shared pursuit of more tangible goals and activities. Community may result from the concrete forms of political, economic, familial, and cultural association among men, but it cannot be willed into existence by exhorting people to immerse themselves in group activity and to find greater significance in their social identities.

The same goes, we might add, for exhorting people to find greater significance in their *interpersonal relationships*. A recent anthology called *The Search for Meaning* asserts (almost tautologically) that "no larger purpose is needed to give meaning to the lives of those who consider personal relationships central to the definition of life." But without a larger purpose, personal relationships lose their meaning: a line connecting two dots doesn't make much of a picture; it takes a detailed larger vision to make the particular connecting lines meaningful. Looking for the meaning of life in personal *relationships* alone is making the same mistake as single-mindedly pursuing the quest for *community*. It's erasing the way that you find what you're after, conceiving of a goal cut off from the ways of reaching it and from what makes it worth reaching. Wrong's analysis of the error in this conception of *community* applies to the current conception of *interpersonal relationships* as well: "the error lies in conceiving of community as a kind of end in itself, apart from the particular activities and functions that actually bind people together, and apart from those values that constitute a truly shared vision of life."

In the case of *community,* what can actually bind people together is an activity like lobbying with neighbors to keep a local school open or cleaning up and replanting a neighborhood park. Working with people on such a project can give you, as a by-product, the desired *community* feeling of belonging and of mutual concern (though, of course, it can also give you other less desirable feelings, like irritation at neighbors' foibles and a sense of being annoyingly stuck — rather than beautifully bound — with people you don't really like). In the case of *interpersonal relationships,* what has traditionally bound two (adult) people together most closely is the shared vision — and the concrete day-to-day work — of marriage. If you're determined to work at helping another person do the best possible job of supporting and raising a family and of contributing in some way to the larger world, it's unlikely that a warm, mutually responsive, personally fulfilling relationship won't result. But if you're determined above all else to have a personally fulfilling relationship, it's likely that the result will be a divorce* — and a feeling more like emptiness than like fulfillment. As with any job or responsibility, doing it well will probably make you feel good, but if you do it mainly in order to

---

* Especially nowadays, when divorce is actually recommended by professionals as a way to improve a relationship. "An enhanced relationship between a married couple might lead to a decision to get divorced," suggests the book *Relationship Enhancement* quite blithely. Certainly some marriages fail, but these failures are nearly always painful for everyone concerned. To celebrate a failed marriage as an enhanced relationship — and even to seek such failure for the sake of what's imagined as a better, more meaningful relationship — is a whacky reversal of values which only an age like ours, which has lost its sense of meaning (lost, we might say, its senses), could contrive.

feel good you'll probably make a mess of it (and, ironically, will end up feeling lousy).

So there's something sadly self-defeating (and *community*-defeating and *relation*-defeating) in the current search for *community* and the running after *relationships* — just as there is, as we've seen in earlier chapters — in the pursuit of *personal growth* and the scramble after *self*. It's in the nature of certain feelings and psychological states to be both deeply desired and directly unattainable: this is as much the case for the warmth of *community* and of *interpersonal relations* as it is for the expansiveness of *personal growth* or the satisfaction of *self-fulfillment*. Put as ends for us to pursue, *community* and *meaningful relationships* are like mirages that dissolve into mist as we rush toward them. Put aside in our minds (held in mind as highly valued and hoped-for treasures) while we pursue some specific goal together, concentrating on what particular good we can do for each other each day, those warm, always welcome feelings of close human *relations* and of *community* can — and often do — come upon us, softly bathing us in the longed-for but elusive values of the heart, surrounding our work with the sense of well-being which (by our very human nature) means so much to us.

15

Environmental *Relationships:*
Interwoven *Relations*

Since the publication of Rachel Carson's *Silent Spring* in 1962, some of the most talked-about *relationships* have been those of the *environment* — and they've continued to be talked about (and often shouted about) in exactly the terms in which Carson presented them. It was Carson's genius, that is (though it certainly wasn't her aim), to have laid out in one stroke the perfect environmentalist prose: a prose evidently so right for its purpose that in the hands of its subsequent users it has remained as pure and inviolate as they wish the natural environment would be.

Carson's vision of *environmental relations* can be seen clearly in the following lines from *Silent Spring:*

> The history of life on earth has been a history of interaction between living things and their surroundings. To a large extent, the physical form and the habits of the earth's vegetation and its animal life have been molded by the environment.

> The earth's vegetation is part of a web of life in which there are intimate and essential relations between plants and animals. Sometimes we have no choice but to disturb these relationships, but we should do so thoughtfully, with full awareness that what we do may have consequences remote in time and place.

This soil community [earthworms, grass, soil bacteria, and so on], then, consists of a web of interwoven lives, each in some way related to the others — the living creatures depending on the soil, but the soil in turn a vital element of the earth only so long as this community within it flourishes.

The balance of nature is not the same today as in Pleistocene times, but it is still there: a complex, precise, and highly integrated system of relationships between living things which cannot safely be ignored any more than the law of gravity can be defied with impunity by a man perched on the edge of a cliff.

What is it about this vision of *Silent Spring* that's especially compelling, so compelling that what we now call "environmentalism" was instantly formed, and has continued to be sustained, in its image? Much of the pull of *Silent Spring* lies, of course, in the pages and pages of carefully described details that justify these general statements about the "balance of nature" and the "web of life": all those pages of tenderly traced lines of interdependence among the actual living things being poisoned by chemical pesticides. ("We spray our elms and the following springs are silent of robin song, not because we sprayed the robins directly but because the poison traveled, step by step, through the now familiar elm leaf-earthworm-robin cycle" — now familiar because Carson has taken us through it, step by step.) And because the damage Carson describes is real, because the balance of nature is indeed upset by chemical pesticides, her vision gets much of its power — as does any accurate exposé of a real and present danger — from the force of truth behind it. But the force of the exposé form is typically a negative force: the exposé condemns what it exposes; it's an attack against its subject. What gives *Silent Spring* its added power is the positive vision propelling its attack: that vision, projected in the lines quoted above, of the *environment* as a highly *integrated* and carefully *balanced system* of *relationships*, a *community* of mutually dependent creatures in continual *interaction*, a *web* of *interwoven* lives. These terms we can now easily recognize as some of the most strongly compelling terms of our time, terms charged with the positive value they've accumulated from their connection with nearly every sort of *relationship* valued in our century. Even positive values that are usually opposed — the emotional value of *community* and the rational value of *integrated systems* — are pulled harmoniously together here, making this vision of *environmental relations* practically irresistable.

Yet while the cumulative positive value of its main terms certainly accounts for some of the appeal of this vision — both its immediate appeal to Carson's first followers and its continuing appeal to much of the general public — the environmentalist view isn't simply imitative or derivative. Partly because of the radically new facts it's confronting, partly because of its characteristic and controversial attitude toward what it sees, the environmentalist view of *environmental relations* has given new significance (of a sort we'll note later) to references to *relations,* and some new, distinctively modern nuances to the meaning of *environment.*

The basic meaning of *environment* (from the French *environ,* "around") is — and always has been — just "surroundings." But starting in the nineteenth century the word began to be identified with particular sorts of surroundings: first, by Carlyle, with natural surroundings like the "picturesque environment" he admired at Baireuth; then, after Darwin, with the natural surroundings to which organisms had to adapt in order to survive; then, in the early twentieth century, with the socio-cultural surroundings of the heredity-vs.-environment debate. These particular associations, as well as the basic general meaning, have all hung on in the word, so that *environment*'s current complete definition as given, for example, by the *American Heritage Dictionary* is:

1. Something that surrounds; surroundings
2. The total of circumstances surrounding an organism or group of organisms, specifically:

    a. The combination of external or extrinsic physical conditions that affect and influence the growth and development of organisms
    b. The complex of social and cultural conditions affecting the nature of an individual or community.

The *environment* with which environmentalists are now concerned is, of course, the particular one of 2a. When they refer to *the environment,* they mean the natural *environment,* seen in this standard Darwinian way. And environmentalism has called so much public attention to its view of the *environment* that its particular meaning of the word has become the main meaning. When we see or hear any mention of *environment* now, we assume — unless our attention is drawn elsewhere by a qualifying adjective ("the business *environment,*" "the urban *environment*") — that it's the natural *environment.*

We also assume, with the environmentalists, that it's the natural *environment* as endangered by man. While environmentalism starts (as in Carson's image that all living things "have been molded by the environment") from 2a's evolutionary assumption that the *environment* "affects and influences" organic growth, it adds its awareness and its sense of alarm that the *environment* is being very much affected and influenced in turn by what we call *our* growth, and that we're not so much "molding" the environment as mangling it. This awareness that the natural environment is threatened by man isn't entirely new. As the *Dictionary of the History of Ideas* points out in its historical survey of the ideas of "Environment and Culture": "That man is an unconscious disturber of nature, an indirect transformer because of his ignorance of the causal chain of interferences, was observed long before the development of modern ecology." But it was previously observed by mavericks — like George P. Marsh, whose view of man as a destroyer of the delicate balance of nature (in *Man and Nature,* 1864) deliberately opposed the traditionally accepted view of man as a weak geological force. What's new since the 1960s is that the view of man as a strong force on nature is the accepted view and also that the main word for man's victim is no longer *nature* but *environment.*

So the word *environment* has suffered quite a change in image in recent years. Once seen, under the initial spell of Darwinism, as a set of unyielding conditions to which every organism had to adapt or else lose the struggle for life, then seen in the Social Darwinist variant as the iron chain of external forces determining one's fate, the *environment* has lost — under the stern environmentalist gaze — both its strength and its separateness and has become part of a weak and fragile *web*. Carson's metaphor of the "web of life," that delicately balanced "system of relationships between living things which cannot safely be ignored," is still the favorite environmentalist image, always extended along the same precarious lines, as in a 1974 *National Wildlife* article called "Our Ecosystem Is an Unraveling Web":

> The radiating strands of the web represent the animal's interrelationships with all the components of the ecosystem — climate, water, and soil . . . plants . . . animals [ellipses, in the original, presumably represent other possible lines to follow in the web], down to the lowest amoeba. Each of the strands, in turn, is interconnected with virtually all of the others.
>
> If any one of these concentric strands is significantly altered, the others will be affected, too, and the whole web may be destroyed.

This new sense of the *environment* as delicate and endangered has practically reversed the meaning of the word's adjectival form. *Webster's* Second Edition in 1941 defined *environmental* as "of, pertaining to, or produced by, environment"; but something more like "produced against, or produced for the protection of, the environment" would be a better definition today. Any "environmental impact" mentioned in the first half of the century, for example, would have been an impact of the environment on (individual) development; today it would be an impact of (industrial) development on the environment. "Environmental questions" asked before the 1960s concerned ways that climate and geography influenced traits and behavior; now, of course, they concern ways that cultural behavior and its by-products influence climate and geography. *Environmental* also has a new set of verbal connections of a political sort that would have made no sense when people were seen as the passive products of *environment:* all the "environmental laws," "environmental regulations," "environmental policies," "environmental groups," and so on that put *environment* in the semantic position of being acted *on* by our standard politically involved substantives. All these compounds, like the "environmental movement" itself, come directly from our new sense of power over and responsibility for a threatened *environment*. So too does the attendant language of protectiveness: the "environmental safeguards" and the "Environmental Protection Agency," as well as the "Environmental Defense Fund," which in turn brings in all the battle lines that seem to come inevitably with a view that what one values is under attack.

Come inevitably, perhaps; but environmentalism does nothing to resist the rhetoric of the self-righteous embattled position, and even aggressively sallies forth with offensive language about "fighting" to save the earth from the "assault" of the "implacable enemy" who is waging "all-out war against the environment." The designated "enemy," meanwhile, is well skilled at wielding rhetorical weapons of its own. Cleverly calling itself the National Environmental Development Association, the industrial force fights back with the claim that it doesn't "destroy" the earth's resources but "develops" them, thus charging ahead under the banner of one of our century's most strongly positive terms.

Battle prose is probably the least persuasive rhetoric we have. Too immoderate to be trusted by any reasonable person, it appeals not to the mind but to the emotions — and to some of the least noble ones — of the people already drawn to either side. Its purpose is to raise not the level of debate but the blood pressure and the level of financial contributions.

Yet human nature and its products are so intriguingly inconsistent that a view promoted, as environmentalism's sometimes is, in the one-sided and imbalanced and inherently unpersuasive language of battle polemic can also be a view presenting one of the most persuasive pictures of harmony and balance around. So persuasive has the environmentalist picture of delicately balanced natural *relations* become that it has done more than give us the new sense, already noted, of relation to and responsibility for our *environment*. It has also given a new sense of importance to our talk about *relations*.

Environmentalism doesn't give this new sense of importance to *relations* by talking about them in new terms. Environmentalism's terms for the *relations* it values are the standard *relationship* terms of our century. As we've seen from the preceding chapters, the twentieth century's most talked-about and most valued *relations* have been those of mutual *interdependence* and reciprocal *interaction* within a *whole* or *total system.* These are the kinds of *relations* carrying special positive value in Gestalt theory and other modern concepts of knowledge, which take the perception of such *relations* as the equivalent of knowledge itself; in the sociological vision, which takes such *relations* as the very definition of society; and in systems thinking, which takes the quantification and control of such *relations* as its ultimate aim. Environmentalism talks about *relations* of *interdependence* and so on too, but it removes them from those rather abstract realms of theory and high-powered thought and brings them strikingly down to earth — making them hit home with unprecedented force.

In their environmentalist connection, that is, the standard words and phrases for talking about *relations* take on a new concreteness, and the grasp of these *relations* becomes a matter of great urgency. The "system of interrelated parts" that seems awfully abstract as a social system, for example, suddenly appears concrete when it's an ecosystem like a coral atoll, or when it's "a natural system in perfect balance" like "the bitter upland plains, the purple wastes of sage, the wild swift antelope, and the grouse" of *Silent Spring.* The "perception of relations" that tends to sound like a mere mind-game when it's the definition of knowledge in some epistemological theory sounds more like a practical imperative when the *relations* needing to be perceived are those of the web of life which in our ignorance we're destroying. Similarly, the goal of learning "enough about a system so as to gain control of it," which can sound Faustian coming from systems analysts, sounds like desperately needed common sense coming from environmentalists who have shown us the danger of letting our power over a natural system exceed our understanding of it.

These examples might be summarized by saying simply that environmental *relations* sound more important than other *relations* we hear about because they refer to something important. Such a statement is, of course, close to a truism, or would be if so much of our language didn't refer to so little. But in this age of nonstop babble which passes for mass communication — this time when the media people whose job it is to send out a constant stream of sound turn most often for their terms to politicians, whose careers depend on keeping their language from referring to anything they could be pinned down on, and to experts in the fields (especially psychology and sociology) notorious for letting their words refer only to each other or to the fuzziest of concepts — in such a time it's almost startling to come across words that refer to definite fact. And startling to be thereby reminded of something so obvious it sounds silly to say it: that when we use language it makes a difference what our words refer to.

For the *interdependence* that environmentalism talks about and tries to impress us with in its vision of "the planet's totally continuous and interdependent systems of air, land, and water" is indeed "not a vision only but a hard and inescapable scientific fact," as the report of the United Nations Conference on the Human Environment claims. We might not accept environmentalism's image of the spider-web-like fragility of this *interdependence*. But we can hardly deny that the interdependence exists — nor that, as the report also emphasizes, taking this environmental *interdependence* into account in the conduct of our national political and economic lives and in the construction of international agreements is of considerable worldwide importance.

This isn't to set environmentalist language up as an ideal, however. Though it has the virtue, rare for popular language, of referring not only to something definite but to something that definitely matters, environmentalist language isn't entirely free from folly. We've already noted environmentalism's unfortunate tendency to get trapped in battle terms; and, like most of us, it sometimes makes use of its powerful connections mainly because they sound impressive. Because *community,* for example, has come — from its connection with closely knit groups of people working cooperatively for the common good — to sound full of the warmly persuasive feeling of comradeship, environmentalism brings in the "environmental community" whenever it wants to persuade us to feel close to and personally responsible for our nonhuman surroundings. And because *system* has come, from popular systems talk, to sound like a specially integrated entity whose interrelated parts are all essential to the functioning of the whole, environmentalist arguments against removing any of the wilderness from the congressionally designated National Wilderness Preservation System make much of the *system* in this designation. They tend to call the object of their concern not "the wilderness" but "the wilderness system," to give a sense of its integral wholeness and inviolability (though it's certainly stretching the meaning of *system* to suggest, as the word does whether or not environmentalists understand the source of the power of their suggestion, that a national wilderness *system* covering over 80 million acres would collapse if a single part were taken away).

So environmentalist language is like other leading language in drawing as much as it can on the persuasive forces gathered elsewhere in its main terms, in order to draw us to its view. What makes environmentalism stand out among the leading modern usages of *relationship* language is, we can say in summary, its ability to draw into a single harmonious vision terms whose values usually conflict (the emotional values of *community*'s warm sense of belonging and the rational values of *system*'s sense of completeness and of detached control) and also its attachment of the usual *relation* terms to an unusually concrete reality. This reality is, furthermore, one whose *relations* are unusually important for us to perceive, to ponder, and to prize. The world would go on fine, I dare say, if epistemological and sociological and systems-analytical and meaningful-interpersonal *relations* were never mentioned; but if we don't talk about and treasure environmental *relations,* the world is in trouble. It's hard even to imagine going through the rest of the century without the language of *interdependence* and *interaction* and *interrelationships* as environmentalism has brought it home to us, although obviously we'll need more than just these terms to get by. (Some of what we need will be suggested at the end of the next chapter and in the epilogue.)

16

Seeing in Terms of *Relations*

When we're told today to "look at the world in terms of relation-ships," as we're told to do by holistic science and sociology and systems thinking and environmentalism alike, what exactly are we being asked to see? A convenient starting point for answering this concluding question about *relationships* is the contents-page ab-stract of a recent *Environment* magazine article, "Forces of De-struction in Amazonia." Drawing on many of the common as-sumptions carried by *relation* terms in our time, the abstract shows us more than what's in this one article; it shows us much of what's in our current vision of *relations,* much of what it means for us to be seeing in terms of *relations* as we do today:

> The present sources of environmental disruption in the Amazon Basin cannot be fully understood without a consideration of the social, political, and economic history of Brazil and its relation-ship to other countries. . . . From the Brazilian experience, we may also learn more about the interdependence of human soci-ety and nature, and the consequences in any century of short-sighted efforts to dominate them.

Though such dull prose might seem to be dozing rather than actually looking at anything, it does project (as all language does) a view of its subject which we can pay attention to even if the prose itself doesn't. What's projected here is, first, the common epistemological view that full understanding of a single fact (in this case, "environmental disruption in the Amazon Basin") requires considering all the *relations* involved. This view is then extended into the Comtian vision that the *relations* involved are those of interconnectedness among the "social, political, and economic" systems as developed both within and beyond the country. It's then extended even further into the modern ecological vision of "interdependence" between this complexly interconnected entity called "human society" and the delicately interwoven web of life called "nature," an interdependence which — as the modern systems view also warns — we must "learn more about" in order to regulate well.

If looking at the world in terms of *relations* means trying to see all this, it's obviously an immense undertaking. With such an extensive vision of *interrelatedness* as the common view of our time, we certainly can't be faulted for not trying to see the whole picture. Yet really trying to trace all the *interdependencies* and *interconnections* whose existence we're vaguely aware of has to put quite a strain on the imagination. There's a limit to how much the ordinary (or even the extraordinary) human mind can grasp, and the entire network of the world's *interrelations* — all of which must be drawn in once we're determined to see anything in all its *relations,* since everything in the world is related in an almost infinite number of ways — is beyond that limit.

Under the pressure to see more than the human mind is made to manage, our minds predictably tend to slip in one of the ways we've noted in previous chapters. Sometimes the slip is toward that reification — which we noted especially where sociological *relations* are concerned — that comes from staring so hard at the conceptual language of *relationships* that abstractions like *whole, interaction,* and *system* start to look more real than the particular concrete things and facts whose relations are being studied. Sometimes the slip is toward the sort of distortion we noted especially in the modern systems method which, being a basically mathematical method, tends to twist the reality it wants control of into quantifiable terms or even to omit altogether — just not see at all — what can't be measured.

Sometimes both sorts of slippage seem to be going on, as in a typical public-policy statement like the following from a political platform:

> An interrelationship exists between all elements and constituents of society. The essential factors in public problems, issues, policies, and programs must always be considered and evaluated as interdependent components of a total system.

The first sentence here sounds innocent and obvious enough. But when an assertion of *interrelationship* slips into an imperative to consider the factors of public problems as *interdependent components* of a *total system,* what sounds at first like a commendably broad view is reduced to a particularly confining one. The abstract *interrelationship* is reified as an *interdependence* that sounds ready (from the "total system" talk) to be reduced to the nearest formula, and the "essential factors" of public policy (which are mainly people) get treated as mechanical-sounding *components* of a system so complex that it can be seen as *total* only by leaving out most of what makes it up. Well-intentioned as such a policy statement may be, it shows what can happen when we insist on seeing "public problems" in terms of *relations,* at least as *relations* are now seen.

Why, though, do we insist so much on seeing in terms of *relations* today? Why do terms like *interrelationship* and *interdependent components* of a *total system* have such pull, such vote-getting appeal, that they'd be put in a political platform? Why does talk about *relationships* have such unquestioned positive value these days?

The answer depends on whether "these days" referred to are those of just recent decades or those of the whole past century. The particular *relationships* that rose in rhetorical value in the 1960s were, as we've found, pushed into prominence by a variety of forces: *systems relations* by the new forces of computer technology and systems engineering, which suddenly filled *systems* with scientific and flashy high-tech value; *environmental relations* by the quite different technological force of the chemical industry, against which the value of environmental relations that suddenly seemed threatened rose in reaction; *community* and *interpersonal relationships* by a combination of socio-political and psychological forces that pushed people out of conventions and onto the streets to express their communal strength and their common feelings. These different forces increasing the value of *relationships* in the 1960s obviously had very little to do with each other; yet their rhetorical effects were so similar — the promotional lines produced by them were so much the same — that the positive value of *relations* (and *interaction* and *systems* and so on) everywhere was reinforced. Familiarity, as we know from watching its impact on other leading language, has a cumulative force of its own: a set of words accumulates positive value, "sounds better," the more we hear it, even if (or maybe even more if) we hear it in very different and apparently disconnected places.

Behind the surge in *relationship* rhetoric since the 1960s there's also the force of a more long-standing familiarity: the century-and-a-half-old assumption that *relations* are especially worth considering, looking for, talking about. Though the existence of relationships among the things of this world has been obvious as long as people have been thinking about such things, the emphasis on *relationships* as we think of them today — and on the word itself as pointing to our particular way of thinking — began in the nineteenth century. The major nineteenth-century intellectual movements of organicism, Marxism, sociology, and Darwinism all insisted that to see the world truly we must see it in terms of its internal *relations;* relations of part to whole, relations of production, relations of the organism or the individual to its natural or social surroundings. This vision of the primary positive value of *relations* was then carried into our century (where it was soon reinforced by Gestalt perceptual values) and up to the present by the modern versions of all these originally nineteenth-century movements.

Yet having noted that our present insistence on the positive value of *relations* goes back to the nineteenth century, we should recall that our present and equally firm insistence on the opposing positive value of the *individual* gets much of its strength from nineteenth-century movements as well. The nineteenth century seems to have responded to the Renaissance and Enlightenment celebration of man the individual in two conflicting ways: by exalting the *individual* even further, raising the separate *self* (as we saw in Part One) on the pedestal of Romanticism; and by squashing all this *self*-indulgence by putting its foot down on the solid ground of *community, interdependence* among individuals, *relationships*.

Today, carrying on both these sets of values, we seem to value *self* and *relations* about equally, although not usually at the same time. We switch back and forth between seeing *self* or seeing *relationship* as our central term; but the switch is less like one between different slides projected alternately on a screen than like a Gestalt switch between different ways of perceiving the same projection, different ways of focusing on the same picture of the world. When we focus on *self* as our prime positive value, we're focusing intently on a single point, the I, so that the rest of the world — seeming to radiate out from that point and to order itself vaguely with respect to it — remains blurred in the background. When we focus on *relationship* as our prime positive value, we're bringing the whole network of worldly interconnections to the forefront and focusing our attention on the interrelations that make the whole more than the sum of separate *self*s, on the web of interdependencies drawing together the otherwise disconnected, *self*-important dots.

In a sense, then, when we shift our focus from the single point of *self* to the interwoven lines of *relationship*, we're adding another dimension to our view of the world. It's still a two-dimensional view, though. There's something definitely flat about the world as seen in terms of today's dominant *relations:* as flat as the famous Gestalt figures that have shaped what we think of as perception; or as flat as the spider's sheet web, which the environmentalist "web of life" calls mainly to mind; or as flat as the ubiquitous flowcharts that we take to represent not only the "total systems picture" but the total picture of almost everything we want to see as a whole. Of course, we know in a way that the world isn't flat: we pride ourselves on our knowledge of the third dimension and even the fourth dimension. But when we try to picture what we mean by knowledge, it's in terms of *relations* imagined along the lines of a *network* or *pattern* or *web*, images which — if not necessarily completely flat — seem to be projected on a practically horizontal plane. Our modern picture of meaningful *relations* * is missing (as we noted in Chapter 11) the vertical dimension that ordered the understanding of earlier eras. Meaning for us doesn't come from above; it lies in the interaction and mutual interdependence among the things of this world, and among these things only insofar as they can be observed or at least measured — only, that is, in their empirical dimension. We sense no need to look beyond the web of worldly dependencies for the meaning of life; we're satisfied that to look at the world in terms of the *interrelations* among observable, measurable elements is to look in the largest possible way.

It is, indeed, to take a much larger view than we can ever get by concentrating our attention on *self*. Seeing in terms of today's dominant *relations* does us great good when it startles us out of *self*-indulgence and pulls us out of *self*-absorptions and parochialisms of all kinds by calling our attention to *community*, to our mutual *interdependencies*, to the interlocking *systems* of life. While not all our dominant *relationship* language does this to the same extent — environmentalist language does it most, talk about *meaningful interpersonal relationships* does it least (since such talk

* Intellectually meaningful *relations*, that is, which include the *relations* that have meaning for sociological, systems, and environmental thinking. The sort of *relation* that has meaning for pop psychology can't be included in these summary comments because, as we found in Chapter 5, such a *meaningful interpersonal relationship* isn't really pictured as much of a *relation* at all: it's seen more in terms of the *self* than in terms of the network of interconnections among people. Taking the *self* as its focal point and seeing human *relations* only as extensions of *self*, it hardly even qualifies as a relational view.

is so *self*-absorbed that it does more to suck us into *self* than to pull us out) — to the extent that our leading *relationship* language does manage to draw us away from *self*-centeredness it's leading us in the right direction.

But there's a limit to how far our currently leading *relationship* terms alone can take us because looking at the world in terms of that network of interrelated lines which is our main way of picturing *relations* is like looking at a road map. A road map can show you all the streets and where they cross and even which are one-way and which are highways and which are service roads and so on, but it can't tell you where you want to go. Once you know the purpose of your trip, once you've decided what kind of drive you want or where you want to end up, a road map is a great help; but it can't help you decide whether you prefer scenery to speed or whether or not you should go to your in-laws. Similarly, our leading *relationship* language can show us *interconnections* and *reciprocal interactions* and *mutual interdependencies*, but it can't tell us what to do once we've seen them. It can lead us to consider social, political, and economic *relationships* and ecological *interdependencies* — and to consider more such *relations* than we could ever really keep in mind — but it can't help us decide which to consider more important. It can lead us to see everything as a *system* comprised of *interrelated* parts; to see the world as an *integrated whole* whose meaning lies in its internal *interrelations;* and to have confidence that we can grasp the meaning of the whole world, and take control of it, by seeing it in these terms. Our leading *relationship* language can take us this far. But it can't tell us what — if we really could get the whole world in our hands — we should do with it.

EPILOGUE

EPILOGUE

Where Does It All Lead?
(and Do We Have To Go Along?)

The leading words we've looked at in the course of this book are all obviously connected. Along the way we've come to particular places where *self* meets *development* (as in *self-fulfillment*); where *personal growth* ties in with *relativity* (at the point where *experience* becomes the source of all values); where *opinion,* merging with *feeling,* fans out into *community consensus;* where *organic growth* and *development* reinforce the *relationship* in an *integral whole,* which in turn slides into the *integration* of *systems;* where *meaningful relationship* moves into *self.* And beneath all these visible connections, all the particular meeting points on the surface of language, these words and the many others that go along with them are connected more deeply by the common concepts they express and the common values they carry, by the underlying assumptions they share.

These assumptions are those of what both its proponents and its detractors now label secular humanism. I use the label neither approvingly, as do the proud signers of a recent document called the Secular Humanist Declaration, nor pejoratively, as do critics like the Moral Majority, but descriptively, to designate the dominant ideology of twentieth-century Western thought. This thought is humanist in the sense (which we noted particularly in Part Two) that it places all its faith in human powers, especially the power of reason, and especially reason as represented by the modern scientific method; and it's secular in the sense (which is really the same sense) that it insists on this world as the exclusive source of all meaning and all values, denies the existence of any transcendent reality, and "places trust [as the Secular Humanist Declaration puts it] in human intelligence rather than in divine guidance." The structure of secular humanist thought is therefore that of a strict and heavily value-laden opposition: between human reason, seen as positive and unlimited in its potential, on one side and divine revelation, seen as negative and even nonexistent, on the other.

To say that we're living in a secular age, in an age dominated by secular thought, is, of course, to say nothing new. But what we see from following some of the main lines of this thought as closely as we've done in the preceding chapters and from tracing the way its main terms tie in not only with each other but also with much of what we do every day is how thoroughly interwoven these lines of thought are with the texture of our lives. The fabric of secular humanist thought isn't just a tapestry hung on some distant wall or a blanket we cover ourselves with during our dreams. It's a widely stretching weave of words and lines that thread their way through our most intense intellectual ponderings, through our public debates, through our daily domestic doings; so that the threads of this fabric *are* our very thoughts, and its patterns are those we follow as we go about our business each day.

Disciples of Marshall McLuhan like to imagine the world as one big but totally interconnected communications network, with the marvels of the electronic media linking us all into a single global village, hooking up all our minds to the same hip concepts, tuning us all in to the same wavelength. There are similarities between the McLuhanite image and my image of the fabric of contemporary thought whose lines weave through our lives; but I don't see that the electronic media have radically changed the nature of communication, as McLuhan insists. The thought of every age, after all, has been drawn together by a communication network, and the electronic media just increase the extent of the network's coverage and the speed at which terms spread along it. Nor am I as sanguine as the McLuhanites are about the implications of the network image. Because rather than seeing the network formed by our current lines of communication as simply connecting us in the state of scintillating "total involvement" celebrated by McLuhan, I see it — as we've seen it throughout this book — pulling all whose minds are attached to it toward its (often confused) sense of purpose and dragging us in the process into a variety of difficulties: into the slipperiness of founding values on our feelings; into the chaos of Adult Development and the perpetual restlessness of pursuing personal growth as a goal; into the logical entanglements and contradictions of relativism; into the distortions of trying to fit business and government operations into quantified systems; into a futile quest for community as an end in itself; into a sense of relationship that (at best) gives us an extensive view of all the interconnections in the world that need managing, but without giving us the values we need to manage them, and (at worse) leads us back to the myopic preoccupations of self.

If we're uncomfortable being pulled along like this, if we don't like where our leading terms are taking us, is there any way we can cut ourselves loose and get free of them? There's no easy way, unfortunately. A reader who has been hoping to find in these final pages a list of approved words, terms guaranteed not to get him into trouble but to lead him to good ends, is going to be disappointed. There's no string of words or line of thought we can just switch to, like switching subway trains, and chug along on comfortably (dozing or absentmindedly reading the newspaper) to salvation.

There are, however, certain words conspicuously missing from the secular humanist network, and we should take note of them before going on to talk about why, although pointing the way out of some of our main modern difficulties, they can't promise us automatic perfection. In a structure of thought dominated, as secular humanism's is, by the strict opposition of "human intelligence" to "divine guidance" and by the insistence that any reference to a transcendent reality is meaningless, obviously most traditional religious terms are going to be missing from respectable discourse (or mentioned only to be demeaned).* So in the list of words deliberately missing from expressions of the currently dominant ideology we'll find, for example, *absolutes, humility, transcendence, truth, wisdom, wonder, soul, sin, grace, gratitude,* and *God.* We've seen many of the specific ways that such words are kept out of our currently dominant discourse: the way *absolutes* are scorned by *relativist* lines, the way *wisdom* and *truth* are displaced by *opinion* and *consensus,* the way *humility* is lost sight of in *systems* thinking, the way *transcendent purpose* is rendered inoperable by *self-fulfilling evolutionary development.* (*Eternity* is even explicitly replaced by *evolution* in a line of Julian Huxley: "Medieval theology urged men to think of human life in the light of eternity — *sub specie aeternitatis:* I am attempting to rethink it *sub specie evolutionis.*") And it's not hard to see how other terms on the missing list are kept out, or their place taken, by our currently leading terms. There's no room for *grace* or *gratitude* in a world where reciprocal and observable *relations* are taken as the whole of what's meaningful and where we think we can have *total control.* Nor is there any place for *sin* in a positive *self*-image permitting only good *feelings;* and the very concept of *soul* is lost in a *psychology* which, though coming in name from the Greek word (ψυχη) meaning both *self* and *soul,* confines its attention now to *self.*

For anyone fed up with or frightened by where our attachment to terms like *self, development, relativity,* and *relationship* is taking us, it's tempting to insist that we all just stop using these words and talk only about *transcendence* and *truth* and *soul* and so on instead. But even if we could somehow legislate a change of popular language, there are no mere words we can count on to remain pure and incorruptible no matter how we use them. Simone Weil

---

* Or sometimes, we should add, kept but deliberately secularized, removed from religious and traditional moral reference: like the *good* that Willard Gaylin defines as "feeling good," or the *duty* that in the Adult Development imperative to *fulfill* one's *potential* is owed only to one's *self.*

believed that there were such words: she named *truth, beauty, justice,* and *compassion* as among those few words "which always, everywhere, in all circumstances express only the good" and so can't possibly "be associated with something signifying an evil." I wish she were right. But it seems to me that human nature being what it is — a mixture of longings for good and lapses into evil — nothing touched by human hands or mediated (as, of course, all language is) through human minds can be guaranteed as incorruptible. We've already seen, in an earlier chapter, an instance of *truth* being turned (in the survey report called "The Truth about Today's Young Men") into a tabulation of opinions and feelings; such *truth* doesn't necessarily signify an evil, but young men's passing opinions can hardly be considered to express a transcendent good either. And while *justice* and *compassion* can, as we noted in the discussion of relativism, point to transcendent ideals if used in the right spirit, they can also easily be used to serve worldly ends and even twisted to defend definitely evil acts. (Torture of political prisoners is always justified by its perpetrators as *justice,* and no one used higher-sounding terms than Hitler.) We have the Moral Majority, too, to remind us that words alone do not a spirit make: that *God* can be called on to defend a narrow chauvinistic militarism; and that, as in the creationism controversy, *truth* can be appealed to with an arrogant ignorance that's far from the spirit of *wisdom.*

We can't, then, simply switch to some ideal set of terms or train of thought and expect that if we ride it religiously, we'll reach the good life automatically at the end of the line. But neither are we simply trapped in those other (currently dominant) terms, simply stuck on the main train of thought of our time. As individuals with free will, we do have the power to get off the going lines at any point. Certainly there are risks in such a departure: we can't predict where we might be stranded; we're likely to be scorned for refusing to have *meaningful relationships* or to go to *stress* workshops or to conform to *community* expectations or to *grow;* we might feel isolated, left with no one to talk to, because we won't *share* our *personal experience* at every group gathering or come up with an *opinion* at every ring of the phone. But actually we needn't feel isolated. In our position deliberately apart from the rapidly running lines of the day, we're in good company: the company of all since Socrates who have leapt off of their society's going lines in order to pose tough questions, from their position of detachment, about where such language was heading; and whose answers have then challenged the adherents of the going language to decide whether they really wanted to keep going along with it.

To put this possibility of detachment from our culture's dominant lines back in terms of my metaphor of the fabric of leading thought that weaves its way through any age and pulls along all minds and activities attached to it, what I'm suggesting is that — no matter how strong the pull and how tightly entangled our thoughts and actions are in its web — we can always shake our heads "no!" to the fabric of currently popular thought and shake our minds loose of its lines, at least loose enough to get a distance on them. From this distance we can see, if we take the trouble to look beneath their surface claims and to draw out their hidden implications, something of where all these leading lines are leading and of what ends their meanings are headed for. And having gotten a glimpse of their implicit ends, we can decide whether these are the ends we indeed want for our lives. Such a decision will be easier the more certain we are of what ends are desirable; if we can point with confidence to the ends handed down through the ages as most worthy of human pursuit, then we can see more clearly how the passing lines of the day arrange themselves with respect to such ends. Those lines that seem to be leading in the desired direction we can hold on to and do our best to follow in our daily pursuits; those that lead elsewhere or that get themselves tangled in confusions we can snip, cut ourselves off from.

But even if our view of life's ends is a bit blurry, we don't have to grab in blind desperation every popular line that comes along. Such lines will always keep coming. It's in the nature of popular culture to produce a nonstop network of attractive and even compelling lines. And it's in our nature as cultural beings to be drawn to them and to have our thoughts and our behavior determined by them to some extent. But it's also in our nature, as individual beings whose thoughts and behavior are to some extent free, to be able to resist the pull of the leading lines if we choose. Although for most of us the leading terms of the time are a given, it's up to each of us how to take them.

Notes

Introduction

6   the change in the value of "simple":
I owe this example to C. S. Lewis's useful book *Studies in Words*
(Cambridge, Eng.: Cambridge University Press, 1967), pp. 170–73.
Elsewhere in the book (p. 282), Lewis imagines the positive values
taken on by words as halos forming over the words' heads.

7   critics of our self-concern:
The most useful critical analyses of our current self-concern that
I'm aware of are, in order of their publication: Peter Marin, "The
New Narcissism," *Harper's*, Oct. 1975, pp. 45–56; Tom Wolfe,
"The 'Me' Decade and the Third Great Awakening," *New York*,
Aug. 23, 1976, pp. 26–40; Edwin Schur, *The Awareness Trap* (New
York: New York Times Book Co., 1976); Paul C. Vitz, *Psychology
as Religion: The Cult of Self-Worship* (Grand Rapids: Eerdmans,
1977); Sally Helgesen, "Students of the Subjective," *Harper's*, June
1977, pp. 26–27ff.; Christopher Lasch, *The Culture of Narcissism*
(New York: Norton, 1978). In Chapter 14, I'll talk about the positive terms that most of these critics set against their negative valuings of our self-concern.

7   the concepts "behind" a word:
The choice of spatial metaphor is unimportant; we can say interchangeably that the concept is "behind" or "over" or "carried by"

or "brought along with" or "in" the word. Words and concepts have no spatial existence, so none of these metaphors for their relation is closer to the truth than the others; all are equally valid (and invalid) analogies in helping us visualize imaginatively something that is essentially invisible.

Chapter 1. From "God sylfa" to "I celebrate myself"

11   Jakob Burckhardt, *Die Cultur der Renaissance in Italien* (Basel, 1860), translated by S. O. C. Middlemore as *The Civilization of the Renaissance in Italy* (London, 1890).

13   The commentator quoted is Thomas Greene, "The Flexibility of the Self in Renaissance Literature," in Peter Demetz, Thomas Greene, and Lowry Nelson, eds., *The Disciplines of Criticism* (New Haven: Yale University Press, 1968), p. 243.

Chapter 2. Psychology's *Self*

19   "concern for the self":
Clark E. Moustakas, ed., *The Self: Explorations in Personal Growth* (New York: Harper and Brothers, 1956), p. xiii.

20   "in psychological discussions":
Ruth C. Wylie, *The Self Concept* (Lincoln: University of Nebraska Press, 1961), p. 1.

20   "currently scores of theories":
George Calhoun, Jr., and William C. Morse, "Self-Concept and Self-Esteem: Another Perspective," *Psychology in the Schools,* July 1977, p. 318.

21   "the self is . . . the center":
Rollo May, *Man's Search for Himself* (New York: Norton, 1953), p. 92.

21   "it indicates that the person":
Willard Gaylin, *Feelings: Our Vital Signs* (New York: Harper & Row, 1979), p. 149.

21   "the archetype of wholeness":
Violet S. De Laszlo, introduction to *The Basic Writings of C. G. Jung* (New York: Modern Library, 1959), p. xxiii.

21   "I speak now of the real self":
Karen Horney, *Neurosis and Human Growth* (New York: Norton, 1950), p. 17.

21 "conceiving ego or self":
Muzafer Sherif, "Social Psychology: Problems and Trends in Inter-disciplinary Relationships," in Sidney Koch, ed., *Psychology: A Study of a Science* (New York: McGraw-Hill, 1963), vol. 6, p. 65.

21 "discovers that he exists":
Carl Rogers, *On Becoming a Person* (Boston: Houghton Mifflin, 1961), p. 110.

21 "the long journey":
May, *Man's Search for Himself*, p. 87.

21 "the maturation of the self":
"Self-Concept in Post-Freudian Psychoanalysis," *International Encyclopedia of Psychiatry, Psychology, Psychoanalysis, and Neurology* (New York: Aesculapius, 1977), vol. 10, p. 108. This work is hereafter referred to as *IEPPPN*.

21 "self-actualization":
Abraham H. Maslow, "Self-Actualizing People: A Study of Psychological Health," in Moustakas, ed., *The Self*, p. 192.

21 "the self now expresses":
IEPPPN, vol. 10, p. 108.

22 Gaylin, *Feelings*, pp. 213, 215.

22 Rollo May, "Contributions of Existential Psychotherapy," in Rollo May, ed., *Existence: A New Dimension in Psychiatry and Psychology* (New York: Basic Books, 1958), p. 64n.

22 Rogers quoted in William P. Alston, "Self-Intervention and the Structure of Motivation," in Theodore Mischel, ed., *The Self: Psychological and Philosophical Issues* (Totowa, N.J., Rowan and Littlefield, 1977), p. 66.

22 *IEPPPN*, vol. 10, p. 100.

22 "when the self is free":
Carl Rogers, quoted in Walter Mischel and Harriet Mischel, "Self-Control and the Self," in Mischel, ed., *The Self*, p. 50. I'm indebted to the Mischels for pointing out this inconsistency of Rogers.

23 Horney, *Neurosis and Human Growth*, p. 17.

23 May, *Man's Search for Himself*, p. 91.

23 Koch, ed., *Psychology: A Study of a Science*, vol. 6, p. 65.

23 Jung, *Basic Writings*, pp. 448–49. The whole passage is: "It is altogether inconceivable that there could be any definite figure capa-

ble of expressing archetypal indefiniteness. For this reason I have found myself obliged to give the corresponding archetype the psychological name of the 'self' — a term on the one hand definite enough to convey the essence of human wholeness and on the other hand indefinite enough to express the indescribable and indeterminable nature of this wholeness. The paradoxical qualities of the term are in keeping with the fact that wholeness consists partly of the conscious man and partly of the unconscious man. But we cannot define the latter or indicate his boundaries." Later Jung adds, "The self is a union of opposites *par excellence*. . . . [It] is absolutely paradoxical in that it represents in every respect thesis and antithesis, and at the same time synthesis" (p. 450).

24   Gaylin, *Feelings*, p. 149.

24   "the self now expresses":
      IEPPPN, vol. 10, p. 108.

24   Rogers, *On Becoming a Person*, p. 108.

24   May, *Man's Search for Himself*, p. 96.

24   Erich Fromm, "Selfishness, Self-Love, and Self-Interst," in Moustakas, ed., *The Self*, p. 67.

25   "From the position of the glorified self":
      IEPPPN, vol. 10, p. 100.

25   "Freud's use of the word *Ich*":
      IEPPPN, vol. 10, p. 106.

25   contradictions inherent in our key terms:
      For speculation on why the key terms of our thought seem necessarily to contain contradictions, see I. A. Richards, *How To Read a Page* (New York: Norton, 1942), passim.

26   a fascinating and disturbing question:
      Efforts to clarify the definition of *self* within the profession of psychology are under way in some quarters. For example, the psychologists and philosophers writing in Theodore Mischel's collection *The Self: Psychological and Philosophical Issues* nearly all decry the vagueness and confusion in the use of *self* in their fields, and devote themselves to sharpening and clarifying the term. Stephen Toulmin's contribution to this end, "Self-Knowledge and Knowledge of the 'Self,' " is an especially rigorous and valuable one.

27   "a man's self may be defined":

Daniel R. Miller, "The Study of Social Relationships," in Koch, ed., *Psychology: A Study of a Science,* vol. 5, p. 672.

27 a slippage in *individual:*
For a concise history of this slippage, see the entry on *individual* in Raymond Williams, *Keywords* (New York: Oxford University Press, 1976). *Keywords* is an extremely useful book for anyone interested in the development of words through, and in interaction with, history.

28 "The struggle to become a person":
May, *Man's Search for Himself,* p. 136.

28 Rogers, *On Becoming a Person,* p. 119.

28 "unless the individual":
May, *Man's Search for Himself,* p. 217.

28 *IEPPPN,* vol. 10, p. 101.

29 James's expansion of the self:
IEPPPN, vol. 10, p. 100.

29 experience "is subdivided":
Kenneth J. Gergen, "The Social Construction of Self-Knowledge," in Mischel, ed., *The Self,* p. 164.

29 *IEPPPN,* vol. 10, p. 99.

29– Rogers, *On Becoming a Person,* pp. 111 ("experiencing of feeling";
30 "fully experiences the feelings"); 17 ("all of these diverse"); 19 ("I have found"; "as having these perceptions"); 115 ("the individual becomes").

31 client / therapist dialogue:
Rogers, *On Becoming a Person,* p. 121.

31 behaviorism:
See, for example, B. F. Skinner, *Beyond Freedom and Dignity* (New York: Knopf, 1971), passim.

32 Rogers, *On Becoming a Person,* pp. 175–76.

32 May, *Man's Search for Himself,* p. 106.

32–33 Gaylin, *Feelings,* pp. 4 ("Feelings are internal"); 216 ("That sense").

33 Rogers, *On Becoming a Person,* p. 22.

33 Gaylin, *Feelings,* p. 213.

Chapter 3. The Power of a Positive *Self*

35–   Gail Sheehy, *Passages* (New York: Dutton, 1974), pp. 21 ("internal
36   life system"); 251 ("you are moving"; "away from external"); 351
       ("one of the great"); 21 ("How do we *feel*").

36   sermons on having a "positive self-image":
       This is the approach recommended to ministers in the "Minister's
       Workshop," *Christianity Today*, May 20, 1977, pp. 32–33. The
       column, titled "Thinking Positively About Self," warns ministers
       that "members of churches that overemphasize sin and underem-
       phasize grace are likely to grow up with very negative self-images"
       and thus to feel that they can "attain a positive self-image only by
       discarding their Christian faith." In order to keep people in church,
       then, pastors are advised to preach sermons "on the importance of
       loving ourselves," which is seen anyway as Christian doctrine: "The
       Bible teaches us to love others as ourselves, which certainly implies
       that there is a sense in which we ought to love ourselves." The
       certainty of this implication is challenged, however, elsewhere in
       Christianity Today. For arguments that the Bible tells us that we
       ought *not* to love ourselves, see, for example, John Piper, "Is Self-
       Love Biblical?" Aug. 12, 1977, pp. 6–9; Philip A. Siddons, "Climb-
       ing Out of the Existential Ditch," Aug. 12, 1977, pp. 8–9; and
       Thomas Howard, "Who Am I? Who Am I?" July 8, 1977, pp. 10–
       13.

36   if we go to medical school:
       If we go, at least, to the University of Rochester Medical School,
       according to an article in the university alumni magazine, reprinted
       in the Rochester *Times-Union*, Dec. 19, 1978, p. 1C.

36   Dr. Wayne Dyer, *Pulling Your Own Strings* (New York: Thomas
       Crowell, 1978), p. 73.

36   Dr. Joyce Brothers's "unique and personal program":
       The quotation is from a review of Brothers's *How To Get What-
       ever You Want Out of Life* in the Rochester *Democrat and Chroni-
       cle*, Jan. 21, 1979. To "increase personal potential," says the re-
       viewer Jean Bell, Brothers "gives practical tips from her own
       experience on . . . breaking loose from conventional thinking to
       develop a unique and personal program." It's hard to avoid notic-
       ing here that nothing is more conventional these days than thinking
       in terms of a "unique and personal program."

37   "Humanist Manifesto II," *The Humanist*, Sept. / Oct. 1973, p. 6.

37   Sheehy, *Passages*, p. 251.

39   Billy Graham, *How To Be Born Again* (Waco, Tex.: Word Books, 1977), pp. 10, 163.

44   the complexity of self-love for both Rousseau and Jesus:
      Rousseau was careful to distinguish vain self-interest (*amour-propre*), which he saw as the root of all evil, from self-love (*amour de soi*), which he saw as the origin of all good. (See, for example, the first few pages of *Emile*, Book IV.) Jesus's command "If a man wishes to come after me, he must deny his very self" is qualified to some extent by his command to "Love your neighbor as yourself" — though the extent of the qualification is open to interpretation. It's useful to note, by the way, that the original Greek does not say *self* in these passages — because it couldn't. Ancient Greek, remember, had no word for *self*, and used reflexive pronouns and middle-voice verbs here to indicate what we now translate (accurately, I think) as *self* — accurately, because we now have a word for the concept that these passages refer to. But the fact that they could refer to it without the word reminds us, again, that we don't need the word *self* in order to be drawn by the force of self.

Chapter 4. The Growth and Development of *Growth* and *Development*

49   "vegetable genius":
      M. H. Abrams, *The Mirror and the Lamp* (New York: Norton, 1958), p. 201. Abrams is a major source for my discussions of the organic metaphor here and elsewhere in the book. Schlegel's line is quoted in Abrams, p. 213.

50   new nineteenth-century concepts of evolution:
      Excellent recent reviews of these concepts can be found in Loren Eiseley, *Darwin's Century* (Garden City: Doubleday, 1958), and in Stephen Jay Gould, *Ontogeny and Phylogeny* (Cambridge, Mass.: Harvard University Press, 1977), and *Ever Since Darwin* (New York: Norton, 1977).

51   Spencer's terms are from his *First Principles* (New York: Appleton, 1862), pp. 146–48.

53   My main source for the early reviews of Darwin's *Origin of Species* is Peter J. Bowler, "The Changing Meaning of 'Evolution,'" *Journal of the History of Ideas*, 1975, pp. 95–114.

56   Julian Huxley, *Evolution in Action* (New York: Harper & Row, 1953), p. 99.

56   Julian Huxley, ed., *The Humanist Frame* (New York: Harper, 1961), pp. 17 ("new pattern of thinking"); 22 ("evolution-centred").

57   "the sole agent":
      Huxley, ed., *The Humanist Frame*, p. 17.

57   Ruth Moore and the Editors of *Life, Evolution* (New York: Time Inc., 1962), p. 172.

57   "Humanist Manifesto II," pp. 4–9.

57   "It is only through possessing":
      Huxley, ed., *The Humanist Frame*, p. 18.

57   "the cosmic process of evolution":
      Huxley, *Evolution in Action*, p. 116.

57   "Today, in twentieth-century man":
      Huxley, ed., *The Humanist Frame*, p. 7.

57   Paul Kurtz, ed., *The Humanist Alternative* (Buffalo: Prometheus Books, 1973), pp. 183–84.

58   "fulfillment seems to describe"; "the struggle for existence":
      Huxley, *Evolution in Action*, p. 125.

59   David Ehrenfeld, *The Arrogance of Humanism* (New York: Oxford University Press, 1978).

61   Grace J. Craig, *Human Development* (Englewood Cliffs: Prentice-Hall, 1976), p. 32.

61   humanistic psychology:
      Erik Erikson, *Childhood and Society* (New York: Norton, 1950), p. 274; Daniel Levinson, *The Seasons of a Man's Life* (New York: Knopf, 1978), pp. 42, 32.

61   Huxley, ed., *The Humanist Frame*, p. 23.

62   The Grant Study is reported on by George Vaillant in *Adaptation to Life* (Boston: Little, Brown, 1977) and in "The Climb to Maturity," *Psychology Today*, Sept. 1977, pp. 34–35ff.

62   Rogers, *On Becoming a Person*, p. 26.

62–   Abraham Maslow, *Motivation and Personality*, 2nd ed. (New York:
63   Harper & Row, 1970), pp. xx ("quite meaningful and researchable concept"); 269 ("Man has an essential nature").

63   Karen Horney, *Neurosis and Human Growth: The Struggle Toward Self-Realization* (New York: Norton, 1950), pp. 17, 15.

64   Erikson, *Childhood and Society,* p. 268.

Chapter 5. The End of *Growth*

67   Julian Huxley, in T. H. Huxley and Julian Huxley, *Touchstone for Ethics* (New York: Harper, 1947), p. 137.

67   George Gaylord Simpson, *The Meaning of Evolution* (New Haven: Yale University Press, 1949), p. 230; Ernst Mayr, *Evolution and the Diversity of Life* (Cambridge, Mass.: Harvard University Press, 1976), p. 396; Theodosius Dobzhansky, *Evolution, Genetics, and Man* (New York: Wiley and Sons, 1955), p. 374; Stephen Jay Gould, *Ever Since Darwin* (New York: Norton, 1977), p. 12; G. Ledyard Stebbins, *The Basis of Progressive Evolution* (Chapel Hill: University of North Carolina Press, 1969); J. Z. Young, "Evolution Toward What?" *New York Review of Books*, Feb. 7, 1980, p. 46.

68   "the evolution of the living world":
Theodosius Dobzhansky, *Heredity and The Nature of Man* (New York: Harcourt Brace, 1964), p. 152.

68   Dobzhansky's and Simpson's tracings of the direction of evolution:
Dobzhansky, *Evolution, Genetics, and Man*, pp. 363–73; Simpson, *The Meaning of Evolution*, pp. 261–62.

68   Gould, "Dreamer," *New York Review of Books*, Oct. 11, 1979, p. 3 ("'progress' of this sort"); and *Ever Since Darwin*, p. 179 ("as a controlling factor").

69   Dale B. Harris, ed., *The Concept of Development* (Minneapolis: University of Minnesota Press, 1957), pp. 3, 109–13.

71   Harris, ed., *The Concept of Development*, p. 3.

71   Haldane's line is quoted by Ernst Mayr in the essay from which Mayr's terms also come: "Teleological and Teleonomic: A New Analaysis," in *Evolution and the Diversity of Life*, pp. 388–403.

72   historical *development:*
While Michel Foucault has tried to oust *development* with his historical *coupure,* and has had some success in converting historians to thinking along structuralist rather than developmental lines, his victory will be incomplete as long as *develop* remains in historical vocabulary.

78   Horney, *Neurosis and Human Growth*, p. 18.

78   psychologists might examine their need for certain metaphors:
      One psychologist, Richard W. Coan, has begun to do this in his
      very useful *Hero, Artist, Sage, or Saint? A Survey of Views on What
      Is Variously Called Mental Health, Normality, Maturity, Self-Ac-
      tualization, and Human Fulfillment* (New York: Columbia Univer-
      sity Press, 1977). Unfortunately, though, Coan sometimes slips from
      his critical position on these terms into the terms themselves: for
      example, treating *growth* as an assumed goal instead of as a con-
      cept he's examining (pp. 285, 295).

79–80 Abrams, *The Mirror and the Lamp*, pp. 174, 220, 221.

80   "there is no limit":
      L. Wolfe, "The Dynamics of Personal Growth," in (of all places)
      House and Garden, May 1976, pp. 90–93.

80   *Psychology Today*, Sept. 1977, p. 110.

81   Skinner, *Beyond Freedom and Dignity*, p. 142.

82   the organic metaphor gives conflicting directions:
      Enthusiastic users of the organic metaphor often appear unaware
      of this conflict. Consider, for instance, Rogers's statement of per-
      sons' "basically positive direction": "The words which I believe are
      most truly descriptive [of this direction] are words such as positive,
      constructive, moving toward self-actualization, growing toward
      maturity, growing toward socialization. . . . Life, at its best, is a
      flowing, changing process in which nothing is fixed. . . . It is al-
      ways in process of becoming" (*On Becoming a Person*, pp. 26–27).
      Rogers seems not to notice that if the direction of growing toward
      maturity were followed and maturity reached, life would no longer
      be at its best, since it would have stopped flowing and changing.
      Or, if he intends the goal of maturity never to be reached, he seems
      to be recommending a direction that leads to frustration rather than
      fulfillment: a Tantalus-like ceaseless striving toward an essentially
      unreachable goal. Maslow, too, seems unclear about whether he's
      directing us to *reach* a certain goal or just to keep heading for it:
      "Full health and normal and desirable development consist in ac-
      tualizing this [inner] nature, in fulfilling these potentialities, and in
      developing into maturity . . ." (*Motivation and Personality*, p. 269).
      The inner confusion of the organic metaphor itself is, we might say,
      actualized here in the ambiguous "-ing" forms: they could be either

present particples (specifying a continuous process) or gerunds (specifying a state, of having completed the process). We have no way of knowing which, nor of knowing whether Maslow was aware of the ambiguity.

83   Stephen Toulmin, *Human Understanding,* vol. I: *The Collective Use and Evolution of Concepts* (Princeton: Princeton University Press, 1972), p. 96. Toulmin, seeing scientific concepts as the product of an ongoing evolutionary process and thus as always in the process of changing, concludes that "intellectual flux, not intellectual immutability, is now something to be expected" — and, he implies throughout his analysis, to be seen as good.

83   Rogers, *On Becoming a Person,* p. 27.

Chapter 6. "You Must Develop"

87   Guillet is quoted in Gould, *Ontogeny and Phylogeny,* p. 155; Cheyney is quoted in Herbert Heaton, "Clio Puts the Question," in Harris, ed., *The Concept of Development,* p. 207; Huxley, ed., *The Humanist Frame,* p. 22; Erikson, *Childhood and Society,* p. 269.

89–   "the seeker after historical laws":
90   Heaton, "Clio Puts the Question," p. 208.

91–   Erikson, *Childhood and Society,* p. 269; Sheehy, *Passages,* pp. 21,
92   100; Levinson, *The Seasons of a Man's Life,* p. 319.

96   P. Vaugh, "Finding the Way to Self-Fulfillment," *Parents Magazine,* Nov. 1977, pp. 68–69; Wolfe, "The Dynamics of Personal Growth," pp. 90–93.

97   "pay the price":
      Levinson, *The Seasons of a Man's Life,* p. 198.

97–98 Horney, *Neurosis and Human Growth,* p. 15.

98   Maslow, *Motivation and Personality,* p. 273.

99   Sheehy, *Passages,* p. 25.

103   W. W. Rostow, *The Stages of Economic Growth* (Cambridge, Eng.: Cambridge University Press, 1960, 1971).

103   Dobzhansky, *Evolution, Genetics, and Man,* p. 72.

104   *development* means only "what happened":
      For example, in Percy Corbett, *The Growth of World Law* (Prince-

ton: Princeton University Press, 1971), p. 3: "This book is a study of the development of legal institutions. . . . It is an account of things that have happened and are happening."

Chapter 7. But I Don't Mean All *That!*

110 Coan, *Hero, Artist, Sage, or Saint?* p. 42.

111 J. Z. Young, "Evolution Toward What?" p. 45.

Chapter 8. *Relativity*'s Lines

118 "Length and time are relative concepts":
Martin Gardner, *Relativity for the Million* (New York: Macmillan, 1962), p. 51.

118– Albert Einstein, *Relativity: The Special and the General Theory* (New
19 York: Crown, 1961), pp. 10, 26. Originally published 1916.

119– Gardner, *Relativity for the Million,* pp. 41 ("there is no meaning");
20 51 ("length and time are relative"); 43 and 51 ("the question of whether . . . his frame of reference").

120 Bertrand Russell, *The ABC of Relativity,* 3rd rev. ed. (New York: Mentor, 1969), p. 35.

121 *Encyclopaedia Britannica,* 1966, vol. 19, p. 103.

122 "One can epitomize":
John W. Tietz, "Relativism and Social Control," in Helmut Schoeck and James W. Wiggens, eds., *Relativism and the Study of Man* (Princeton: Van Nostrand, 1961), p. 206.

122 L. Pearce Williams, ed., *Relativity Theory: Its Origins and Impact on Modern Thought* (New York: Wiley and Sons, 1968).

123 critical analyses of the error of interpreting relativity's *observer* as "subjective":
Philipp Frank, *Philosophy of Science* (Englewood Cliffs: Prentice-Hall, 1957), pp. 140–43, and *Einstein: His Life and Times* (New York: Knopf, 1972), p. 263; Hans Reichenbach, "The Philosphical Significance of the Theory of Relativity," in Paul Schilpp, ed., *Albert Einstein: Philosopher–Scientist* (New York: Tudor, 1949), pp. 294–96; Russell, *The ABC of Relativity,* p. 138.

123– Werner Heisenberg, *Physics and Philosophy* (New York: Harper
24 and Brothers, 1958), pp. 5–53. Heisenberg's choice of expansive

terms here was deliberate. He enjoyed drawing out the epistemo-logical implications of the Uncertainty Principle and of physics gen-erally, and insisted repeatedly in *Physics and Philosophy* that while "quantum theory does not contain genuine subjective features," it starts, like classical physics and like all human thought, "from the division of the world into the 'object' and the rest of the world" and so is "already a reference to ourselves."

124– Gardner, *Relativity for the Million,* p. 38; Russell, *The ABC of*
25   *Relativity,* p. 16.

125   "the theory of relativity has altered . . . the world":
       Russell, *The ABC of Relativity,* p. 58. While Russell does nothing
       to push his *world* beyond the boundaries of physics, Ortega and
       Bachelard do everything to pull it as far as their breathless hyper-
       bole can carry it: relativity theory becomes "the initiation of an
       entirely new attitude to life" (José Ortega y Gasset, *The Modern
       Theme* [New York: Harper & Row, 1961], p. 149, originally pub-
       lished 1931) and causes a Nietzschean " 'upheaval of concepts,' as
       if the earth, universe, things, possessed a different structure" (Gas-
       ton Bachelard, "The Philosophic Dialectic of the Concepts of Rel-
       ativity," in Schilpp, ed., *Albert Einstein: Philosopher–Scientist,* p.
       565).

125   Stuart Chase, *The Tyranny of Words* (New York: Harcourt Brace,
       1938), p. 117.

126   "Historic truth is relative and subjective":
       Edward Hulme, "The Personal Equation in History," *Pacific His-
       torical Review,* June 1933, pp. 129–40, quoted in Hugh I. Rodgers,
       "Charles A. Beard, the 'New Physics,' and Historical Relativity,"
       Historian, Aug. 1968, pp. 545–60. Rodgers's article is the source
       for many of my comments in this section.

128   the "very facts themselves":
       Carl Becker, "Detachment and the Writing of History," *Atlantic,*
       Oct. 1910, quoted in Rodgers, "Charles A. Beard . . . ," p. 546.

128   John Dewey, quoted in Cushing Strout, *The Pragmatic Revolt in
       American History* (New Haven: Yale University Press, 1958), p. 27.

128   "true relatively to the needs":
       Becker, "Detachment and the Writing of History," p. 546.

129   Becker, *Everyman His Own Historian* (New York: F. S. Crofts,
       1935), p. 252.

129   Reichenbach, "The Philosophical Significance of the Theory of Relativity," pp. 295–96. Russell makes the same point in *The ABC of Relativity*, p. 22: "Just as you can estimate a man's fortune in different currencies without altering its relations to the fortunes of other men, so you can estimate a body's motion by means of different reference bodies without altering its relations to other motions. And as physics is entirely concerned with relations, it must be possible to express all the laws of physics by referring all motions to any given body as the standard."

130   "Evaluations are relative to the cultural background out of which they arise":
      Melville Herskovits, *Man and His Works* (New York: Knopf, 1948), p. 63.

130   Tylor's definition of culture (1891):
      Quoted in "Culture: The Concept of Culture," *International Encyclopedia of the Social Sciences* (New York: Macmillan, 1968), vol. 3, p. 527. This work is hereafter referred to as *IESS*.

131   Herskovits, *Man and His Works,* pp. 63, 76.

131   textbook definition of cultural relativism:
      Roger M. Keesing, *Cultural Anthropology* (New York: Holt, Rinehart and Winston, 1976), glossary.

134   " 'Right' and 'good' are relative terms":
      "History of Ethics," *Encyclopaedia Britannica*, 1966, vol. 8.

135   Julian Huxley, in T. H. Huxley and Julian Huxley, *Touchstone for Ethics*, p. 256.

135– Edward Westermarck, *Ethical Relativity* (London: Kegan Paul,
36   1932), pp. xviii ("defense"); 183 ("Ethical relativity implies"); 141 ("there are no moral truths"); xvii (moral judgments); 135 (" 'good' is a concept"); 109 (moral judgments).

136   "there are no objectively sound procedures":
      "Problems of Ethics," *Encyclopedia of Philosophy* (New York: Macmillan, 1967), vol. 3, p. 125.

137   John Dewey, *Human Nature and Conduct* (New York: Random House, 1930), p. 51. Originally published 1922.

138   Joseph Fletcher, *Situation Ethics* (Philadelphia: Westminster Press, 1966), p. 76.

138– Harvey Cox, *The Secular City*, rev. ed. (New York: Macmillan,
39 1966), pp. 27 ("the awareness" and "secular man's values"); 30 ("the relativization of values"); 31 ("can accept the fact").

Chapter 9. *Relativity*'s Tangles and Other Troubles

146 Alexis de Tocqueville, *Democracy in America*, vol. 2 (New York: Vintage Books, 1945), Book II, chap. 2.

147 "Freedom of Choice for Inner-City Parents," *National Review*, July 25, 1980.

148 Cox's "should not be tampered with" and Herskovits's "need" for tolerance were quoted in Chapter 8. Herskovits says "the very core of cultural relativism is the social discipline that comes of respect for differences — mutual respect," in "Cultural Relativism and Cultural Values," 1955, reprinted in *Cultural Relativism* (New York: Random House, 1972), p. 33.

148 Max Black, "Linguistic Relativity: The Views of Benjamin Lee Whorf," *Models and Metaphors* (Ithaca: Cornell University Press, 1962), p. 256.

148 "how Marxism alone":
"Georg Lukacs, *Encyclopedia of Philosophy*, vol. 5, p. 103.

148 "Cultural Relativism," *Encyclopedia of Anthropology* (New York: Harper & Row, 1976).

148 "the main claim of relativism":
Larry Briskman, "Historicist Relativism and Bootstrap Rationality," *The Monist*, Oct. 1977, p. 518.

149 "it is equally logical":
"Cultural Relativism," *IESS*, vol. 3, p. 547.

149 "Ethical Relativism," *Encyclopedia of Philosophy*, vol. 3, p. 76.

150 "Relativism is not a position one can ultimately live with":
Keesing, *Cutlural Anthropology*, p. 179.

151 American Anthropological Association statement:
Quoted in Lowell D. Holmes, *Anthropology: An Introduction* (New York: Ronald Press, 1971), p. 414.

152 belief in the superiority of democratic values could not be defended:
Nevertheless, the founding cultural relativist, Melville Herskovits, still tried to defend it. In his 1942 essay "On Cultural Values,"

reprinted in *Cultural Relativism,* Herskovits refused to budge from his relativist position and tried bewilderedly — in the face of the Nazi assault on democracy — to defend democratic values without claiming them superior.

152   "cultural relativism leads us into moral impotence":
Keesing, *Cutlural Anthropology,* p. 179.

152   "cultural relativism remains . . . indefinite":
"Cultural Anthropology," *IESS,* vol. 1, p. 319.

152   "the moral corollary":
Eric R. Wolf, *Anthropology* (Englewood Cliffs: Prentice-Hall, 1964), p. 21.

153   "the ideal of objective historical knowledge":
Maurice Mandelbaum, *The Problem of Historical Knowledge: An Answer to Relativism* (New York: Liveright, 1938), p. 177.

153   Linton's findings were reported in "Universal Ethical Principles: An Anthropological View," in Ruth Anshen, ed., *Moral Principles of Action* (New York: Harper and Brothers, 1952).

154   "there is an actual common core" which "may be called absolutes as well as universals":
"Cultural Relativism," *IESS,* vol. 3, p. 546. Actually, Linton hadn't called his universals *absolutes.* But the eagerness among others to recall *absolutes* to anthropological vocabulary was a response to a technical distinction insisted on by cultural relativism, which recognized cultural *universals* (defined as mere general categories like morality or beauty) but denied the existence of *absolutes* (defined as fixed moral principles — like the prohibition of incest — held by all cultures at all times).

154   "some individual patterns":
Leonard Carmichael, "Absolutes, Relativism, and the Scientific Psychology of Human Nature," in Schoeck and Wiggens, eds., *Relativism and the Study of Man,* p. 9.

Chapter 10. It's All Relative Still, in Some Cases

158n   Harris's remark is quoted in Michael Wheeler, *Lies, Damn Lies, and Statistics* (New York: Liveright, 1976), p. 253.

159   "Some people feel":
A 1972 Michigan Survey Research Center questionnaire, quoted in *Public Opinion Quarterly,* Spring 1978, p. 83.

161   National Opinion Research Center poll quoted in *Public Opinion Quarterly*, Spring 1981, p. 37.

161– Gallup poll reported in George H. Gallup, "Human Needs and Sat-
62   isfactions: A Global Survey," *Public Opinion Quarterly*, Winter 1976–77, pp. 459–67.

163   Louis E. Raths, Merrill Harmin, and Sidney B. Simon, *Values and Teaching*, 2nd ed. (Columbus: Charles Merrill, 1978) originally published 1966; Sidney B. Simon, Leland W. Howe, and Howard Kirschenbaum, *Values Clarification* (New York: Hart, 1972). All quotations on Values Clarification are from these two books, along with "In Defense of Values Clarification," Kirschenbaum, Harmin, Howe, and Simon, *Phi Delta Kappan*, June 1977, pp. 243–46.

167   Steven Muller, "Universities Are Turning Out Highly Skilled Barbarians," *U.S. News and World Report*, Nov. 10, 1980, pp. 57–58.

167– All quotations are from the Commission's report in Suzanne Burk-
68   holder, Kevin Ryan, and Virgil E. Blanke, "Values, the Key to a Community," *Phi Delta Kappan* Mar. 1981, pp. 483–85.

171   Sidney J. Harris, syndicated column, *Democrat and Chronicle* (Rochester, N.Y), Aug. 10, 1980.

172   religious institutions unable to keep from flirting with a denial of *absolutes:*
    A recent example of Cox-like relativist confusion within the Christian church is the publication by the Episcopalian Seabury Press of *The Sex Atlas* (1978). "There is no objective way of making ethical choices," the atlas announces with typical relativist fervor. "The final arbiter will be experience, not some unquestioned religious dogma" — a bewildering proclamation to issue from a religious press, as an understandably exasperated Episcopal Church member points out in *National Review*, May 1, 1981, pp. 490–93.

Chapter 11. Wholistic *Relationships:*
Relations Perceived as Meaningful *Wholes*

179   J. C. Smuts, *Holism and Evolution* (New York: Macmillan, 1926), pp. 99 ("the ultimate principle"); 101 ("not merely put together"); 104 ("in a specific internal relatedness"); 103 ("more than the sum of its parts").

180   These "holistic medicine" terms are taken from Harold H. Bloom-
field and Robert B. Kay, *The Holistic Way to Health and Happiness* (New York: Simon & Schuster, 1978), p. 46, but they can be
found in the publications and pronouncements of Holistic Health
Centers everywhere. The "holistic science" language is from a review by David Kolb of Morris Berman's *The Reenchantment of the
World* and Fritjof Capra's *The Turning Point* in *Commonweal,* June
18, 1982.

181   "what happens to a part":
Max Wertheimer, quoted in Kurt Koffka, *Principles of Gestalt Psychology* (New York: Harcourt Brace, 1935), p. 683. Wertheimer,
Koffka, and Wolfgang Köhler are considered the original Gestalt
psychologists.

182   "understanding" as "an awareness":
Solomon Asch, "Gestalt Theory," *IESS,* vol. 6, p. 162. Asch has
done much both to explain Gestalt thinking to American audiences
and also to extend it into the area of social psychology.

182   "intelligence" as "the perception of relations":
Paraphrase of Köhler in Edwin G. Boring, *A History of Experi-
mental Psychology,* 2nd ed. (New York: Appleton-Century-Crofts,
1957), p. 596.

182   "productive thinking" as "the development":
Asch, "Gestalt Theory," p. 163.

182   "a whole is meaningful":
Wertheimer, in Willis D. Ellis, *A Source Book of Gestalt Psychology* (New York: Harcourt Brace, 1938), p. 16.

182   "Gestalt Psychology," *Encyclopaedia Britannica,* 1966, vol. 10, p.
370.

182   Colderidge quoted in Abrams, *The Mirror and the Lamp,* pp. 171
("nothing more"), 174 ("dependence . . . on its parts").

184   "making gestalts . . . into wholes":
Joel Latner, *The Gestalt Therapy Book* (New York: Julian Press,
1973), p. 194.

184   California's brand of *holism:*
For a delightful analysis of the *self-*centered content of the California *whole,* see Shiva Naipaul, "The Pursuit of Wholiness," *Harper's,* Apr. 1981, pp. 20–25.

184   Ruth Benedict, *Patterns of Culture* (Boston: Houghton Mifflin, Sentry edition, 1959), p. 47. Originally published 1934.

184–   A. R. Radcliffe-Brown quoted in "Culture: The Concept of Cul-
85   ture," *IESS*, vol. 3, p. 530.

185   Anthropology "considers an 'explanation' achieved":
       "Culture: The Concept of Culture," *IESS*, vol. 3, p. 533. Actually,
       there's less agreement among anthropologists about what is considered "explanation" than this summary statement suggests; but
       according to this encyclopedia's survey, both of the main competing
       theories are "holistic theories" (both the social structure theory,
       which "assigns basic explanatory value to social relations," and the
       pattern theory, which focuses on the "over-all configuration" of a
       culture).

185   summary of Carl Becker:
       Strout, *The Pragmatic Revolt in American History*, p. 34.

186   relativity physics as "systems of relations":
       "Relativity Theory, Philosophical Significance of," *Encyclopedia of
       Philosophy*, vol. 7, p. 134.

186   "a thing derives its nature":
       Tietz, "Relativism and Social Control," p. 206.

186   structuralism's "meaning of individual elements":
       Michael Lane, *Introduction to Structuralism* (New York: Basic
       Books, 1970), p. 35. Structuralism traces its *relational* view to the
       early twentieth-century linguist Ferdinand de Saussure, who —
       according to Wade Baskin, the English translator of Saussure's
       Cours de linguistique générale (1915) — saw language not as "simply an inventory or mechanical sum of the units used in speaking"
       but as a "self-contained system whose interdependent parts function and acquire value through their relationship to the whole"
       (*Course in General Linguistics* [New York: McGraw-Hill, 1959],
       p. xii).

Chapter 12. Sociological *Relationships:* Reified *Relations*

190   C. Wright Mills, *The Sociological Imagination* (New York: Oxford
       University Press, 1959), p. 137; Robert A. Nisbet, *The Sociology
       of Emile Durkheim* (New York: Oxford University Press, 1974),
       p. 73; "Sociology: The Field," *IESS*, vol. 15, p. 1; Donald Light,
       Jr., and Suzanne Keller, *Sociology* (New York: Knopf, 1975), p. 13.

191   Emile Durkheim, *The Rules of Sociological Method* (New York: Free Press, 1938), p. 102. Originally published 1895.

192   Comte's terms are from his *Cours de philosophie positive* (1830–42), translated by Stanislav Andreski, in *The Essential Comte* (New York: Barnes & Noble, 1974), pp. 153, 160.

192   Max Weber, *The Protestant Ethic and the Spirit of Capitalism*, translated by Talcott Parsons (New York: Scribner's, 1958), p. 91. Originally published 1904. Weber, by the way, rarely uses the word *relation* in this masterpiece of complex relational thinking.

194   "The *social system*" and the "general patterns of norms" are from the *IESS* article "Sociology: The Field," quoted at the beginning of this chapter. The other lines are from Talcott Parsons's extremely influential and obsessively abstract work *The Social System* (New York: Macmillan, 1951), p. 25.

195   The "specific reality" that Durkheim saw in social forces was so far from concrete that he was accused of mysticism. But some of Durkheim's influential *Rules of Sociological Method* is probably partly responsible for the subsequent reification of sociology's *relations*. When he asserts that "the social fact is a thing distinct from its individual manifestation" (p. 7) and that "the first and most fundamental rule is: consider social facts as things" (p. 14), he certainly sounds as if he's pushing the social relations whose reality he's insisting on toward a concrete thing-ness.

195   the sociologist will see *interrelations* and a *system:*
Radical sociologist Alvin Gouldner claimed that traditional sociologists automatically see in society not only *interrelations* and *system* but *equilibrium* and *mutual interdependence* as well; and Gouldner criticized the conservative bias of this functionalist assumption that all the parts of the social system are neatly interrelated and naturally balanced. In his 1959 essay "Reciprocity and Autonomy in Functional Theory," reprinted in *For Sociology* (New York: Basic Books, 1973), Gouldner proposed talking instead about the "functional autonomy" of parts of the social system, so as to focus in good 1960s fashion on "tension-producing relationships" among the parts. This is indeed a politically radical shift of terms, but it conserves sociology's larger concepts: Gouldner still sees society as a *system* and still focuses on *relationships*. So do nearly all sociologists of all schools. In Margaret Poloma's recent wide-ranging and extraordinarily fair-minded review of sociological theory, *Contemporary Sociological Theory* (New York: Macmillan,

1979), the terms *system, structure, interaction,* and *relation* appear as constants through all the ups and downs of sociological emphasis and all the ins and outs of sociological debate. As sociologist Daniel Bell (the exception who proves the rule) puts it: "almost all of contemporary social science thinks of society as some unified 'system' " (*The Cultural Contradictions of Capitalism* [New York: Basic Books, 1976], p. xi).

195 "the fundamental and inescapable subject matter":
Robert Nisbet, *The Social Bond* (New York: Knopf, 1970), pp. 45–46.

196 Hannah Arendt, *The Human Condition* (Chicago: University of Chicago Press, 1958), p. 23. I owe this reference, as well as the other observations in this paragraph, to the generous correspondence of Michael Nill.

197 definite structures in which we live and move and have our being:
Deliberately playing on the biblical "For in Him [God] we live and move and have our being" (Acts 17:28), an early sociology text even puts human interaction explicitly in place of God: "We live and move and have our being as parts of each other" (*General Sociology,* 1905, quoted in Tietz, "Relativism and Social Control," p. 214).

Chapter 13. *Systems* Analysis: Quantified and Controlled *Relations*

200 The five steps of the systems approach here are a composite from many sources, including the 1982 *Encyclopedia Americana* articles on "Systems Analysis" and "Systems Engineering" (vol. 26, pp. 198–200) and various systems engineering textbooks.

201 Johnson's lines are from speeches in 1965 and 1967, quoted in Ida Hoos, *Systems Analysis in Public Policy* (Berkeley: University of California Press, 1972), pp. 68–69. I've drawn freely throughout this chapter on Hoos's book, which provides not only a wealth of what were the going *systems* lines of the 1960s but also a whipping of them which is, while maybe too harshly unforgiving of human follies, still persistently sharp and witty and right on the line in its strikes.

201 Simon Ramo, *Cure for Chaos* (New York: Iland McKay, 1969).

201 Senator Gaylord Nelson's speech is quoted in Hoos, *Systems Analysis in Public Policy,* p. 87.

203   Humphrey's speech, quoted in Hoos, *Systems Analaysis in Public Policy*, p. 88, continues: "There is no checkbook answer to the problems of America. There are some human answers and the *system analysis approach* that we have used in our space and aeronautic programs — that is the approach that the modern city of America is going to need if it's going to become a livable social institution. So maybe we're pioneering in space only to save ourselves on Earth. As a matter of fact, maybe the nation that put a man on the Moon is a nation that will put man on his feet right here on Earth. I think so." "The man-on-the-moon magic" is Hoos's phrase.

206   The "problems of today's complex organizations" are repeatedly evoked when *systems* are being promoted. "Coping with complexity" is listed as one of ten reasons "why systems analysis pays off" in Richard F. Neuschel, *Management Systems for Profit and Growth* (New York: McGraw-Hill, 1976), p. 16, which also asserts that PPBS gave the Defense Department "a clear sense of direction in the face of unparalleled complexity" (p. 31). "In today's complex organizational world," echoes the textbook *Management*, it's hard to see the whole picture without "the application of systems theory" (Michael Meson et al. [New York: Harper & Row, 1981], p. 55). A recommendation of "the systems-analysis approach" by Ford Motor Company President Arjay Miller states that "computers and other technical devices" used by systems analysis "have extended greatly our ability to understand and cope with the complex problems we face in today's world" (quoted by M. Ways in F. E. Emery, ed., *Systems Thinking* [Harmondsworth: Penguin, 1969], p. 376). And so on.

207   "controlling implies measurement":
       Harold Koontz and Cyril O'Donnell, *Management: A Systems and Contingency Analysis of Managerial Functions* (New York: McGraw-Hill, 1976), pp. 634, 785. Elsewhere this book inadvertently illustrates a problem that management *control* talk tends to run into. The chapter "Controlling," after starting off with an apparently firm sense of *control* as "the function that closes the loop in the system of managing" and then going through pages of pronouncements about "feedforward control systems" and "logistic systems as control devices," considerably relaxes its *control* by concluding that, after all, "the most direct form of control is assurance of the quality of managers." Such a lapse into the larger looser sense of the word is almost inevitable whenever a common word takes on a technical meaning. Despite the earnest effort by manage-

ment to tighten up *control* and make it a matter of measurement and automated feedback, the word still carries its looser common sense, which can descend at any moment and crush all the scientific hopes and technical control devices in its vague general meaning.

207   "the basis of control is information":
      George Miller, "Management Guidelines: Being in Control," *Supervisory Management*, June 1981, p. 25.

208   "The gist of the control process":
      V. Vemuri, *The Modeling of Complex Systems* (New York: Academic Press, 1978), p. 342.

208   "Future-directed control" is given as the purpose of "feedforward control system" in Koontz and O'Donnell, *Management*, p. 646. "A better grip on the future" and "a whole new way of . . . testing in advance" are from M. Ways, "The Road to 1977," in Emery, ed., *Systems Thinking*, pp. 376–77. "Factors such as chance" and "predict and compare the outcomes" are from Wayne C. Turner et al., *Introduction to Industrial and Systems Engineering* (Englewood Cliffs: Prentice-Hall, 1978), p. 282.

209   Theodore Willoughy and James Senn, *Business Systems* (Cleveland: Association for Systems Management, 1975), p. 21.

210   "the analyst can specify":
      Vemuri, *The Modeling of Complex Systems*, p. 343.

210– Alice Rivlin, *Systematic Thinking for Social Action* (Washington,
 11   D.C.: Brookings Institution, 1971), pp. 50 ("in important areas");
      74 ("most people suspected").

211   William C. Byham, "Applying a Systems Approach to Personnel Activities," *Training and Development Journal*, Dec. 1981, pp. 60–65.

212   Gerald L. Arffa, "Making Waves: Change Management That Works," *Supervisory Mangement*, June 1981, pp. 19–24.

212– *The Logic of Social Systems* is a massive abstract construct by
 13   A. Kuhn (San Francisco: Jossey-Bass, 1974), which "takes a few central system concepts, adapts them to the social context, and elaborates them" (p. 9). In the process of elaboration, people become "controlled systems, presumably designed by the process of biological evolution" (p. 38). Further elaboration produces statements like: "Man is a controlled system. His behavior can be understood (to the extent it can be understood at all) only by

knowing the processes and content of his detector, selector, and effector and possibly *their* respective subsystems" (p. 102).

213   Willoughby and Senn, *Business Systems,* p. 11.

215   "the notion of system":
The abstract theorist quoted is A. Kuhn, *The Logic of Social Systems,* p. 20. The lines surrounding Kuhn's "notion" are revealing: "Systems analysis has two distinct advantages. First, the notion of system is widely applicable to many kinds of things. Second, generalizations developed from observing one kind of system are often discovered to be valid for other, sometimes discrepant, kinds of systems." Of course! If you see anything *as* a *system,* your generalizations about *systems* will apply to it.

215   "Almost all life is a system":
This sad attempt to apply the general *systems* view to particular examples is by Koontz and O'Donnell, *Management,* p. 19.

215   A sampling of *systems* with *components:* in an engineering textbook, "we shall define a system as a set of components related by some form of interaction or interdependence working together for a common purpose" (Turner et al., *Introduction to Industrial and Systems Engineering,* pp. 366–67); in a management article, "a system is an interrelated organization of component parts" (Arffa, "Making Waves: Change Management That Works"); in a theoretical treatise, a "comprehensive" definition of system is "any set of interrelated or interacting components" (Kuhn, *The Logic of Social Systems,* p. 4).

216   "a synthesis of scientific knowledge":
Russell L. Ackoff, quoted in Ludwig von Bertalanffy, *General System Theory* (New York: Braziller, 1968), p. 9.

216   The "new scientific categories" are Bertalanffy's, touted by him everywhere (for example, in *General System Theory,* p. 5).

216   the general system "world view":
All general system theorists promote *systems* as a "world view." See, for example, Ervin Laszlo, *Introduction to Systems Philosophy: Toward a New Paradigm of Contemporary Thought* (New York: Gordon and Breach, 1972), p. 13. The claim of coming from von Bertalanffy is made not only by von Bertalanffy, whose ego is as large as his projected systems view, but by most general system theorists. Yet the similarity of Gestalt and general system theory lines is obvious. For instance, Laszlo's demand "for 'seeing things

whole' and seeing the world as an interconnected interdependent field" (p. 6) is an old Gestalt demand. And the characteristic Gestalt line that "the whole is more than the sum of its parts" reappears uncredited as "a system is more than the sum of its parts" in a recent systems book (Russell L. Ackoff, *Redesigning the Future: A Systems Approach to Societal Problems* [New York: Wiley, 1974], p. 13), where the line is italicized as if shaking its head in amazement at such radically new arithmetic.

Chapter 14. Human *Relationships*: Longed-for, Heartfelt *Relations*

219– Ferdinand Tönnies, *Gemeinschaft und Gesellschaft*, translated by
20   Charles P. Loomis (London: Routledge & Kegan Paul, 1955), p. 38.

221   William Safire's comment is in *On Language* (New York: Times Books, 1980), p. 97, where he says: "Since 'community' had a warmer connotation than 'establishment,' generals and spooks have been moving to 'the defense community' and 'the intelligence community.' "

221   "idea of community":
      Daniel Yankelovich, *New Rules: Searching for Self-fulfillment in a World Turned Upside Down* (New York: Random House, 1981), p. 227.

222   Marin, "The New Narcissism," pp. 45–46.

224   Carl Rogers, "Being in Relationship," in Bobby R. Patton and Kim Giffin, *Interpersonal Communication* (New York: Harper & Row, 1974). Psychologists and psychiatrists with whom I've consulted agree that Rogers alone isn't responsible for pop psychology's *relationship*, but they can't put their finger on any single other source either. Evidently, *relationship* emerged as *meaningful* in the current sense from several sources at once: from the human potential movement's *self* psychology, of which (as we'll see) *relationship* is an extension; from Fritz Perls's Gestalt therapy, which urges us to "experience ourself as intimately related" to everything in the world; and from the social trends of the sixties.

225   The Practice Home Session sheet is in Bernard G. Guerney, Jr., et al., *Relationship Enhancement* (San Francisco: Jossey-Bass, 1977), p. 378.

225 Patton and Giffin, *Interpersonal Communication*, p. 360.

225– Helen Harris Perlman, *Relationship: The Heart of Helping People*
26   (Chicago: University of Chicago Press, 1979), pp. 23 ("Relationship is a human being's feeling"); 24 ("minimally responsive"); 28 ("again one sees"). Perlman's book is much better than these quotations make it sound. Addressed primarily to members of the "helping professions" like doctors and social workers, the book is a perceptive, mostly down-to-earth, and certainly useful reminder to them that the people who come for their professional help are often distressed, and that loving attention to the feelings of a distressed person can be as much help as attention to the particular problem causing the distress.

226 May, *Man's Search for Himself*, p. 108.

226–27 Guerney et al., *Relationship Enhancement*, p. 12.

227 Rogers, *On Becoming a Person*, pp. 17–18 ("result which seems to grow"), and "Being in Relationship," p. 477 ("real interpersonal relationships").

227 "to increase the psychological":
     Guerney et al., *Relationship Enhancement*, p. 1.

228 "community and caring relationships":
     Yankelovich, *New Rules*, p. 11.

228 *community* as a "biological necessity":
     Gaylin, *Feelings*, p. 54.

229 George Bach and Laura Torbet, *A Time for Caring: How To Enrich Your Life Through an Interest and Pleasure in Others* (New York: Delacorte, 1982).

229 Yankelovich, *New Rules*, pp. 249–59.

229 Marin, "The New Narcissism," p. 55.

230 Nisbet's terms are from his extremely useful analysis of "community" as one of the basic "unit-ideas of sociology" in *The Sociological Tradition* (New York: Basic Books, 1966), chap. 3.

230 Yankelovich's lines are from *New Rules*, p. 250; Marin's from "The New Narcissism," p. 48.

232 Dennis Wrong, "The Idea of 'Community': A Critique," *Dissent*, May–June 1966; reprinted in *Skeptical Sociology* (New York: Co-

lumbia University Press, 1976), pp. 79 ("the achievement of community"); 78 ("the error lies").

232 Richard F. Hettlinger and Grace Worth, eds., *The Search for Meaning* (Washington, D.C.: National Council on the Aging, 1980).

233n Guerney et al., *Relationship Enhancement*, p. 87.

Chapter 15. Environmental *Relationships*: Interwoven *Relations*

235– Rachel Carson, *Silent Spring* (Boston: Houghton Mifflin, 1962), pp.
36   5 ("the history of life"); 64 ("the earth's vegetation"); 56 ("this soil community"); 246 ("the balance of nature"); 189 ("we spray our elms").

239 Lee M. Talbot, "Our Ecosystem Is an Unraveling Web," *National Wildlife*, Apr. 1974, p. 24.

240 The bellicose terms about "fighting" to save the earth are mainly from the fund-solicitation letters of the deceptively peaceful-sounding Friends of the Earth.

241 "a natural system in perfect balance":
Carson, *Silent Spring*, p. 66.

241 learning "enough about a system":
Vemuri, *The Modeling of Complex Systems*, p. 342.

242 The report of the United Nations Conference on the Human Environment was published as Barbara Ward and Rene Dubos, *Only One Earth* (New York: Norton, 1972). The quotations are from the book's final pages, which put their concluding argument almost entirely in terms of the *relations* with which we're now so familiar: *interdependence, community, the total system*, and, of course, *environment*. The pages are a plea for "full realization of planetary interdependence," for the "recognition of our environmental interdependence" which could "give us the sense of community, of belonging and living together" that we need in order to survive, for the view that "we do indeed belong to a single system, powered by a single energy, . . . depending for its survival on the balance and health of the total system."

Chapter 16. Seeing in Terms of *Relations*

244 "Forces of Destruction in Amazonia," *Environment*, Sept. 1980.

246 The platform statement made in terms of *relationships* is from a Canadian political platform of the 1960s, quoted enthusiastically by Ludwig von Bertalanffy in *General System Theory*, p. 4.

247 Marxism:
Though definitely relational in its language, Marxist thought has hardly been mentioned in these chapters on *relations* because — despite Marxism's considerable (mostly indirect) influence on American social and economic thought and despite its considerable direct influence on political thought and behavior in other parts of the world — it doesn't seem to be one of the sources of the popular American talk about *relationships,* which is the subject of this part of the book.

Epilogue: Where Does It All Lead?
(and Do We Have To Go Along?)

254 "places trust in human intelligence":
"A Secular Humanist Declaration," *Free Inquiry,* Winter 1980 / 81, p. 1.

256 Huxley, *Evolution in Action,* p. 118.

256 For a thorough critique of psychology's current devotion to a *soul-less self* see Vitz, *Psychology as Religion.*

257 Simone Weil, *The Simone Weil Reader,* ed. George A. Panichas (New York: David McKay, 1977), p. 328.

Index